D0928037

FROM CONTACT TO CONQUEST

From Contact to Conquest
Transition to British Rule in Malabar, 1790–1805

Margret Frenz

OXFORD
UNIVERSITY PRESS

OXFORD
UNIVERSITY PRESS

YMCA Library Building, Jai Singh Road, New Delhi 110 001

Oxford University Press is a department of the University of Oxford. It furthers the University's objective of excellence in research, scholarship, and education by publishing worldwide in

Oxford New York

Auckland Bangkok Buenos Aires Cape Town Chennai
Dar es Salaam Delhi Hong Kong Istanbul Karachi Kolkata
Kuala Lumpur Madrid Melbourne Mexico City Mumbai Nairobi
São Paulo Shanghai Taipei Tokyo Toronto

Oxford is a registered trade mark of Oxford University Press
in the UK and in certain other countries

This is the revised edition of the Ph.D. dissertation first published by the South Asia Institute of the Heidelberg University as Volume No. 188 of the series 'Beitraege zur Suedasienforshung' through Franz Steiner Verlag, Stuttgart/Wiesbaden, Germany, 2000.

Published in India
By Oxford University Press, New Delhi

© Oxford University Press, 2003

The moral rights of the author have been asserted
Database right Oxford University Press (maker)

First published 2003

All rights reserved. No part of this publication may be reproduced, stored in a retrieval system, or transmitted, in any form or by any means, without the prior permission in writing of Oxford University Press, or as expressly permitted by law, or under terms agreed with the appropriate reprographics rights organization. Enquiries concerning reproduction outside the scope of the above should be sent to the Rights Department, Oxford University Press, at the address above

You must not circulate this book in any other binding or cover
and you must impose this same condition on any acquiror

ISBN 0 19 566321 7

Typeset by Wordcraft, Delhi 110 034
Printed by Pauls Press, Delhi 110 020
Published by Manzar Khan, Oxford University Press
YMCA Library Building, Jai Singh Road, New Delhi 110 001

In memoriam

Victor

Contents

	Acknowledgements	viii
	Abbreviations	ix
ONE	Meeting Malabar Malabar in the Eighteenth Century • Pre-colonial Social Order • Pre-colonial Land Law	1
TWO	Legitimation of Rule Religious Legitimation • The Model of the *Little Kingdom* and Its Modification • *Contact Zone* as a Model of Interaction	30
THREE	In Search of Black Gold Economic Attractiveness of Malabar • The Portuguese, the Dutch and the French • Initial Contacts with the British • The Invasions of Haidar Ali and Ṭippu Sulttān	62
FOUR	Clash of Sovereignty Maisūrian Policy Meets Resistance in Malabar • British Policy towards Malabar after 1792 • Conflicts between the Local Élite and the Colonial Administration	92
FIVE	Concept of Rule Kōṭṭayaṃ—a *Little Kingdom*? • *Contact Zone* Malabar • The Aftermath in the Nineteenth Century	141
SIX	Transformation of Rule in Malabar	170
	Notes on Sources and Transliteration	175
	Appendix Maps • Place Names	179
	Glossary	184
	Bibliography	188
	Index	203

Acknowledgements

From the first time I visited Kēraḷa, it became my personal ambition to undertake a study of this region so neglected in research. It is my intention that this book, which is a revised version of my Ph.D. dissertation submitted in 1999 at the South Asia Institute, University of Heidelberg, should contribute towards focusing attention and interest on the region of southern India.

There are many to whom I owe a deep debt of gratitude, and without whose support this work would not have been possible. I have to restrict myself to naming only a few. In particular, my gratitude goes to my thesis supervisor Dietmar Rothermund for his untiring willingness to listen and his expert advice. Also to secondary examiner Hermann Kulke, whose constructive criticism sharpened the development of my thesis.

In addition, I would like to express my thanks to Scaria Zacharia, M.G.S. Narayanan, A.P. Andrewskutty, K.K. Marar, Christopher Bayly, Susan Bayly, David Arnold, Georg Berkemer, Tilman Frasch, Fabian Heitsch, and Anna Schmid as well as the staff of the following archives and libraries: the Tamil Nadu State Archives in Ceṉṉai, the Kerala State Archives in Tiruvanantapuraṃ, the Regional Archives in Kōḻikkōṭu, the Oriental and India Office Collections of the British Library in London and the National Library of Scotland in Edinburgh. For her assistance with map-drawing my gratitude extends to Helga Nischk. I am grateful to Sanjay Subrahmanyam, Ines G. Zupanov, and Christophe Z. Guilmoto, who encouraged the idea of an English edition of the book. Special thanks are due to Paul Allen who translated the present study from the German original into English.

Abbreviations

BC	Board's Collections
BRP	Bombay Revenue Proceedings
CIS	*Contributions to Indian Sociology*
EIC	East India Company
HMS	Home Miscellaneous Series
IESHR	*Indian Economic and Social History Review*
JAAS	*Journal of Asian and African Studies*
JAS	*Journal of Asian Studies*
JIF	*Journal of Indian Folkloristics*
JIH	*Journal of Indian History*
KSA	Kerala State Archives (Tiruvanantapuraṃ)
MAS	*Modern Asian Studies*
MCR	Malabar Collectorate Records
ME	Malayāḷaṃ Era
MLTMT	Mackenzie Local Tracts Malabar in Tamil
NLS	National Library of Scotland (Edinburgh)
OIOC	Oriental and India Office Collections, British Library (London)
PCB	Public Consultations Bombay
PR	Palaśśi Rēkhakaḷ
RAK	Regional Archives Kōlikkōṭu
SPP	Secret and Political Proceedings
TNSA	Tamil Nadu State Archives (Ceṉṉai)

One

Meeting Malabar

Spices that were native to India and which are still harvested along the coast of Malabar have, to a great extent, created the 'myth of India'. Since ancient times, merchants from across the globe had been drawn to pepper, 'black gold'. The coast of Malabar is conventionally understood as the south-west coast of India ranging from Mumbai to Tiruvanantapuraṃ. However, the cultivable land for spices itself is in the heart of the Malabar coast, the area of Malabar which, in the strict sense, is located in what is now the north of Kērala. Here, on a small scale, the 'myth of India' as 'Eden' or 'God's Garden'[1] was sustained in a 'myth of Malabar', emerging from the description of this area by those Europeans who had settled there. In 1498, during the 'age of discovery', Vasco da Gama arrived near the town of Kōḻikkōṭu which resulted in a change of previous relations in the Indian Ocean and on the coast of Malabar. The trade that had been maintained on a personal level between individual merchants up until this point, became institutionalized and geared towards long-standing trade relations. The Europeans—particularly the Portuguese, the Dutch, the French and the British—were the driving forces behind this development. Besides attempting to secure trade monopolies, they also increasingly sought to gain control over goods production and the political make-up of Malabar. It is in this way that the spice trade presents Malabar as an important gateway, rich in tradition, between India and Europe. Yet despite Malabar's prominent role in the history of India, relatively little academic study has been undertaken on this region.

As an interface between Europe and India, Malabar—henceforth to be understood in its strict sense, i.e. the northern part of today's Kērala—had to go through major transformations during the transitional period from pre-colonial to colonial rule. Despite the importance of this region in the Indo–European commercial relations, the south of the subcontinent has scarcely been the focus of research. The present study draws attention on hitherto little known historical phenomena of south India, contributing at the same time to the large debate concerned with the complex interaction between European colonial powers and indigenous forces.

Different views that conceptualize the contact and interactions between Indian and European powers can be traced in the historiography of southern India. These arguments have developed from rather extreme poles. Roughly speaking, we can distinguish between two lines of argumentation taken by historians of South Asia with regard to the contact between Europe and India: on the one hand the 'orientalist' approach referring to Edward Said's influential study,[2] in which the agency of the British is seen as the central force behind the formation of the decisive discourse patterns that give India a specific shape whereas Indians are perceived as subordinates playing a comparatively passive role. Representing this view, Nicholas Dirks in his recent monograph on caste, considers the achievements of colonialism as the major coining features of modern India. He argues that caste as it is understood today is the product of the attempt of the British to systematize Indian social relations in order to consolidate their rule.[3]

On the other hand we find advocates for a 'dialogic' character of processes in the period of colonial rule between locals and Europeans. One of the first historians who argued in this line was Holden Furber who held the view that European and Indian merchants from about 1500 to 1750 traded as partners. Furber coined the term 'age of partnership'.[4] Elaborating on this aspect is Eugene Irschick when he describes the interaction between locals and the British as a 'dialogic process'.[5] Christopher Bayly, too, follows this line in his study *Empire and Information.* He perceives the establishment of an information system in north India during the nineteenth century as emerging from a process based on dialogue. He emphasizes the continuity of pre-colonial forms of information even though a 'more sophisticated' information system was built up by the British.[6]

Illustrating political, economic and social processes in early modern south India, Sanjay Subrahmanyam investigates the contacts between Europeans and locals taking an attitude in between the 'dialogic' and the 'orientalist' approach. He labels the centuries of colonialism as 'age of contained conflict',[7] thereby emphasizing the mutual influence of the different forces in the game with clear dominance of the Europeans. Subrahmanyam concludes that violence is used by any European nation on the Indian subcontinent; they differed just in the extent to which they used it as a means to reach their goals. In his recent study *Penumbral Visions,* Subrahmanyam adds one more dimension that is often neglected in the context of the interface between European and Indian contact: the interactions amongst Indians themselves. Usually this dimension does not figure prominently, although it is an important factor in the interaction of locals and the Europeans in pre-colonial as well as in colonial times.[8]

Taking into account the different perspectives on Indian historiography, the 'orientalist' as well as the 'dialogic' approaches do not seem to offer a satisfactory analytical frame, since they are one-sided and do not take into consideration the whole spectrum of ideas, concepts and possibilities of contact between Indians and Europeans. Whereas the 'orientalist' persepective emphasizes the European agency to a maximum extent, the 'dialogic' idea overestimates the local agency.

In the present study I take a somewhat different stance from the described attitudes. For the analysis of the situtation in Malabar in particular, but also for the broader context concerning the transition from pre-colonial to colonial India, I prefer to work with the model of the *contact zone*. In contrast to the 'orientalist' as well as the 'dialogic' approaches, both of which assume either the power of the British overwhelmingly dominating Indian politics, administration, cultural and social life or, respectively, the ability to discuss and compromise matters as relatively 'equal partners', the *contact zone* model provides us with a framework in which contacts and negotiations take place without implicitly defining the nature of the negotiations *a priori*. The main advantage of this model, having been introduced into the debate by Mary L. Pratt on the basis of eighteenth-century travel journals on America,[9] and modified in the following study, is its neutrality offering a broad framework for the analysis of encounters between any kind of forces—may they be external or internal, foreign or local. Within this frame, the nature of encounters may range from peaceful negotiations to armed skirmishes, the interactions always being dependent on the contextual coordinates of power they are taking place in.

Besides analysing the 'colonial' encounters within the framework of the *contact zone*, the aim of the present study is to look into the transitional phase between the modes of indigenous and of colonial administration. Which concepts of state lay behind the forms of local and colonial rule respectively? I shall examine, whether the model of the *little kingdom* proves to be suitable for the classification of historical phenomena in Malabar. This approach was originally formulated in the 1960s by Bernard S. Cohn to explain the Mahārājā of Benares' behaviour towards the Navab of Avadh in the eighteenth century. Within the last thirty years, the research of Nicholas Dirks, Georg Berkemer and Burkhard Schnepel has developed the model of the *little kingdom* from a pure typology of the hierarchy of rule into a processual model of dynamic relationships of dependence and exchange.[10] From a Eurocentric viewpoint, this concept of rule appears to constitute a labile and baffling network of relationships, but an inside viewpoint shows it to be a stable and constantly adaptable structure within the participation in power, which is manifested by military force as well as religious and political ritual. Dirks related his model to the rulers of Putukkōṭṭai in Tamiḻnāṭu. Berkemer extended it in such a way that it can be applied to other regions in India. Schnepel was able to adapt the *little kingdom* approach to a non-Hindu context in his work on the jungle kings of Orissa. The present work investigates whether the *little kingdom* model can be applied to the matrilineal society in Malabar, and which new parameters need to be introduced in order to get a deeper insight into the situation in eighteenth-century Malabar.

As aforementioned, although Malabar had been one of the pivots between orient and occident, this region has been remarked upon only fleetingly in academic literature. Most depictions of Malabar breathe the spirit of nineteenth-century historiography and are of a generally descriptive nature. There is a marked lack of specialist study on the area. William Logan's *Malabar* is still regarded as the standard work that not only examines the historical background, but also the political, economic and social situation of nineteenth-century Malabar.[11] K.K.P. Menon's *History of Kerala* also gives a broad account of the history of Kēraḷa, providing a detailed commentary of the social, political and economic issues in their historical context on the basis of letters written by a European traveller.[12] More recent monographs on the history of Kēraḷa[13] are generally based on Logan's work, known in the vernacular as the 'Malabar Manual'. Further research was carried out by C.K. Kareem on historical events of eighteenth-century Kēraḷa at the time of the Maisūr rule, and by Rajendran on the establishment of the British in Malabar.[14] Any reasonably extensive assessment of the role of land laws, and their significance to the political and economic development of Kēraḷa has not been undertaken yet, for the primary reason that hardly any concrete source seems to exist on this topic for the eighteenth century. We can only have recourse to Logan's Malabar, to Baden-Powell's work on Indian land laws that, however, when dealing with Kēraḷa more often than not refers to Logan, and a more recent article on eighteenth-century economic conditions in Kēraḷa by K.N. Ganesh.[15] There are two studies on the interrelation of economic and social structures in nineteenth- and twentieth-century south India by Dharma Kumar and T.C.Verghese.[16] Regarding the social context of Malabar especially the Nāyar and Nampūtiri communities, the works of Christopher Fuller, who investigates the socio-political structures within the Nāyar community, Melinda Moore, who concentrates on the interrelation of economic and familial connections within Nāyar house-and-land-units, and Joan Mencher, who examines traditional structures within the Nampūtiri community, have to be mentioned. Looking at the Māppiḷḷas, Stephen Dale reduces their political and economic activities to being motivated almost entirely by religion, aiming at establishing a Māpiḷḷa-Rāj. However, he does not take the multiple range of factors decisive for the Māppiḷḷas' various activities into account. Roland Miller acknowledges other factors shaping the Muslim community, though in his study also Islam plays the major role.[17]

In contrast to Malabar—coming under direct British rule at the turn of the eighteenth to the nineteenth century—the political development in the princely state Tiruvitāṃkūr (Travancore) took a different route. During the eighteenth century, both Martanda Varmma (1706/7–1758) and Rama Varmma (1724/5–1798) were able to rearrange political and administrative affairs in Travancore, thereby creating a 'modern' state.[18] In the following centuries as well, Malabar and Tiruvitāṃkūr were worlds apart regarding the political structure: whereas the direct rule of the British meant a fundamental change in Malabar's political and social landscape, the rulers of Tiruvitāṃkūr were able to keep the main political agency, although the British influenced the major decisions through indirect rule. A comparison between Tiruvitāṃkūr and Malabar in the early modern period is still a desideratum.

In the Indian context, the region of Malabar exhibits particularities in its socio-political, social and economic structure.[19] This study will address the issue of the construction and legitimation of a ruling élite in Malabar. Further, the way in which the Malabar élite reacted to the invasion of forces from abroad, and to their claims to power, will be analysed. The first such invasions to be addressed are those of the rulers of Maisūr, Haidar Ali (1728–82) and Ṭippu Sulttān (1750–99), who had been making repeated attempts to gain hegemony over Malabar since the mid-eighteenth century. The British had been seeking to convert their trading posts, which had been in existence on the Malabar coast since 1684, into permanent territorial rule since the last decade of the eighteenth century. Consequently, fundamental social, economic and political changes occurred in Malabar, which have endured through colonial times and are still perceptible to the present day. The negotiation between Europeans and indigenous rulers provided the setting for the upheavals. Questions may be raised as to which structural changes emerged on a socio-political and economic level in the collisions between British colonial powers and the people of Malabar. Of particular note is the problematic nature of the various constructs of power, how this power was exercised, and of the resulting relationship of tension between the Malabaris and the British. In defence of their sovereignty, certain local élite were in favour of putting up resistance to British claims to power, whereas others cooperated with them. A close examination of two rulers and their reaction to the new political situation in the eighteenth century will be presented here as an example. The leading figure of the resistance in Malabar was the ruler of

Kōṭṭayaṃ, Kēraḷa Varmma Paḻaśśi Rājā, whose death in 1805 signalled a loss of momentum for the resistance movement. Paḻaśśi Rājā's conception of rule merits closer examination, for he was the most significant personage in the conflict between the British, in their attempt to gain territorial rule, and the Malabaris. The methods he employed to legitimize and manifest his rule have to be investigated. It will be of particular interest to assess whether or not he displays characteristics indicative of a *little king*. Investigation is also required here into Vira Varmma of Kurumpranāṭu, who was the political opponent of Paḻaśśi Rājā. At this stage internal interactions are the topic of interest and analysis—a hitherto only marginally examined phenomenon.

Malabar in the Eighteenth Century

Since no systematic account exists on the social structure of northern Malabar, we have to start with a sketch of its most important features in order to be able to assess the changes brought about by the Maisūrian and British intrusion.[20] Descriptions and data collections made by the colonial administration in the nineteenth century allow us to reconstruct an approximate picture of the social structure in the eighteenth century. It should still be borne in mind, however, that this reconstruction is in no way complete; it can merely be a depiction of the essential features of the most important forms of organization.

What did northern Malabar, the almost legendary 'Eden', look like? At the turn of the nineteenth century, the area of Malabar was bordered in the north by South Kanara, in the east by Kurg, Maisūr, the Nīlagiris and Kōyamputtūr, and in the south by Kocci. The name Malabar means hill country. Its inhabitants originally called it Malayaṃ or Malayāḷaṃ.[21] Nowadays, Malayāḷaṃ is used to indicate the language spoken by the people of this coastal region. In the eighteenth century, Malabar was not a single political unit but comprised several small principalities and kingdoms. The most significant political units of historic Malabar were Ciṟakkal, Kannūr, Kōṭṭayaṃ (not to be confused with the town of Kōṭṭayaṃ nor the district Kōṭṭayaṃ in central Kēraḷa), Katattanāṭu, Kōḻikkōṭu and Kurumpranāṭu. Malabar as a district, created by the British, initially belonged to the Bombay Presidency and was annexed to the Madras Presidency in 1800. The British Malabar Province contained not only Malabar itself but also smaller units in Tiruvitāṃkūr, as well as the islands of Lakkadives and Minicoy. In 1802, an estimated number of 465,594 inhabitants lived in the British province of Malabar.[22]

The Ghat mountains adjoin the narrow coastal strip of Malabar in the east, running parallel to the coast at an average distance of 30 kilometres. The mean height of the mountains is 1,530 metres above sea level, with the highest peaks reaching a height of 2,440 metres. One of the most interesting formations in this mountain range is the natural opening of the massif on the plane around Pālakkāṭu in today's Middle Kēraḷa, which extends over some 25 kilometres and has thus provided a propitious connecting path for trade with the neighbouring Tamiḻnāṭu right up to the present day. The British province of Malabar reached a maximum width of roughly 110 kilometres at Pālakkāṭu, while the narrowest point, in the southern part of the Ponnāni district, barely measured 10 kilometres across. One of the best-known mountains of the West Ghats, which occupies a position off the coast, is the Ēḻimala (260 metres above sea level). The mountain lies a few kilometres to the north of Kannūr, and has served as an aid to orientation for sailors since days of old, for it could already be spotted from approximately 35 kilometres out at sea. Thus it became the landmark for Malabar. Even Marco Polo mentions the Ēḻimala, and Vasco da Gama is also said to have taken his bearings from this mountain when he landed on the Malabar coast in 1498.[23]

The connecting arteries between the mountains and the coastal land are the rivers, which run east to west from their sources in the Ghats, and flow into the Indian Ocean. The majority of rivers in Kēraḷa are shorter than 100 kilometres and carry sufficient water from the months of June to November to be navigable. The shipment of goods in a north–south direction relies on the *kāyal*s, known by the British as *backwaters*, which link the rivers together. The nature of these connections, so created to run both cross-country and north-to-south, still makes for an excellent transport system today. In pre-colonial times the network of water-routes provided an ideal basis for communication and transport between settlements.

We shall outline the most significant courses of the rivers here—moving from north to south—in order to give an idea of the extended fluvial topography in Malabar. The Nīlēśvaraṃ river actually lies partly in Dakṣiṇa Kannaḍa, but it also provides northern Malabar with water, and forms Malabar's northern border with south Karnāṭaka in certain sectors. The Ēḻimala river is roughly 50 kilometres in length and branches out in the lowlands into several river arms around Ēḻimala. The so-called *sulttāntōṭu*, the sultan's canal, connects the Ēḻimala river to the lagoon which forms the mouth of the Taḷippaṟambu and Valapaṭṭaṇaṃ rivers, both situated a little to the south of the Ēḻimala river. The canal runs roughly three kilometres in length and was constructed in 1766 on the instructions of Haidar Ali under the supervision of the Ali Rājā of Kannūr. The canal linked the Taḷippaṟambu, Valapaṭṭaṇaṃ and Ēḻimala rivers all year round.[24] The Añcarakaṇṭi river became highly important in the sixteenth century;[25] some 65 kilometres after its source, it splits into two river arms that flow round the island of Dharmaṭaṃ (Dharmapaṭṭaṇaṃ), which was fortified by the English in 1734 and 1789 respectively.[26] It was important because one could sail up the Añcarakaṇṭi river to the hinterland—into the heart of the pepper-growing area of Kōṭṭayaṃ. In Añcarakaṇṭi itself the British laid out a model garden to cultivate a number of tropical plants, including some kinds of spices.[27] Like the Añcarakaṇṭi river the Kōṭṭa river is navigable right up into the Ghats; up to Kūtiyāṭi to be precise. There the land and water routes met with the moutain pass to north Vāyanāṭu. Prior to the arrival of the British, the fort, which was located at the mouth of the Kōṭṭa river was known as a hideout for pirates.[28] Even in the dry season, the Bēppūr river is navigable up to 50 kilometres; ships with a weight of up to 300 tonnes can moor at its estuary.[29] This river provides water to extended areas in the Vāyanāṭu Ghats and Nīlagiris.[30] All these rivers connected the coast, lowlands, and Ghats well, making trade between coast and hinterland fairly easy. Today, Kēraḷa has a navigable network of water routes running more than 2,000 kilometres in length, which is still in use and represents roughly 20 per cent of the length of water routes in all of India.[31]

Since rivers alone do not make trade, let us turn to the ports. The entire stretch of coastline was actively involved in trading right up to the nineteenth century. One clear advantage enjoyed by the ports along the Malabar coast was the fact that those ports situated offshore at the level of Pālakkāṭu were connected directly to the hinterland by the aforementioned river system, where goods were both being produced and delivered. A second advantage were the *kāyal*s, stretching over more than 300 kilometres, at whose estuaries ocean-going ships could be put in. This provided an ideal network with a sufficient number of set-down points to enable trade between Indian and non-Indian merchants.

The ports located along the coastline differ from one another in their geographical features, and have been of varying importance over the centuries to the Malabar trade around the globe. Kannūr, for example, was already an active port in Roman times, known at the time as Naura. One of the most important archaeological findings of Roman coins of the time of the emperors Tiberius, Claudius, and Nero was made in Kannūr.[32] Since Kannūr was of strategic importance on the Malabar coast, the Portuguese built a fort close to the port between 1502 and 1505.[33] This fort was taken over by the British in the eighteenth century. Still in the 1880s, trade in Kannūr boomed: Logan reports an annual figure of 459,250 tonnes per transhipped total cargo for ships at anchor in the port of Kannūr. The value of the imports amounted to an approximate average of 2,144,700 rupees, with exports valued at 1,387,750 rupees.[34]

Talaśśēri's harbour provided a sheltered anchorage, that afforded ships sufficient protection even during the south-westerly monsoon. Despite the poor connection of the port with the river system into the interior of the country, the port of Talaśśēri had been an active emporium since the sixteenth century.[35] The old trading port of Dharmaṭaṃ would have been better suited to this purpose, but the British preferred to trade from Talaśśēri because the port in Dharmaṭaṃ had been the subject of dispute with three local rulers since the beginning of the eighteenth century. The British chose Talaśśēri as the centre point for the pepper trade, a market which they strove to control. Indeed, Talaśśēri was considered one of the principal trading bases for the East India Company right up to 1792. In the 1880s, the mean value of imports effected there amounted to 4,263,270 rupees, with rice and salt as the most frequently imported goods; the mean value of exports totalled 7,305,700 rupees—pepper and coffee being the most important exports. The transhipped total cargo for ships at anchor in Talaśśēri amounted to an average of 601,400 tonnes per annum.[36] The small town Mayyaḻi is situated a few kilometres south of Talaśśēri, which was dominated by the French and had held an active port since the sixteenth century.

The port of Kōḻikkōṭu had been an important emporium for goods since ancient times—according to Logan, Kōḻikkōṭu's popularity had been on the increase since the eleventh century. However, it steadily decreased in importance after the arrival of the Portuguese. Nor did the era of British rule see any complete recovery from the port's demise, which could be put down in the main to the more attractive location of Kocci and the preferential treatment it received from the Portuguese, the Dutch, and later from the British. Nevertheless, in the 1880s, Kōḻikkōṭu was considered to be one of the largest ports in the Madras Presidency. At that time, the annual transhipment tonnage in the port of Kōḻikkōṭu amounted to approximately 902,100 tonnes. The mean value of imports, consisting primarily of cereals, salt and packaged goods, totalled 6,843,000 rupees. The mean value of exports amounted to 14,437,600 rupees; exports were composed chiefly of coffee, pepper, teak and ginger.[37]

The port of Bēppūr, situated to the south of Kōḻikkōṭu, was established by Ṭippu Sulttān. Previously, the port of Caliyaṃ, located on the opposite bank, had occupied the prominent position at the estuary of the Bēppūr river up into the seventeenth century. The port of Bēppūr was favourably connected to the hinterland by the Bēppūr river, on which wood for shipbuilding was floated from the forests to the coast. For a considerable period of time right up until the final takeover of administration by the British, this was the shipbuilding centre of Malabar.

Let us now turn our attention to on-land transport connections. There is every probability that roads, in the European sense, were scarcely to be found in Malabar in the olden days since 'the climate, the physical character of the country, and, in most places, the nature of the road materials are all unfavourable to road-making in Malabar'.[38] Road-building was not accorded any real urgency either, because an excellent transport system already existed over water, which ensured that settlements and trading centres were connected to one another. Consequently, there was a markedly low number of roads; those that existed were primarily intended for pedestrian traffic and less for transports made by cattle wagon or the like.[39] Thus, the transport of goods on land was a complicated affair, and additionally the danger posed by bandits when using such a means of transport, plus the dangers of political instability in certain regions, were too great to be risked.[40]

Road-building on a bigger scale only began in Malabar with the invasions of Haidar Ali and Ṭippu Sulttān. All of the Maisūrian rulers' road-building projects intersected at Śrīraṅgapaṭṭaṇaṃ; from there, the roads also led to Kēraḷa, which helped to bring the army to its destinations. The following roads in Malabar were apparently built by Ṭippu: Malapuraṃ–Tamaraśśēri, Kōḻikkōṭu–Tamaraśśēri, Fārūkhābād–Kōyamputtūr, Pālakkāṭu–Tiṇṭukal, Veṅkatakōṭṭa–Kōyamputtūr.[41] In the Ghats, it had been necessary to construct passes on the routes in areas that were difficult to access and that had to be crossed on the journey from Maisūr to Malabar. Thus, it also became possible for the army and baggage supply trains to travel through the passes of Pēriya, Tamaraśśēri and Karikkūr.[42] These roads, which had been planned and the majority of which had been built by Ṭippu Sulttān, were taken up by the British once they had gained an administrative foothold in Malabar in 1792. From the Europeans' point of view the scarcity of roads was a hindrance to their taking possession of the whole country. Besides the lack of roads, locomotion and transport were obstructed further by the fact that more than two-thirds of the land surface in northern Malabar was covered by forests at the end of the eighteenth century.[43] These forests constituted an obstacle to 'extensive rule' for British EIC staff and officers and, at the same time, provided opponents of the British with ideal conditions for hiding-places and ambushes.

The limited size of Malabar in geographical terms and in its associated scope for action, produced a corresponding effect on the economic, social and religious structures of the country. This also influenced the range and intensity of power exerted by a ruler. The ecology of rule in eighteenth-century Malabar is depicted thus: the range of a prince's power was restricted to a relatively small area by geographical factors, such as the Ghats and the course of rivers, but the intensity of his power was generally high within this area. The limited size and relative isolation made it possible for pre-colonial structures in Malabar to be preserved, and was thus well suited to small units of power. As a consequence, the rulers had largely a free hand in matters political and economic and were thus independent de facto. This marked a fundamental difference between Malabar and the east coast and the north of India, where large alluvial land levels supported a ruler's dominance with sizeable resources.

Pre-colonial Social Order

During the eighteenth century, the social, administrative, ritual and family structures of society were closely interconnected. The stability of the Malabar social system can be explained by the absence of any great political or social pressure from outside. As long as the political stucture had been kept intact, this system proved to be adaptable enough to accommodate new social and economic influences, such as the merchants coming in from Arabic countries and Jews settling on the Malabar coast. Eventually the system began to break down during the eighteenth century in the transition from local to colonial rule.

The basic institutions of pre-colonial social order were family groups, which regulated affairs within the villages and districts of a principality. The administrative units in Malabar, and thus in Kōṭṭayaṃ, were usually run by a number of Nāyar families, whose position in society marked them as the dominant group.[44] Numerically speaking, they also constituted the largest group in the population.[45] Many Nāyars, who had taken on functions in local institutions or a higher position, no longer referred to themselves as Nāyar but as Sāmanta. *Sāmanta* had originally been a title that the king bestowed upon Nāyars of outstanding merit. Over the centuries, however, the title developed into a caste name.[46] Besides them, there were Nampūtiris, the Kēraḷa Brahmins, who lived together in patrilineal family groups[47] and who were responsible for temple duties. In their role as landowners, they were often closely linked to the Nāyars by land-leasing. The Māppiḷḷas constituted an important section of the population; they were Arab merchants who settled in Malabar in the seventh century. It was the Nāyars, along with the Sāmantas and the Nampūtiris, who exerted the most notable influence within the pre-colonial social order. Since it was primarily the Nāyars who adopted key positions as warriors and defenders of the ruler we shall provide a closer, more detailed look into the Nāyars' internal structure.[48] In the present study this is of special importance since the members of the royal family of Kōṭṭayaṃ, who were part of the Nāyar community, take a central position in the argument.

The Nāyars in general and also the royal family in Kōṭṭayaṃ followed the matrilineal principle of succession. The sons of the king's sister, in order of their seniority, were in line to inherit the throne irrespective of the *kōvilakaṃ* (branch of the family) they belonged to.[49] The head of the family was the eldest male, who held the position of *rājā*, whilst the three eldest members of the other kōvilakaṃs stood by him as vice-regents.[50] Kēraḷa Varmma Paḷaśśi Rājā, one of the kings under scrutiny in this study, ruled in Kōṭṭayaṃ at the end of the eighteenth century. He came from the *paṭiññāru kōvilakaṃ* (the western branch) of the royal family of Kōṭṭayaṃ, which also comprised a *kiḷakku* (eastern), a *tekku* (southern) and a *malayaṭi kōvilakaṃ* (at-the-foot-of-the-mountain branch).[51] The headquarters of the paṭiññāru kōvilakaṃ were approximately 15 kilometres away from Talaśśēri in a place called Paḷaśśi, the birthplace of the ruler Kēraḷa Varmma who added its name to his, calling himself Paḷaśśi Rājā. Paḷaśśi Rājā was probably born at the end of the 1750s or the beginning of the 1760s. His political opponent Vira Varmma of Kurumpranāṭu came from the tekku kōvilakaṃ of the Kōṭṭayaṃ family; he was a first cousin of Paḷaśśi Rājā on his mother's side, the son of his mother's sister. Vira Varmma had been adopted by the original Kurumpranāṭu Rājā after whose death he took over rule in Kurumpranāṭu. He thereby dropped out of the line of succession in Kōṭṭayaṃ.[52] The mothers of Vira Varmma and Paḷaśśi Rājā were sisters of the old Kōṭṭayaṃ Rājā, who was probably somewhere between 70 and 80 years of age by the end of the eighteenth century. Yet in spite of his old age, he was still the highest point of authority in many affairs regarding the governance of the country.

The Nāyar family groups, the *taṟavāṭu*s, usually resided in a large house situated in the centre of their landed property. Since the taṟavāṭu can be regarded as a microcosm for the macrocosm of a principality, it is of particular interest to this study to get an idea, on the one hand, of internal relations within a taṟavāṭu and, on the other hand, of the taṟavāṭu's relations with life outside the house, within the village and with regard to larger administrative units. The taṟavāṭus were run by the eldest, male member of a family, the *kāraṇavar*, who had the responsibility to see that the prescribed religious ceremonies of the taṟavāṭu were carried out.[53] Where it was not possible for any male member to regulate the affairs of the taṟavāṭu it was left to the eldest female of the house, the *kāraṇavarti*, to take over responsibility.[54]

The ownership of the taṟavāṭu was a joint property in the name of its female members. Leasing or selling was only possible when all members agreed upon it. Such decisions were made in the *taṟakūṭṭaṃ* (see below), in which all members of the taṟavāṭu were entitled to vote, including the women.[55] Since taṟavāṭus constituted independent, economic units,[56] this style of joint organization enabled the ownership of a taṟavāṭu to be retained in times of war when the men went into battle. Within certain limits, men and women alike had the right to carry out 'private' business that was unrelated to their joint ownership. The taṟavāṭu distinguished itself as an economic factor through purchases and sales, and also through cultivation of land. Where property was to be sold, not only the right to cultivate land could be put up for sale but also titles associated with the land, such as water rights or ritual authority.[57]

When speaking of the connection of land property and ownership in a taṟavāṭu, the anthropologist Melinda Moore refers to a 'house-and-land unit'.[58] This term expresses appropriately the unit comprised by the economic and social connections within the taṟavāṭu. In the event of a taṟavāṭu being divided up, the 'house-and-land unit' was split up into equal parts in the newly formed taṟavāṭu branches.[59] The new branches, called *tāvaḻis*, were each set up by a woman with a male relative, such as her brother, her husband or her children under the condition that a woman shared in the setting up of the tāvaḻi since she had the nominal rights to land and property.[60] A further possibility existed whereby a woman could start a tāvaḻi and still retain her rights to the 'house-and-land unit' of the original taṟavāṭu.[61] It also made no difference towards inheritance whether the woman had set up the new taṟavāṭu with her brother, husband, or children since the inheritance of property took the maternal line. This right of inheritance is known as *marumakkattāyaṃ*, which literally means 'sister's son's inheritance'.[62] According to Moore, this compound word can be derived etymologically in two ways: firstly from *marumakan* and *dāyaṃ*—'sister's son' and 'gift', and secondly from marumakan and *āyaṃ*—'sister's son' and 'property'. The same derivation applies equally to *makkattāyaṃ*, the inheritance that takes the paternal line. Both etymologies indicate that these terms are used in Malayāḷaṃ to express inheritance regulations and not family relationships. This in itself suggests that a taṟavāṭu was regarded as an economic unit within which the members shared certain family relationships with one other and that contrary to the interpretation of this term by Fuller and Gough, it was not a purely genealogical classification.[63]

Besides the economic aspect, the ritual aspect of the taṟavāṭu unit is accorded great importance: the rites of passage, and the annually recurring sowing and harvesting festivals took place within the framework of the family. The taṟavāṭu thus served a plethora of functions that affected every aspect of life. The studies by Moore and Arunima show that a taṟavāṭu stood out on account of the great diversity of its functions, that the house which belonged to the taṟavāṭu was its centre, and that the family could adapt itself flexibly to new situations.[64]

Looking more closely at the role of women within the taṟavāṭu, we get the following picture: Although it was possible for a woman to occupy an eminent position within the framework of the family group—for example, as a founder and testatrix of a taṟavāṭu—she rarely held an important position outside of the taṟavāṭu. Public posts were occupied mostly by men, for example the post of the kāraṇavar. A prominent exception to this rule was the Bibi (queen) of Kannūr, who controlled the destiny of the ruling family in Kannūr at the end of the eighteenth century.[65]

Another distinctive feature of the Nāyars was their military training.[66] It was common for all children, girls included, to be trained in the art of fencing, *kaḷarippayaṟṟu* in the *kaḷari*s [67] from the age of seven. The children were also taught reading and writing. Their military skills put the Nāyars in the position to defend themselves if threatened, and to assert their claim to titles and honours, if necessary, by force; they were thus able to defend their practically incontestable position in society. With this training, the Nāyars gained the requisite knowledge to carry out the tasks that the king envisaged for them. In the *Kēraḷōlpaṭṭi*,[68] a historical narrative, these are the elements assimilated from Malabar heroic ballads, called 'the hand', 'the eye' or 'the order', and are described as follows: The Nāyars were charged with protecting the civilian population against enemies ('hand'), supervising the *kāṇaṃ* ('eye'), and with collecting the share of the rājā's profits as tax ('order'). A certain potential for conflict was inherent amongst the Nāyars on account of their military training and the relatively great extent to which they had the right to share in decisions, and it was possible for clashes to occur.

Attention can now be turned to the public institutions of pre-colonial Malabar society. The *taṟakūṭṭaṃ*, the assembly of the kāraṇavar, stood at the head of a *taṟa*, i.e. a group of taṟavāṭus. There the guidelines for local social, economic and political affairs were discussed and decided upon.[69] The political body up from the taṟa was the village, *dēśaṃ*. At its head stood the *dēśavāḻi*, the village elder. It was his responsibility to monitor the civilian, military and religious affairs of the village, and he was therefore the most powerful man in the village.[70] Among many other tasks, he conducted the ceremonies of the village shrine and managed the village's respective estates, he commanded the defence of the village, and also gave out police orders.[71] In this way the dēśavāḻi was an important person, being present at all the main functions of the locality.

Two or more dēśaṃs constituted a *nāṭu*, a kind of district or small province. At the head of the nāṭu was the *nāṭṭukūṭṭaṃ*, which was formed by representatives of the villages and chaired by the *nāṭuvāḻi*.[72] The responsibilities of the nāṭuvāḻi were similar to those of the dēśavāḻi, albeit at a higher level, and included the collection of the rājā's share of profits in the harvest, and the command of his nāṭu's army, which was raised in the event of war. His status thus lay somewhere between that of the dēśavāḷi and the rājā. Indeed he was entitled to a small share of the rājā's tax. Yet while dēśavāḷi and nāṭuvāḷi occupied important positions within the aforementioned assemblies, they were not able to act without the consent of their respective assembly. In this respect, the interdependence between those who had functions to perform and society itself is reflected; an interdependence that also bound the rājā to the top-level associations (see below).

Above the nāṭṭukūṭṭaṃ was the *Malabarkūṭṭaṃ*, the assembly of rājās. Since no mahārājā had ruled in Kēraḷa since the ninth century, the Malabarkūṭṭaṃ sat under the chairmanship of one of the rulers—from the thirteenth century, this was customarily the Tāmūtiri of Kōḻikkōṭu. Provided that there were not any extraordinary affairs to be discussed, the association of rājās convened every twelve years during the Mahāmakhaṃ festival in Tirunāvāya in southern Malabar. Affairs that had implications for the whole of Malabar were discussed and decided upon here. In 1743 the Malabarkūṭṭaṃ obviously convened for the last time. It seems most likely that any subsequent assemblies came to an end in the turbulence of the second half of the century.[73]

Despite the fact that it did not occupy the highest level of the kūṭṭaṃ, it was the nāṭṭukūṭṭaṃ which formed the highest point of authority within the hierarchy. According to the *Kēraḷōlpaṭṭi*, the nāṭṭukūṭṭaṃ had been established originally by Brahmins as a monitoring body for the rājā so as to put a quick stop to the theoretically conceivable scenario of a rājā pursuing a 'despotic' way of rule. Thus, it was to this assembly that the rājā himself was accountable, and to whose decisions he was bound.[74] In this way, the kūṭṭaṃ formed an opposite or corrective pole to royal decisions, which meant that, as a rule, the rājā was not able to make decisions without first obtaining sanction from the kūṭṭaṃ. The rulers did not have absolute power to control the activities of people under them; they had to look for the help of local chieftains to enforce their authority. Taking into account the relatively great extent to which Nāyars present in the nāṭṭukūṭṭaṃ enjoyed the right to share in decision-making, the rājā depended strongly on having loyal Nāyars in the area over which he ruled.

The apparently pyramidal structure of the country's government gives the initial impression that a high level of involvement by the population would be guaranteed. Yet we have to keep in mind the fact that 'only' the Nampūtiris and the Nāyars participated in the assemblies, with the remaining village population not involved in decisions of great consequence in any way at all. Various historians are often keen to use the term 'democracy' where there is an absence of a central authority in the social structure and where associations exist that enjoy a certain degree of participation in decision-making. This interpretation, however, gives the reader the wrong impression. The Nāyars, who constituted a clear counterbalance to the ruler thanks to their extensive numbers in the assemblies and also their military training, were particularly well represented within the democratic elements. This ultimately meant that the rājā depended upon the good will of the representatives of the different assemblies.

In this sense, Palaśśi Rājā had to rely upon the consent of the nāṭṭukūṭṭaṃ, should he have wanted to carry through reforms in Kōṭṭayaṃ. The Malabar-kūṭṭaṃ, which was made up of the Bibi of Kannūr, the Rājā of Ciṟakkal, and Vira Varmma of Kurumpranāṭu among others, decided on the fortune of the Malabar region. From the above account it becomes clear that relatively autonomous structures had developed due to Malabar's limited size, structures signifying a high degree of participation in the decisions of the rājā for a certain section of the population.

Pre-colonial Land Law

The following section will focus on the most important elements of pre-colonial land law in Malabar. This will provide us with the necessary background in the economic situation to assess the changes resulting from the establishment of British colonial administration as fundamental interventions in the society's structure. The outline will also enable us to recognize the conflicts that arose subsequently as a problem of two cultures coming into contact with one another. We shall see that the conflict was inevitable, since the structure of their respective political, economic and social contexts were formed in completely different ways. The sources of friction and the differences between the Malabar-Indian and the Anglo-Saxon parties become particularly apparent in respect to the land law.

Pre-colonial land law in Kēraḷa was either termed *janmakāran-kuṭiyān-sampradāyan* or *janmaṃ-kāṇaṃ-maryyāda*. The first term refers to the relationship between landlord and tenant, the second to the relationship of the rights and obligations of the landlord with those of the tenant. Any explanation of their characteristics depends on how one interprets the terms *janmakāran*, proprietor or landlord, *kuṭiyān*, farmer or tenant, and *maryyāda*, rules and customs of society. In 1856, the proceedings of the Sadr Adalat in Madras stated that there were no less than 24 different kinds of land lease in Malabar—there were reported to have been over 100 kinds in Tiruvitāṃkūr.[75] For the purposes of this study, it will suffice to present the basic forms of land lease in order to provide the reader with an overview of the socio-economic conditions in Malabar, which were associated with the land law.

Janmaṃ[76] denoted the piece of land which was inherited by birth from ancestors, and on which no payments were levied by the rājā at all.[77] The janmakāran was entitled to sell or retain the land as he desired, thus he could 'lose' it if he handed it over or sold it to another person. He could offer his services to a rājā, a temple, or to the mahārājā provided that he considered homage to these persons or bodies to be appropriate on political and/or economic grounds. It was also possible for him to gain additional land by paying rent or charges, but this land was taken into separate consideration to that of janmaṃ. In his report to the Board of Revenue for 1801, the British official Thomas Warden estimated a figure of 44,378 for the the total number of estates in Malabar identified as janmaṃ.[78]

The question of ownership of janmaṃ still raises a number of controversies within the academic debate, as the janmaṃ is the key element to understand pre-colonial land law. Geneviève Lemercinier endorses the opinion of Francis Buchanan, who states that only Nampūtiris would have owned janmaṃ and that they leased it as kāṇaṃ (see below) to Nāyar families. These families did not always farm the land themselves but leased it on to farmers or to employed workers on their fields.[79] Alexander Walker, a salaried employee of the EIC, refers in his report explicitly to the fact that anyone who had a sufficient amount of money available was able to gain ownership of janmaṃ.[80] Innes and Evans also emphasize that the Nāyars could be both owners of land (janmakāran) as well as leaseholders (*kāṇakkāran*): '[...] the janmis, who then included Māppiḷḷas, Tiyans and Mukkuvans in their number as well as Nāyars and Brahmans, as being in fact in the position of landlords, and the kanamdars in the position of tenants, [...].'[81]

An interesting interpretation is made by Kathleen Gough, who claims that one could sell freely not only the rights of janmaṃ but also those of kāṇaṃ. The local kūṭṭaṃ had to give its consent to a transaction before it could be considered legally binding. Thus a kāṇakkāran could not be forced into giving up his kāṇaṃ as long as he had the kūṭṭaṃ on his side. According to Gough, it was not unusual in northern Malabar for Nāyars both to own land and to farm it themselves, and thus to be scarcely dependent on landowning Nampūtiris at all.[82] This view, however, openly contradicts Lemercinier's stance, which subjects the categories of land law to a one-dimensional division. Yet this one-dimensionality does not do justice to the complex contexts and mutual dependencies which are characteristic of pre-colonial land law in Malabar. To exemplify the many different forms that the system could incorporate, it is worth mentioning that Nampūtiris frequently had the function of the janmakāran but that this was certainly not always the case. Nāyars could adopt the role of a landowner as well as that of a farmer.[83]

However, the decisive element within the land law of eighteenth-century

Malabar was not landownership, but land lease. Cultivable land was leased in two ways: firstly, by the kāṇaṃ; secondly, by the *vērumpāṭṭaṃ*, which was a temporary lease without any right to ownership and which was granted to a farmer by a kāṇakkāran—or, mainly in the north of Malabar, directly by the janmakāran—for the cultivation of the land.[84]

In Malabar, the kāṇaṃ was the most common form of land right that was defined by land law. Initially, it was mainly the Nāyars whose task it had been to take charge of the land. In course of time, the kāṇaṃ, the right of supervision had turned into a form of factual ownership. In the eighteenth century, the kāṇaṃ could be compared to a mortgage: the land still remained redeemable for the janmakāran, who repaid the money which he had received originally from the kāṇakkāran as a security for his land.[85] The durations of leases, restricted to twelve months from the fifteenth to the seventeenth century, apparently increased up to a period of forty-eight years in the eighteenth century; in some cases they were lifelong agreements.[86]

Besides the different forms of land law, there were also various taxes. The *pāṭṭaṃ* was the share of the yield that had to be handed over to the respective janmakāran. It was to some extent comparable to the tithe in medieval Europe. The pāṭṭaṃ was collected by the Nāyars either in natural produce, cash, or a mixture of the two. As a rule, the pāṭṭaṃ was made up of a fifth of the harvest going to the janmakāran, or of a combination of a tenth to the janmakāran and a tenth to the rājā.[87] The top rate of pāṭṭaṃ could amount to a third of the yield.[88] From around the thirteenth century, an increasing number of estates were given to temples as *dēvasvaṃ*, temple property, in order to avoid paying such a high level of tax—this resulted in the tax burden being decreased to a sixth or an eighth of the yield.[89] Yet according to the report of the Malabar Land Tenures Committee, no pāṭṭaṃ was collected from land belonging to temples.[90] It is unlikely that these contradictory statements about land owned by temples can ever be fully resolved, since the sources which would be required to make a clear reconstruction of the situation do not exist any more.

At times when janmakārans experienced a shortage of cash, it was common for them to borrow this money from their respective kāṇakkārans.[91] To redeem the borrowed sum of money, the kāṇakkāran deducted this sum plus the interest rate incurred from the janmakāran's pāṭṭaṃ from the pāṭṭaṃ that he himself owed. This could also be paid back in instalments for which the interest was fixed at certain rates. To ensure that the janmakāran could receive any share of the yield at all, in some cases only the interest on the amount borrowed was paid off by fixed methods of repayment.[92] If the interest rate for the amount borrowed had become so high that the entire share of the janmakāran's yield (pāṭṭaṃ) was used up in the repayment, then the kāṇakkāran's share or demand for interest on the janmakāran's land (which the kāṇakkāran had leased originally, and which was intended to be his security against the janmakāran) was handed over as *oṭi*[93] to the ownership of the kāṇakkāran. Nevertheless, in losing his share of the yield, the janmakāran had not lost everything he owned, since, besides the share of production, he was also entitled to legal titles and honours, *sthānamānaṅṅaḷ*, which were closely connected to his land.[94] Such titles and honours included water rights and bondmen who worked on the land. Counted among such people were the Cērumārs and Pulayārs, who worked mainly in agriculture. It was seemingly less common to see bondsmen in northern Malabar than in the south of Kēraḷa.[95]

The transfer of the sthānamānaṅṅaḷ in parts was used towards the repayment of debt. If the janmakāran wanted to reoccupy the oṭi which the kāṇakkāran had claimed from him, he had three possibilities which were graded by scale: Firstly, the *oṭṭikuṃ purameyullakāṇaṃ*,[96] a mortgage, with the aid of which the janmakāran borrowed 10 per cent or more of the amount received from the kāṇakkāran for the right to the oṭi; secondly, the *nīrmutal*,[97] which enabled the janmakāran to borrow an additional 10 per cent of the money which he had already received for the rights to the oṭi and *oṭṭipuraṃ*.[98] He thereby undertook to transfer the water right to his creditors. Thirdly, the *janmappaṇayaṃ* or the pawning of the rights of the janmaṃ, and the settlement of another advance payment—in addition to the amount of money already borrowed. Once he had exhausted all these options, the janmakāran's only choice was to give up the very right to be janmakāran, which involved the transfer of all sthānamānaṅṅaḷ.[99] *Janmanīr* denoted the complete loss of janmaṃ and its associated rights.

This meant in practice that a janmakāran first mortgaged his own share of the yield up to the full value. As soon as this was used up, he was forced to pay the interest from his resources of legal titles and other symbolic entities of authority. It was important that the janmakāran did not actually mortgage the ground itself, but only his share of the yield and, in emergencies, parts of the sthānamānaṅṅaḷ, on which his status as a janmakāran was based. The land itself changed owners only very rarely. The British did not take these facts into account when they made a close inspection of their acquired provinces and changed the existing structures at their own discretion. They assumed that the Malabar janmakāran would correspond to the concept of the Roman dominus in matters relating to his ownership, rights and responsibilities. Thus a significant area of conflict between the British and the Malayalis was already imminent.

The size of the advance which the kāṇakkāran granted to the janmakāran was determined at regular intervals, meaning that it was usually revised with each new generation. Either 13 per cent of the advance was discounted and a new document was made out with the credit reduced by this percentage, or the janmakāran presented a sum of money to the kāṇakkāran which corresponded to the 13 per cent discount, and the original document was confirmed. The latter method was more beneficial to the kāṇakkāran since, contrary to the former method, the mortgage for the issued 13 per cent remained intact. Such a revision to the contract was, therefore, usually applicable. The renewal charge received in this case by the janmakāran constituted one of the regular sources of income for the king in his function as a janmakāran. The logic behind the revision was to exempt the share of the janmakāran's yield from the mortgage in regular instalments, something which redounded to the janmakāran's and kāṇakkāran's advantage.[100] This method of leasing the land placed the janmakāran and kāṇakkāran in a fruitful and mutual relationship of dependence: 'The system was admirably conceived for binding the two classes together in harmonious interdependence.'[101] The historian Ganesh describes the mutual dependency of the two classes as a dichotomy. On the one hand there was the janmakāran, who held the traditional rights of ownership including the ritual authorities, and on the other side was the kāṇakkāran, the one who really exercised control of the land. Although this state of affairs might suggest a conflict of interests, Ganesh also comes to the conclusion that this dichotomy existed for the mutual benefit of all those involved.[102]

Another method of dividing up the yield was *kuḻikkāṇaṃ,* which applied to the development of jungle land into cultivated farm land. The farmer (*kuṭiyān* or *pāṭṭaṃkār*) who cultivated the land had to pay a particular amount to the janmakāran once a certain number of years had elapsed, usually twelve years after he had started to farm. Up to that point, the kuṭiyān received the entire yield of the land which he had recently put to plough, with the exception of a symbolic amount from the first harvest which he handed over to the janmakāran as kuḻikkāṇaṃ. Once the appointed time period had elapsed, the janmakāran could collect the pāṭṭaṃ, i.e. the rent, from this new land by giving the kuṭiyān a redemption fee for the land. Usually, however, no money was actually handed over, and the janmakāran instead received over the years a smaller amount of pāṭṭaṃ than the amount to which he would otherwise be entitled from this land.[103] The problem of the redemption fee was resolved in this way. Since Malabar was home to hilly and in parts impassable terrain, conditions for cultivating the land were fraught with difficulties. In Kōṭṭayaṃ, for example, only 21 per cent of the land surface was cultivated at the beginning of the twentieth century; in Vāyanāṭu it was even less: viz. 12 per cent.[104]

Thus the cultivation of land and the associated leasing rights were of the utmost importance to the agrarian development of the country, and especially to the additional acquisition of farmland.

The conditions and forms of the lease depended upon the established traditions and laws for the respective region. The rights of the janmakāran to the land and the responsibilites of the leaseholders were laid down by the maryyāda—there were many locally differing variations of the maryyāda. The economic authority of the landholding group also expressed itself in its political authority. This meant that the janmakārans and kāṇakkārans were often charged with public functions, such as the post of dēśavāḻi or nāṭuvāḻi, and thereby carried a corresponding amount of weight in politics. Contrarily, the kuṭiyāns had fewer chances to have their say on account of their status. The kuṭiyāns could be both leaseholders of land who had their land cultivated by others and simple farmers.[105]

Originally, there had not been any land revenue in Malabar in the sense of extensive tax payment made by all inhabitants of the country.[106] The rājā therefore had to draw his income from different sources, including his janmaṃ, *cuṅkaṃ* (toll route), mint duties, fines for criminal activites, as well as from property by intestates and confiscated goods. Nobody could adopt an heir without the rājā's consent—in order to receive the king's blessing it was possible to pay him for the permission to adopt. In addition, he received presents from his subjects on the main public holidays and at festival times, most of all at Oṅaṃ and Viṣu, and he enjoyed prerogatives over gold, elephants, ivory and teak.[107] The king also received particular kinds of animals, for example cows with three or five teats.[108]

> [...] those Raja's rights in general did not then extend to the exaction of any regular settled or fixed revenue from their subjects; [...] and the Rajas held also large domains of their own, which, with the Customs on Trade and Mint duties, might have been sufficient for the maintenance of their ordinary state; [...][109]

Probably due to the geophysical situation in northern Malabar, the different ways of leasing land were not marked by such a great degree of differentiation as those in southern Malabar. Furthermore, the forms of ownership and control were less dynamic. Overseas trade did indeed contribute to an increase in a ruler's resources, as exemplified by the rulers of Kannūr and Kōḻikkōṭu, but a transformation in the agrarian structure could not be prompted in this way.[110] Here I have again to point to the specific features of the narrow, hilly landscape of Malabar due to which the described forms of economic patterns evolved, in turn influencing the kind of governance exerted over the country by the rulers. The relatively intense power of the traditionally divided authorities only began to decrease with the invasions in the mid-eighteenth century by

Haidar Ali and Ṭippu Sulttān, whose policies resulted in heavy and unequally distributed taxes for the population in Malabar.

With this overview of the pre-colonial social order and economic conditions, the political and social background in Kōṭṭayaṃ can now be discussed. In Chapter Two, attention will be primarily focused on Kōṭṭayaṃ's network of temples which constituted one of the foundations and modes of legitimation of the Malabar rājās' rule. The model of the *little kingdom* will be critically examined as will the model of the *contact zone*; these will be considered in relation to the situation in Malabar and will provide an analytical framework for the events that occured in the eighteenth century. The subject of Chapter Three will be the foreign policy relations that were cultivated by Malabar before and during the eighteenth century, and what consequences these had for the long-term prospects of Malabar's development. Chapter Four will deal with the administrative measures that were introduced by the British after they seized power, and the subsequently varying reactions of the local rājās, which exhibited a wide range of patterns of conduct from cooperation at the one extreme through to active resistance at the other. Chapter Five will be used to discern whether any modifications are required in the case of Malabar when applying the models of the *little kingdom* and the *contact zone*. The conclusions of the study will be summarized in Chapter Six.

NOTES

1. For example, in a letter by Hermann Gundert to his parents, dated 18.11.1838, Deutsches Literaturarchiv Marbach, A: Hesse-Gundert, and in his travel journal dated 24.1.–10.2.1839 to the Committee of the Basel Mission, Archives of the Basel Mission, regional acts C-1.

2. Said, Edward W., *Orientalism*, New York, 1979.

3. Dirks, Nicholas B., *Castes of Mind: Colonialism and the Making of Modern India,* Princeton, 2001. He claims to have gone 'much further than Said'. Ibid., p. 304.

4. Furber, Holden, 'Asia and the West as Partners before "Empire" and After', *JAS* 28,4 (1969), pp. 711–21.

5. Irschick, Eugene, *Dialogue and History: Constructing South India, 1795–1895*, Berkeley and Los Angeles, 1994.

6. Bayly, Christopher A., *Empire and Information: Intelligence Gathering and Social Communication in India,* 1780–1870, Cambridge, 1996 (Cambridge Studies in Indian History and Society 1).

7. Subrahmanyam, Sanjay, *The Political Economy of Commerce: Southern India 1500–1650*, Cambridge 1990 (Cambridge South Asian Studies 45), pp. 252–4.

8. Subrahmanyam, Sanjay, *Penumbral Visions: Making Polities in Early Modern South India*, New Delhi, 2001, pp. 186–219.

9. Pratt, Mary Louise, *Imperial Eyes: Travel Writing and Transculturation,*

London and New York, 1992. Also see her article 'Linguistic Utopias', in: Nigel Fabb et al. (eds.), *The Linguistics of Writings: Arguments Between Language and Literature*, Manchester, 1987, pp. 48–66.

10. Dirks, Nicholas B., *The Hollow Crown: Ethnohistory of an Indian Kingdom*, Ann Arbor, 2nd edn., 1993. Berkemer, Georg, *Little Kingdoms in Kalinga: Ideologie, Legitimation und Politik regionaler Eliten,* Stuttgart, 1993 (Beiträge zur Südasienforschung 156). Schnepel, Burkhard, *Die Dschungelkönige: Ethnohistorische Aspekte von Politik und Ritual in Südorissa/Indien*, Stuttgart, 1997 (Beiträge zur Südasienforschung 177). In Chapter 1, Schnepel provides an overview based on the historical theory of the model of the *little kingdom* and on the state in India. Schnepel, *Die Dschungelkönige*, pp. 13–73.

11. Logan, William, *Malabar*, 2 vols., Madras, 1887, reprint New Delhi and Madras, 1989.

12. Menon, K.P. Padmanabha, *History of Kerala: Written in the Form of Notes on Visscher's Letters from Malabar,* 4 vols., reprint New Delhi and Madras, 1989.

13. For example, Leela Devi, Rangaswami Pillai, *History of Kerala,* Kottayam, 1986; Menon, A. Sreedhara, *A Survey of Kerala History,* Madras, 1988; idem, *Kerala History and its Makers,* Madras, 2nd edn., 1990; Gangadharan, T.K., *Kerala History,* Calicut s.a.

14. Kareem, C.K., *Kerala under Haidar Ali and Tipu Sultan,* Ernakulam, 1973; Rajendran, N., *Establishment of British Power in Malabar* (*1664 to 1799*), Allahabad, 1979. Further there is an unpublished dissertation on the establishment of British rule in Malabar, whose main focus is the representation of the history of events, and a comparison with the establishment of British colonial power in Africa. Swai, Bonaventure, 'The British in Malabar, 1792–1806', unpublished dissertation, University of Sussex, 1974.

15. Baden-Powell, B.H., *The Land-Systems of British India: Being a Manual of the Land-Tenures and of the Systems of Land-Revenue Administration Prevalent in the Several Provinces,* 3 vols., Oxford, 1892, reprint Delhi, 1988, vol. 1, p. 95. Ganesh, K.N., 'Ownership and Control of Land in Medieval Kerala. Janmam-Kanam Relations During the 16th–18th Centuries', *IESHR* 28,3 (1991), pp. 299–323.

16. Kumar, Dharma, *Land and Caste in South India: Agricultural Labour in the Madras Presidency During the 19h Century*, Cambridge, 1965, reprint New Delhi, 1992; Verghese, T.C., *Agrarian Change and Economic Consequences: Land Tenures in Kerala 1850–1960*, Bombay et al., 1970.

17. Fuller, Christopher J., *The Nayars Today,* Cambridge, 1976; Moore, Melinda A., 'A New Look at the Nayar Taravad', *Man* (n.s.) 20 (1985), pp. 523–41; Mencher, Joan P., 'Namboodiri Brahmins: An Analysis of a Traditional Elite in Kerala', *JAAS* 1 (1966), pp. 183–96; Mencher, Joan P. and Goldberg, Helen, 'Kinship and Marriage Regulations Amongst the Namboodiri Brahmans of Kerala', *Man* (n.s.) 2 (1967), pp. 87–106. Dale, Stephen Frederic, *Islamic Society on the South Asian Frontier: The Māppiḷas of Malabar 1498–1922*, Oxford, 1980; Miller, Roland E., *Mappila Muslims of Kerala: A Study in Islamic Trends,* 2nd, ext. edn., Hyderabad, 1990.

18. De Lannoy, Mark, *The Kulasekhara Perumals of Travancore: History and State Formation in Travacore from 1671 to 1758*, Leiden, 1997.

19. Mukherjee and Frykenberg also stress the ecological and social characteristics of Malabar, which differ fundamentally from other provinces of the Madras Presidency. Mukherjee, Nilmani and Frykenberg, Robert E., 'The Ryotwari System and Social Organization in the Madras Presidency', in: Robert E. Frykenberg (ed.), *Land Control and Social Structure in Indian History*, Madison and London, 1969, pp. 217–26, p. 218.

20. Northern Malabar differs from southern Malabar in various political and cultural structures; the dividing line is usually given as the river Kota. Cf. Miller, Eric J., 'Caste and Territory in Malabar', *American Anthropologist* 56,1 (1954), pp. 410–20, p. 416.; Fuller, Christopher J., 'The Internal Structure of the Nayar Caste', *Journal of Anthropological Research* 31,4 (1975), pp. 283–312, p. 284.

21. Logan, *Malabar*, vol. 1, p. 1. Cf. also Gundert, Hermann, *A Malayalam and English Dictionary*, Mangalore, 1872, reprint Kottayam, 1992, p. 798, col. 2; p. 799, col. 2.

22. Clementson, P., *A Report on Revenue and Other Matters Connected with Malabar: Dated 31st December 1838*, Calicut, 1914, p. 3. In 1871 in Kōṭṭayaṃ, then a district of the British province of Malabar, the number of inhabitants totalled 143,761. Logan, *Malabar*, vol. 2, p. ccciv.

23. Marco Polo noted the 'kingdom of Eli'. No kingdom of this name actually existed, yet we can be sure from additional accounts that he must have meant the region surrounding the Ēḷimala. Yule, Henry and Cordier, Henri, *The Book of Ser Marco Polo,* 2 vols., Paris, 3rd edn., 1903, reprint New Delhi, 1993. In the report about Vasco da Gama's travels to India, it is noted that a mountain range north of Kōḻikkōṭu was first spotted on the Indian subcontinent. Cf. Ravenstein, E.G. (trans. and ed.), *A Journal of the First Voyage of Vasco da Gama 1497–1499*, London, 1898, reprint New Delhi and Madras, 1995, pp. 47, 198.

24. Cf. Logan, *Malabar*, vol. 1, p. 9f.

25. Cf. Deloche, Jean, *Transport and Communications in India Prior to Steam Locomotion*, 2 vols., Delhi, 1993/94 (French Studies in South Asian Culture 7), vol. 2, p. 83.

26. The first fortification of Dharmaṭaṃ by the English took place in 1734, the second after having lost and recaptured Dharmaṭaṃ in 1789. Cf. Sewell, Robert, *Lists of the Antiquarian Remains in the Presidency of Madras*, vol. 1, s.l. 1882, reprint Delhi and Varanasi s.a. (Archaeological Survey of Southern India 7), p. 243.

27. It would exceed the scope of this study to present a detailed description of the garden-grounds at Añcarakaṇṭi; they were founded in 1799 and run shortly after by Murdoch Brown (1750–1828). The treaty between the Malabar Commission and Murdoch Brown is published in Logan, William, *A Collection of Treaties, Engagements and Other Papers of Importance Relating to British Affairs in Malabar*, s.l., 2nd edn., 1891, reprint New Delhi and Madras, 1989, ii, CLIX, pp. 286–9. The plantation is described briefly in Logan, *Malabar*, vol. 1, p. 522 and Nightingale, Pamela, *Trade and Empire in Western India 1785–1806*, Cambridge, 1970 (Cambridge South Asian Studies 9), p. 102f.

28. Cf. Logan, *Malabar,* vol. 1, p. 11f. In his commentary on Periplus, Schoff assumes that southern Kanara and northern Malabar had contained pirates' dens from time immemorial right up into the nineteenth century. Schoff, Wilfried H. (transl and ed.), *The Periplus of the Eythraean Sea: Travel and Trade in the Indian Ocean by a Merchant of the First Century,* New York, 1912, reprint New Delhi, 1974, p. 203.

29. Cf. Deloche, *Transport,* vol. 2, p. 89.

30. Cf. Logan, *Malabar,* vol. 1, p. 13.

31. Cf. Singh, R.L., *India: A Regional Geography,* Varanasi, 1971, reprint Varanasi, 1998, p. 913.

32. Cf. Schoff, *Periplus,* p. 204.

33. For more information on the construction and function of Fort St. Angelo in Kannūr see Kurup, K.K.N., 'Fort St. Angelo', in: M.G.S. Narayanan and K.K.N. Kurup (eds.), *Kerala Historical Studies,* Calicut, 1976, pp. 44–6. Cf. Schoff, *Periplus,* p. 204.

34. Logan, *Malabar,* vol. 1, p. 70.

35. Cf. Deloche, *Transport,* vol. 2, p. 83.

36. Cf. Logan, *Malabar,* vol. 1, p. 70f.

37. Cf. Logan, *Malabar,* vol. 1, p. 73. Sewell also mentions the chequered history of the port in Kōḻikkōṭu. Cf. Sewell, *List of Antiquarian Remains,* p. 246.

38. Logan, *Malabar,* vol. 1, p. 62.

39. Buchanan reports: 'In Malabar even cattle are little used for the transportation of goods, which are generally carried by porters', in: Buchanan, Francis, *A Journey from Madras through the Countries of Mysore, Canara and Malabar, Performed under the Orders of the Most Noble the Marquis Wellesley, Governor General of India, etc.,* 3 vols., London 1807, vol. 2, p. 434.

40. Cf. Chaudhuri, Kirti N., *Trade and Civilisation in the Indian Ocean: An Economic History from the Rise of Islam to 1750,* Cambridge, 1985, p. 138.

41. Report by Shamnaut in: Logan, *Malabar,* vol. 1, p. 63. In the letter by the British officer responsible for the routes, the following routes are included amongst those through which artillery could be transported: from the Bēppūr river via Tanūr to Koṭuṇṇalūr (five rivers could be crossed with boats), from Tanūr via Pālakkāṭu to Kōyamputtūr. Logan, *Malabar,* vol. 1, p. 63f.

42. Cf. Deloche, *Transport*, vol. 1, p. 78.

43. Cf. Ganesh, '*Ownership*', p. 319.

44. Cf. Jeffery, Robin, *The Decline of Nair Dominance: Society and Politics in Travancore 1847–1908,* New Delhi, 2nd edn., 1994, p. xix.

45. Cf. Menon, K.P.P., *History of Kerala,* vol. 1, p. 251.

46. Cf. Gundert, *Dictionary,* pp. 1052–3, coll. 2 and 1: Head of a district, regent; Son of a Brahman by a Kśatriya mother. Cf. also Moore, Lewis, *Malabar Law and Custom, Madras,* 3rd edn., 1905, p. 423: Caste which, according to its members, lies between that of Nāyars and Nampūtiris. Contrary to this, Arunima speaks only of *sāmanta* in the context of certain Nāyars, who had been granted this title by the king as reward for their exceptional service to him. Arunima, G., 'Multiple Meanings: Changing Conceptions of Matrilineal Kinship in Nineteenth- and Twentieth-Century

Malabar', *IESHR* 33,3 (1996), pp. 283–307, p. 287. In the sphere of interstate affairs, sāmantas can be understood as neighbouring princes. Cf. Kulke, Hermann, 'Die frühmittelalterlichen Regionalreiche: Ihre Struktur und Rolle im Prozeß staatlicher Entwicklung Indiens', in: idem and Dietmar Rothermund (eds.), *Regionale Tradition in Südasien,* Wiesbaden, 1985, pp. 77–114; Gopal, Lallanji, 'Sāmanta—Its Varying Significance in Ancient India', *JRAS* 5 (1963), pp. 21–37; Gopal, Krishna Kanti, 'The Assembly of the Samantas in Early Medieaval India', *JIH* 22,1 (1964), pp. 241–50.

47. Cf. MLTMT, Ms. 77, No. 19, in: T.V. Mahalingam (ed.), *Mackenzie Manuscripts: Summaries of the Historical Manuscripts of the Mackenzie Collection*, 2 vols., Madras, 1972, vol. 1, p. 304.

48. The reader might refer to the corresponding literature for equivalent information on the other social groups. Thurston, Edgar and Rangachari, K., *Castes and Tribes of Southern India*, 7 vols., Madras, 1909.

49. Report by Alexander Dow dated 2.10.1796, in BRP, OIOC P/366/19. Other royal families in Malabar also followed the matrilineal principle of succession. Cf. MLTMT, Ms. 77, No. 9, in: Mahalingam, *Mackenzie Manuscripts,* vol. 1, p. 298.

50. Examination by P. Cantu on 25.5.1798 in Calicut, in SPP, OIOC P/380/70. Cantu reports that the government of the land was originally divided up between the four eldest women and the men. This custom was abandoned, however, over the course of the seventeenth century to the men's favour.

51. Examination by P. Cantu on 25.51798 in Kōḻikkōṭu, in SPP, OIOC P/380/70; Report by Alexander Dow dated 2.10.1796, in BRP, OIOC P/366/19. *The malayaṭi kōvilakaṃ* has died out. Information given by a descendant of the *kilakku kōvilakaṃ,* September 1998.

52. *Reports of a Joint Commission from Bengal and Bombay, Appointed to Inspect into the State and Condition of the Province of Malabar, in the Years 1792 and 1793. With the Regulations thereon Established for the Administration of that Province,* 3 vols., Bombay s.a., reprint: 2 vols., Madras 1862, § XXX, XCII. Contrary to the genealogical information given here, Dilip Menon considers Vira Varmma to be an uncle of Kēraḷa Varmma Paḷaśśi Rājā. Menon, Dilip M., 'Houses by the Sea: State Experimentation on the Southwest Coast of India 1760–1800', in: Neera Chandhoke, *Mapping Histories: Essays Presented to Ravinder Kumar*, New Delhi, 2000, pp. 161–86, p. 171.

53. Cf. Balakrishnan, P.V., *Matrilineal System in Malabar,* Kannur, 1981, p. 43.

54. Cf. Panikkar, T.K. Gopal, *Malabar and Its Folk: A Systematic Description of the Social Customs and Institutions of Malabar*, Madras, 3rd edn., 1929, p. 17; Raj, Kaleeswaram and Suchitra, K.P., *Commentaries on Marumakkathayam Law,* Payyanur, 1995, p. 27; Trautmann, Thomas R., *Dravidian Kinship*, New Delhi, 1981, p. 417. Buchanan reports of taṟavāṭus which were led in principle by women. Buchanan, *Journey*, vol. 2, p. 513.

55. Cf. Panikkar, T.K., *Malabar and its Folk,* p. 15f. The discussions on this were held in assemblies at *kāvus*, snake shrines. Iyer, L.A. Krishna, *Social History of Kerala,* 2 vols., Madras, 1970, vol. 2 (*The Dravidians*), p. 93.

56. Cf. Fuller, *The Nayars*, p. 2. See also Trautmann, *Dravidian Kinship*, p. 418f.

57. Cf. Arunima, 'Multiple Meanings', p. 291.

58. Moore, M., 'A New Look', p. 525. For more information on the function of the taṟavāṭu as a community of residence and land, cf. Moore, Melinda A., 'Taravad: House, Land and Relationship in a Matrilineal Hindu Society', unpublished dissertation, University of Chicago, 1983.

59. Cf. Panikkar, T.K., *Malabar and its Folk*, p. 15.

60. Cf. Moore, M., 'A New Look', p. 529.

61. Cf. Arunima, 'Multiple Meanings', p. 291.

62. Balakrishnan compares the taṟavāṭu with the Roman *gens*, whose fundamental difference lies in inheritance law: In the gens the line of succession followed the male side. Cf. Balakrishnan, *Matrilineal System*, p. 34.

63. Gough, Kathleen, 'The Nayar Taravad', *Journal of the M.S. University of Baroda* 1,2 (1952), pp. 1–13, p. 5. Gough, Kathleen, 'Nayar: Central Kerala', in: idem and David M. Schneider (eds.), *Matrilineal Kinship*, Berkeley and Los Angeles, 1961, pp. 298–384, pp. 323, 343. Fuller, 'Internal Structure', p. 284. Cf. also Unni, K. Raman, 'Visiting Husbands in Malabar', *Journal of the M.S. University of Baroda* 5,1 (1956), pp. 37–56, p. 40.

64. For example, the matrilineal line of succession only crystalized itself within the taṟavāṭu in the sixteenth/seventeenth centuries. Cf. Elamkulam, Kunjan Pillai, *Studies in Kerala History*, Kottayam, 1970, pp. 292–323. Possibilities to develop further were also taken in the eighteenth century, cf. Fuller, 'Internal Structure', p. 303; Moore, 'A New Look', p. 525f. and Arunima, 'Multiple Meanings', p. 289. Miller, on the other hand, regards the eighteenth century as a relatively static period. Miller, E.J., 'Caste and Territory', p. 412. This thesis is not tenable, since it was precisely in the eighteenth century, through the frequent conflicts with foreign powers, that the flexibility of the people and their social structures was challenged and changed. For more information on the revolutions of the eighteenth century, cf. Bayly, Susan, 'Hindu Kingship and the Origin of Community: Religion, State and Society in Kerala, 1750–1850', *MAS* 18,2 (1984), p. 177–213, p. 177f.

65. Cf. Arunima, 'Multiple Meanings', p. 292. For literature on the Bibi see: Logan, *Malabar*, vol. 1, pp. 442–4, 464–71; Buchanan, *Journey*, vol. 2, pp. 553–5. The rule of Bibi goes far to disprove Mayer's thesis that no women were regents: Mayer, Adrian C., 'Rulership and Divinity: The Case of the Modern Hindu Prince and Beyond', *MAS* 25,4 (1991), pp. 765–90, p. 765.

66. Cf. Fuller, *The Nayars*, p. 1.

67. Details are given in Zarrilli, Phillip B., *When the Body Becomes all Eyes: Paradigms, Discourses and Practices of Power in Kalarippayattu, a South Indian Martial Art*, Delhi et al., 1998.

68. Cf. MLTMT, Ms. 83, in: Mahalingam, *Mackenzie Manuscripts*, vol. 1, p. 339; Wilson, H.H., *The Mackenzie Collection: A Descriptive Catalogue of the Oriental Manuscripts, and Other Articles Illustrative of the Literature, History, Statistics and Antiquities of the South of India; Collected by the Late Lieut. Col. Colin Mackenzie, Surveyor General of India*, Madras, 2nd edn., 1882, pp. 347–62.

69. Cf. Menon, K.P.P., *History of Kerala,* vol. 1, p. 260f.; Santha, E.K., *Local Self-Government in Malabar (1800–1960),* New Delhi, 1994, p. 3.

70. Cf. Santha, *Local Self-Government,* p. 4.

71. Cf. Menon, K.P.P., *History of Kerala,* vol. 2, pp. 376–80.

72. Cf. Gundert, *Dictionary,* p. 540, col. 1: governor; one who had approximately 100 Nāyars under his supervision. Cf. also MLTMT, Ms. 77, No. 12, in: Mahalingam, *Mackenzie Manuscripts,* vol. 1, p. 300: 'A chief of 100 Nāyars is a *Nadvali*'.

73. Cf. Menon, K.P.P., *History of Kerala,* vol. 1, p. 251, 265f. For information on the Mahāmakhaṃ festival, cf. also MLTMT, Ms. 77, No. 15, in: Mahalingam, *Mackenzie Manuscripts,* vol. 1, p. 302; Logan, *Malabar,* vol. 1, pp. 164–6.

74. Cf. Menon, K.P.P., *History of Kerala,* vol. 1, p. 252.

75. Cf. Chopra, Pran N., Ravindran, T.K., and Subrahmaniam, N., *History of South India,* 3 vols., New Delhi, 1979, p. 183.

76. Cf. Gundert, *Dictionary,* p. 402, col. 1: birth, inherited property. The term janmaṃ is derived from Sanskrit and replaced the originally used Malayāḷaṃ term *pēṟu,* birth, from the nineteenth century. The act of passing down inheritance was performed in the majority of cases with water. Cf. Logan, *Malabar,* vol. 1, p. 599.

77. Cf. Ganesh, 'Ownership', p. 300.

78. Cf. Extract of the Report of Thomas Warden, in: Panikkar, K.N., *Peasant Protests and Revolts in Malabar,* New Delhi, 1990, p. 27.

79. Cf. Buchanan, *Journey,* vol. 2, p. 360; Lemercinier, Geneviève, *Religion and Ideology in Kerala,* New Delhi, 1984, p. 136.

80. Cf. Walker's Report on the Land Tenures of Malabar, 1801, in: Innes, C.A. and Evans, F.B., *Malabar and Anjengo,* Madras, 1908 (Madras District Gazetteers), p. 290.

81. Innes and Evans, *Malabar,* p. 303f.; Cf. also Logan, *Malabar,* p. 601; Walker's Report on the Land Tenures of Malabar, 1801, in: Innes and Evans, *Malabar,* p. 290.

82. Cf. Gough, Kathleen, 'Changing Kinship Usages in the Setting of Political and Economic Change Among the Nayars of Malabar', *JRAI* 82 (1952), pp. 71–81, pp. 75, 78.

83. Cf. Kieniewicz, Jan, 'Pepper Gardens and Market in Precolonial Malabar', *Moyen Orient & Océan Indien* 3 (1986), pp. 1–36, p. 13.

84. Cf. Strachey, J., *Report on the Northern Division of Malabar: Dated 7th March 1801,* Calicut, 1908, § 17, p. 4: 'The Tenant cultivates an Estate, leased to him upon a reserved rent, for a term of years, or from year to year.'

85. Cf. Extract from the Report of Thomas Warden to the Board of Revenue, 19 March 1801, in: Panikkar, K.N., *Peasant Protests,* p. 14.

86. Cf. Ganesh, 'Ownership,' p. 307.

87. Cf. Elamkulam, *Studies,* p. 343f.

88. Cf. Extract from the Minute of Thomas Warden, in: Panikkar, K.N., *Peasant Protests,* p. 15.

89. Cf. Elamkulam, *Studies,* p. 343f.

90. Cf. Report of the Malabar Land Tenures Committee, Madras 1887, in: Innes and Evans, *Malabar,* p. 296. Cf. also Chopra et al., *History,* vol. 3, p. 179.

91. In the nineteenth century, the janmakārans had often become debtors of the

kāṇakkārans; they appeared to the British as farmers in debt. Cf. Rothermund, Dietmar, *Government, Landlord and Peasant in India: Agrarian Relations under British Rule 1865–1935,* Wiesbaden, 1978 (Schriftenreihe des Südasien-Instituts der Universität Heidelberg 25), p. 161.

92. Cf. Logan, *Malabar,* vol. 1, p. 604.

93. Cf. Gundert, *Dictionary,* p. 175, col. 1: a piece of land; also *uṭa.* This example shows the misunderstanding displayed by the Europeans towards the Indian practice of land law; the proportional right to the land can be meant here, depending on the context.

94. One can take Logan's published certificate no. 9 as an example where not only the material value of a piece of land or building, but also the associated legal titles and honours, were handed over. Here, the dēśaṃ itself plus the authority in the dēśaṃ and, together with the temple, the honorary position within it, and the management of temple affairs, were all handed over. Logan, *Malabar,* vol. 2, Appendix XII, p. cxxx.

95. Cf. Buchanan, *Journey,* vol. 2, pp. 173, 370. Kumar, *Land and Caste,* p. 26. Gough, Kathleen, 'Nayar: North Kerala', in: David M. Schneider and eadem (eds.), *Matrilineal Kinship,* Berkeley and Los Angeles, 1961, pp. 385–404, p. 386. For more information on agricultural work within the relationship of dependency, at least for the nineteenth century, cf. Hjejle, Benedict, 'Slavery and Agricultural Bondage in South India in the Nineteenth Century', *The Scandinavian Economic History Review* 15,1–2 (1967), pp. 71–126.

96. Summarized from *oṭi, puraṃ, kāṇaṃ*—understood as a mortgage on a piece of land and a house.

97. Cf. Gundert, *Dictionary,* p. 572, col. 1: *nūr. water, nūrmutal*: property.

98. Abbreviated form for *oṭṭikuṃ purameyullakāṇaṃ.*

99. Cf. Logan, *Malabar,* vol. 1, p. 604f.

100. Cf. Extract from the Report of Thomas Warden, in: Panikkar, K.N., *Peasant Protests,* p. 23; Logan, *Malabar,* vol. 1, p. 605.

101. Logan, *Malabar,* vol. 1, p. 606.

102. Ganesh, 'Ownership', p. 310f.

103. Cf. Strachey, *Report* 16, p. 4; Logan, *Malabar,* vol. 1, p. 606.

104. Benson, C. and Majoribanks, N.E., *A Statistical Atlas of the Madras Presidency,* Madras, 1908, p. 613.

105. Cf. Ganesh, 'Ownership', pp. 302–4.

106. Cf. Logan, *Malabar,* vol. 1, p. 601. Cf. also Thackeray's Report to the Board of Revenue, dated 4 August 1807, cited in Innes and Evans, Malabar, p. 291: 'There is no proof that any land-tax existed in Malabar before Hyder's invasion.'

107. Cf. *Reports of a Joint Commission* § X; Extracts from the Minute of the Board of Revenue about Ryotwar Settlement, 5 January 1818, in: Panikkar, K.N., *Peasant Protests,* p. 19.

108. Cf. Innes and Evans, *Malabar,* p. 307f.

109. *Reports of a Joint Commission,* § X.

110. Cf. Ganesh, 'Ownership', p. 320.

Two

Legitimation of Rule

Religious Legitimation

The network of temples was of utmost importance to the rule of an Indian *rājā,* because temples and their respective festivals were instrumental in the religious legitimation of the ruler. The temples could also function as places of refuge and accommodation both when a rājā was touring the country, and when external circumstances forced him to take flight. In this capacity, the temples formed a network over and above their religious function, whose importance could grow with the escalating decline of a rājā's power and with his associated retreat into more remote areas of his country. It will be our task to find out more about the religious legitimation of the rulers of Malabar, taking as an example the legitimation policy of Kēraḷa Varmma Paḷaśśi Rājā of Kōṭṭayaṃ. The location of the temples within Paḷaśśi Rājā's sphere of influence will be described in the following paragraphs in order to mark out the geographical arena in which he operated. An examination will then be made of the linking of temples to a network, and how he and the population made use of this network.

Bhagavati Worship in Malabar

In Kēraḷa, and especially in Malabar, the goddess Bhagavati is considered to be one of the most important deities. She is described by Sarah Caldwell as the 'matron goddess of Kerala'.[1] In the majority of towns in Malabar there is a shrine of Bhagavati. This shrine is usually known by the place where it is situated. Many other deities besides Bhagavati are also worshipped in the region, including deities of the Sanskritic tradition, such as Śiva and Viṣṇu. The term 'Bhagavati' is used on a number of different levels with differing connotations, which may result in some confusion. Despite the highly inadequate state of sources, an attempt will be made here to consider the levels seperately so as to construct a conceptual framework for the use of the term. This will be based on records of reverence for Bhagavati collected during my research in India, and on references to her worship which can be found dispersed in literature.

Bhagavati is regarded firstly as a goddess in her own right, to whom temples are dedicated. In this form Bhagavati embodies both 'dark'—meaning cruel, frightening—and 'light'—meaning peaceful, benevolent—aspects; the 'dark' aspects of Bhagavati are reflected in her cruelty and frightening appearance, whilst her 'light' aspects portray her benevolence and peaceableness.[2] The temple of Varakkal Bhagavati in Kōḻikkōṭu can be taken as an example of the positive side of Bhagavati: The temple is positioned to protect Kēraḷa's coasts on the Arabian Sea and was allegedly founded by Paraśurāmā, the mythical father of Kēraḷa.[3] According to K.K.N. Kurup, Bhagavati is depicted here with autochthonous, tribal features but is also integrated into the pantheon of Hindu gods.[4] One document reports that the Brahmins ordered the reverence of Bhagavati.[5]

Secondly, Bhagavati is meant in the sense of *dēvī*, or *durgga*, as a generic term for different goddesses, with both 'light' as well as 'dark' aspects.[6] In the Devīmāhātmyam, Bhagavati is used as a synonym for dēvī.[7]

In a third sense, Bhagavati is taken as a synonym for Kāḷi or Bhadrakāḷi.[8] In this representation, she only portrays the dark, cruel side of the goddess. 'Bhagavati, the predominant deity of Kerala, is a form of the pan-Indian goddess Kālī. As Bhagavati she is a benevolent protectress, but in her more common angry and violent form, she is referred to as Bhadrakāḷi.'[9]

Fourthly, Bhagavati is connected to Śiva, for she is identified with the married goddess Parvati. In this form, she is considered to be the female half of Śiva—more precisely, to be Siva's wife or daughter.[10] Hermann Gundert argues that this is also indicated in the etymology of her name: Bhagavati is the feminine form of *bhagavān*—the blessed, the glorious, he who is to be worshipped—which is used for Śiva or Viṣṇu.[11] Here, Bhagavati embodies the 'light', peaceful side of the goddess, and is thus described in the Periyapurāṇam: 'This beautiful woman was called Bhagavati; / Chaste and submissive, her life was married harmony.'[12] In the Piśarikkāvu temple of Pantalāyini, for example, Bhagavati is revered alongside Śiva.[13]

In a fifth way, Bhagavati can be seen as a philosophical principle. She is either understood as *prakṛti*, the 'primordial matter', from which everything originates, or she is regarded as *ādiparaśakti*, the (female) highest principle of the Śaivasiddhānta, in which everything is united and from which everything originates. The creation of mankind is attributed to her in this way: '[...], we may draw the inference that she who is *bhagavati*, in addition to being beneficent, is the creatrix of humanity or, more precisely, it is through her who is *bhagavati* that Manu is creative.'[14] In this sense the attributes of Bhagavati are all-embracing: 'Bhagavatī combines in herself knowledge, affluence, riches, fame and strength.'[15]

Whenever Bhagavati is discussed, it becomes apparent just how many different levels of understanding exist for her. Bhagavati is revered in a form which involves autochthonous or local rites on the one hand, but in which, on the other, she is also placed in the common Hindu context. Her most striking aspect is her ambivalent character. Whilst she is a benevolent and peaceful goddess, she is also violent and frightening. It should be noted here that these two aspects, frequently portrayed as conflicting concepts, are in fact two sides of the same coin. Despite the ritual portrayal of her differing functions, both positive and negative, she represents a unity. It is possible in this context to talk of two complementary facets of Bhagavati.[16] The reverence shown for Bhagavati has social relevance as a shared common ground between the different social groups. To a certain extent, Bhagavati can be said to unite the different communities in Kerala, at least at the time of her festival, for all the groups are involved in the yearly festival, each with specific functions according to their standing within the village.[17] Each form of Bhagavati is worshipped in a special Teyyaṃ, a dance in praise of the goddess.[18] The dancer of the Teyyaṃ—who becomes the personification of Bhagavati—acts, while in a trance-like state, as the mouthpiece of the goddess.[19]

What relationship did Paḻaśśi Rājā have to the ritual worship of Bhagavati? In his letters to the EIC it becomes clear that religious ceremonies occupied an important place within his way of rule. He tried to ensure that festivals which were threatened by unrest still went ahead even if this meant that negotiations with the British had to be cancelled as a consequence. He was backed by the senior rājā of Kōṭṭayaṃ who also asked the British to give financial support towards the religious festivals, since he had to deliver all money-making products of the country to the British and was therefore unable to pay for costs incurred by the ceremonies. Paḻaśśi Rājā considered it impossible to stay in Kōṭṭayaṃ, or Vāyanāṭu, without being able to keep up religious obligations.[20]

The country above the Ghauts (Waynaad) being mine, and myself straitened for subsistence by remaining here, the celebrations of religious rites at Tricherakuna or Mantanna being indispensable, my own birthday to be held, and devotion to be performed at Tirunelly, all these reasons as well as a consideration of the distresses of that country's inhabitants which I wish to alleviate, urge me to ascend the Ghauts, and having comforted them personally to return.[21]

'Perumal Bhugwady'[22] and 'the god and goddess Perumal',[23] which can probably be regarded as family deities (*kuladaivaṃ*) denote Śiva and his wife Bhagavati. The reason given by Paḻaśśi Rājā for his and the local people's active role in the fight against the British was the fear of revenge by the goddess Perumāḷ Bhagavati.[24] The addition *perumāḷ* denotes a title given to the goddess—it means 'the Great' and was used for gods as well as for the ancient rulers of Kēraḷa.[25]

Despite the fact that the majority of Paḷaśśi Rājā's letters and notes only exist as English translations, and on the assumption that each translator's own interpretation will influence the text in some way, it is still possible to recognize how great an importance the rājā attached to the adherence to religious ritual obligations. As far as it was in any way possible for him to do so he kept up these obligations. The observance of these ceremonies enabled the rājā to achieve the religious legitimation of his rule. Furthermore, he was able to increase the glory of Bhagavati by adhering to the cyclically recurring festivals, something which ultimately stood him in good stead.

The festival of the chiefdom goddess was often the culmination of a series of lesser festivals for the separate village goddesses. It was from the goddess of his temple that the chieftain was held to derive his power—and especially his success in battle. His power, of course, confirmed the prestige of his goddess.[26]

Location of the Temples

Since the network of temples was of such considerable importance to the rule of Paḷaśśi Rājā, I shall give a brief description of the most important temples (the exact locations of the temples are marked on the map in the appendix). Again, the difficulty when studying the temples is the almost complete lack of written literature. Although the quality of art objects in these temples is not inferior to those of other regions of India, they have attracted only little attention by academics so far.[27]

Muḷakunnu

The temple in Muḷakunnu is dedicated to the goddess Śrī Mṛdaṃgaśailēśvari, also known as Durgga or Śrī Pōrkāḷi. This is the chief temple of the Kōṭṭayaṃ dynasty. On its four sides, the royal family built four palaces that were occupied by one *kōvilakaṃ* (branch) of the family each. Accordingly, the kōvilakaṃs were known by the four points of the compass: *tekku* (southern), *paṭiññāru* (western), *malayaṭi* (at-foot-of-the-mountain) and *kiḷakku* (eastern) palace. After the four branches of the Kōṭṭayaṃ dynasty had left Muḷakunnu, the kilakku and the tekku kōvilakaṃ settled in Kuttupaṟambu near the temple situated there, while the paṭiññāru kōvilakaṃ settled in Paḷaśśi. The goddess Śrī Mṛdaṃgaśailēśvari is the traditional family goddess of the Kōṭṭayaṃ dynasty. It is a sign of her importance that her statue is made from a special alloy of five metals. As an illustration of the power exerted by the goddess, locals today tell those visiting the temple that her statue has been stolen five times within the last decade, but that it has always found its way back to the sanctum sanctorum of the temple in Muḷakunnu.[28]

Muḷakunnu is also home to the *kaḷari,* where the members of the royal family learned the traditional Kēraḷan art of warfare, the *kaḷarippayaṟṟu,* from the head of the Pindāli-*taṟavāṭu.* It was customary for a new ruler to come to this spot at Navarātri for political and ritual ceremonies. He received a sword from the head of the Pindāli-taṟavāṭu, and had to perform a kaḷari-payaṟṟu. Only after this ritual could the new ruler be invested.[29] According to information given by one local, at least ten different kinds of sword are kept within the kaḷari. However, these are only shown at the time of Navarātri or, on the occasion of the Teyyaṃ, performed to celebrate the glory of the *kaḷarripparadēvata* (in this case the Raktacāmuṇḍi), which is the deity belonging to the kaḷari.[30]

When questioned by the British, Paḷaśśi Rājā's disloyal subject, Palavīṭṭil Cantu, mentioned Muḷakunnu as being one of the most important temples in Kōṭṭayaṃ. On that occasion, he also included the temples of Maṇattaṇa, Tōṭṭikkalaṃ and Kuttupaṟambu, and others.[31] A letter written by Paḷaśśi Rājā in 1797 to his governor in Muḷakunnu, in which he gives instructions for tax collection, shows the involvement of that place in his political and ritual activities. The subsequent report was said to have been sent to him in Tōṭṭikkaḷaṃ.[32]

Tōṭṭikkaḷaṃ

Originally a two-storey temple built in the traditional Kēraḷan style, which was partially destroyed during the battles of 1796/97, the Śiva temple in Tōṭṭikkaḷaṃ still bears a number of impressive frescos. There are more than 150 paintings, presumably dating back to between the sixteenth and eighteenth centuries, on forty panels which cover a surface area of approximately 65 square metres. The depictions are mainly myths of Śiva and Viṣṇu. There is also a scene with a king, perhaps from the Kōṭṭayaṃ dynasty, in which he is paying homage to a goddess.[33] It is likely that this temple dedicated to Rudra was established by Hariścandra Perumāḷ, the ruler of Puraḷimala and founder of the Kōṭṭayaṃ dynasty.[34]

Locals related how this temple was reported to have been a favourite place of retreat for Paḷaśśi Rājā; it seems probable that a palace or palatial building of sorts in which he could hold meetings was located in the vicinity.[35] The British files of administration report that Tōṭṭikkaḷaṃ was a place of retreat for Paḷaśśi Rājā,[36] where he stayed from October to December 1796[37] and to which he retired in spring 1797 after negotiations with the British had ended abruptly.[38] In July 1797, the Britons Jonathan Duncan and James Stuart reported that Paḷaśśi Rājā could be found in the temple at Tōṭṭikkaḷaṃ, where he was performing ceremonies on the anniversary of his mother's death. In 1797, a battle took place between the rebels and the British in Tōṭṭikkaḷaṃ in the immediate vicinity of the temple, which resulted in the large-scale destruction of the temple itself. It was for this reason—to save the remains of the temple—that Paḷaśśi Rājā is reported to have ordered the retreat to Maṇattaṇa.[39]

Maṇattaṇa

There are two Bhagavati temples located in Maṇattaṇa, one of which is called Bhagavati Kulottuṅṅara temple. Unfortunately, access is only granted to certain persons[40] and I am not aware of any literature about this temple. Sewell mentions an 'ancient and important temple' in Maṇattaṇa to which Europeans were not allowed access because of daily *pūjā*.[41] According to one Brahmin from Kōṭṭayaṃ this was the seat of the god and goddess Perumāḷ:

> They are the Guardians and rulers of the Cotiote Country under whose influence the Moota (elder) and Ellia (younger) Raja act in their Government of it. These Rajas,... holding the reins of Government as Viceregents of the god and goddess Perumal, derive their support from Office.[42]

It was customary for the rājā to bear the costs of temple festivals. According to the reports of P. Cantu the costs for a festival, held in peacetime in the temple at Maṇattaṇa, came to 12,000 *iṭaṅṅali*s[43] of rice, approximately 5,000 silver *paṇaṃ*s.[44] In a report to the British, P. Cantu wrote that the temple in Maṇattaṇa had been demolished by Ṭippu Sulttān, and its surrounding land destroyed by fire.[45] At the end of March 1798, a *harkārā* (messenger, courier)[46] reported that Paḷaśśi Rājā had retired to Maṇattaṇa to perform religious ceremonies.[47]

In 1796, the British considered Maṇattaṇa to be the place over which Paḷaśśi Rājā exerted the greatest influence. Strategic considerations were the reason for their plan to open a station[48] there from where they aimed to direct the continued pursuit of Paḷaśśi Rājā.[49] The British station in Maṇattaṇa must already have been functioning by June 1796, since a proclamation was issued from there which concerned the flight of Paḷaśśi Rājā.[50] Paḷaśśi Rājā reported to an ally in 1800 that, in spite of his attempts to prevent it, the British had gained control of roads to Maṇattaṇa and Kaṇṇotta, and that soldiers were taking up positions there.[51] The strategic and logistic importance of Maṇattaṇa was also reported in the nineteenth century.[52]

Tirunelli

Tirunelli, also known in the vernacular as the Benares of the south,[53] is situated approximately 15 kilometres north-east of Mānantavāṭi, on a mountain plateau that juts out from the Brahmagiri mountains and the forests of Vāyanāṭu. The Mahāviṣṇu temple of Tirunelli is also known by the name Āmalakam temple or Sidha temple. According to the legend surrounding its foundation, Brahma dedicated the temple to Viṣṇu. Viṣṇu is also revered here as Dēva Dēvāsan and Tirunelli Perumāḷ. Seven sources of holy water are located in the vicinity of the temple, of which the most important is the Pāpanāśini; it is said that sins can be washed away in its water.[54]

Shrines were built around the temple at each of the four points of the compass, with the most important one, the Vaḷḷiyūrkāvu Bhagavati temple, located on the south side (see below). The temple and the water-pipes, which were laid above ground from the sources into the temple, suffered large-scale destruction in the conflicts of the eighteenth century. Remains of the fortress, which had been built near the temple, can also be seen today. They are said to have been destroyed during Ṭippu Sulttān's invasions of Malabar.[55]

Thomas H. Baber, the subcollector at Talaśśēri at the beginning of the nineteenth century, was also said to have visited the hermits of the Tirunelli temple;[56] it seems likely that he paid this visit whilst looking for Paḻaśśi Rājā. According to today's temple priest, underground tunnels run into the mountains, in which Paḻaśśi Rājā is said to have taken refuge with his supporters.[57] In 1798, Paḻaśśi Rājā was residing in Tirunelli so that he could perform ceremonies there. The country was in turmoil and Paḻaśśi Rājā thus considered it his primary duty to restore at least a minimum of order by adhering to religious ceremonies.[58]

Vaḷḷiyūrkāvu

Two closely connected temples are located in Vaḷḷiyūrkāvu: one of them on a hill top and the other at the foot of the same hill. Both temples are dedicated to Bhagavati. The festival to celebrate the glory of Bhagavati is held there in March. On this occasion, statues of Bhagavati, but also of Śiva, are brought to the temple from the surrounding area and carried along in a procession.[59] One thesis about the foundation of the temple suggests that Vaḷḷiyūrkāvu was lined up with the Tirunelli temple as one of the aforementioned four shrines; the other stems from a legendary account, which connects the Vaḷḷiyūrkāvu temple with the temple in Koṭuṅṅalūr.[60] According to that legend the temple is said to have been founded by *veḷiccappāṭu*s from Koṭuṅṅalūr. These pilgrim devotees of Bhagavati acted as her medium from time to time.[61] Although there is no direct evidence about visits of Paḻaśśi Rājā to the Vaḷḷiyūrkāvu temples, it is likely that he had passed through this place as it lies on the route from Tirunelli to Mānantavāṭi.

Mānantavāṭi

The Paḷḷiyaṟa temple, located on the outskirts of Mānantavāṭi, is dedicated to Bhadrakāḷi, one of the forms of Bhagavati. In conversation, the temple priest affirmed that the kings of the Kōṭṭayaṃ dynasty—including Paḻaśśi Rājā—stayed overnight in the room next to the sanctum sanctorum when they passed through on their travels.[62] Nowadays, it is Ayyappan (also known as Śāsta) who is worshipped in this room. It seems likely that Paḷaśśi Rājā also used the temple of Mānantavāṭi as a place of retreat during the times of conflicts with the British.

Sulttānbaṭṭēri

The land for the Māriyamman temple in Sulttānbaṭṭēri is said to have been given by Paḷaśśi Rājā to a tribal chief who had supported him in the clashes with the British.[63] The annual festival takes place from 20 Mīnaṃ and lasts for seven days (in February). The statue of the deity is brought out of the sanctum sanctorum and carried along in a procession. It is performed by women who wear traditional Kēraḷan dress and carry with them coconut halves, flowers and lamps.

Tiruvaṅṅāṭu

The story behind the emergence of the Śrī Rāmasvāmi temple of Tiruvaṅṅāṭu, nowadays a part of Talaśśēri, is not to be found in any written source, but is based on oral tradition handed down through several generations.[64] Besides the chief deity Viṣṇu, reverence was also paid in this temple to Bhagavati who, as the legend goes, had been brought here following a bet between a temple priest and a *marar*, a temple drummer.[65] During the eighteenth century, the temple enjoyed an extremely varied history; amongst other purposes, it served as a refuge for the people fleeing Haidar Ali; in the 1780s the walls and a seven-storey tower were destroyed by Ṭippu Sulttān's army. For unknown reasons the British established a positive relationship with the temple. It is said that the abovementioned subcollector, Thomas H. Baber, became a devotee of Rāma and visited the temple on regular occasions.[66] A contrary view, in which the temple is said to have been an outpost of the fort during the eighteenth century, was expressed by Innes, a British official living in Malabar at the end of the nineteenth century.[67] Interestingly enough, the wall surrounding the temple and its neighbouring plot of land were paid for and built on the instructions of Baber; such is the inscription on the outer wall: 'The wall around this pagoda was constructed under the supervision and patronage of T.H. Baber esq. in 1815.' This is the very same Baber who had pursued Paḷaśśi Rājā with tenacity. The fact that Innes mentioned the Tiruvaṅṅāṭu temple as an outpost of the fort makes it clear that strategic relevance must have been attached to the fact that Baber had the wall built.

The basic principles of religious legitimation of Malabar rājās, exemplified here by the case of Paḷaśśi Rājā, were the adherence to and performance of religious ceremonies, as well as temple patronage. The temples formed a network which enabled the rājā, on the one hand, to fulfil his religious duties and which served, on the other hand, as places of refuge come times of need.

Just why the ritual tasks of the rājā were attached such supreme importance in the social system will become clear with the analysis of the power structure in Malabar.

The Model of the *Little Kingdom* and its Modification

Nicholas Dirks' model of the *little kingdom* aims to describe the period when colonial rule was established in southern India, from the viewpoint of the Indian rulers. This model is of particular importance since its bases are authentic Indian source texts; this feature distinguishes it from other models. Methodologically, Dirks classifies his study as *ethnohistory*, a term which he understands as the reconstruction of the history of a region and of a people who do not have any written history themselves. Accordingly, *ethnohistory* is the application of anthropological theories and methods to practical experience from history, which should use a critical and reflective technique to question existing, preconceived opinions.[68] The following account will focus on the extent to which elements of Dirks' opinion actually fit in the structure of a *little kingdom*, and in which respect the rule of a *little king* is legitimized and manifested.[69]

A Critique of Dirks' Approach

On the basis of the history of Putukkōṭṭai in today's Tamiḻnāṭu, presented in *The Hollow Crown*, Dirks aims to develop a model for the state formation prevailing in eighteenth-century India. This model describes political units before fundamental changes to its overall administrative, political, ritual, social and economic structure were introduced by the colonial power. Dirks examines the role of the *pāḷaiyakkārar*s (known by the British as *poligar*s) who originally ruled over fortified villages, and who developed over the course of time into the rulers of local centres. Within their territory they were called rājā and they exercised a level of authority comparable to that of a king, but their authority was not as important nor as wide-ranging as that of the particular kinds of '*great king*s', such as the kings of Vijayanagara for example. It is for this reason that Dirks refers to them as *little kings*.[70] He borrowed the term *little kingdom* from Bernard Cohn who had introduced it in his essay 'Some Notes on Law and Change in North India',[71] and who had modified it in 1962 in a study of Benares.[72] This term, which had been applied for northern India, is transferred by Dirks to the context of southern India and, based on this, he develops certain criteria which comprise the nature of the *little kingdom* as a model of the state. These criteria, however, are found as isolated aspects spread throughout his entire work and he does not provide us with a concise definition.

In his study, Dirks refers essentially to the examination of political and ritual conditions in the *little kingdom*. In doing so he assumes that political and religious domains were neither superordinate nor subordinate to one another, but that they were on the same level, something which became evident in how they appeared in practice: 'Ritual and political forms were fundamentally the same.'[73] Within the *little kingdom*, the kinship system was the basis and expression of social and political relations, which found their symbolic representation in the redistributive system of the *little kingdom*—i.e. the exchange of gifts between the *little king* and his subjects. These relations formed the 'building materials' for all social and political networks in the *little kingdom* above the village community, as well as for all transregional political systems.[74] The redistribution clarified the relations of those involved and illustrated their hierarchical solidarity. Thereby the centre was identified as well as strengthened and the mutual relations between the centre and the periphery were articulated.[75]

In colonial times, Dirks claims, the king was regarded as the creator, definer, and protector of 'culture' at the head of society: '[he] had full powers to construct the sets of relations and categories that made up the social and political system.'[76] Here, the size of the territory over which a *little king* ruled did not play any role in determining his authority. That was defined by the share of power which he wielded over the land and the people. Dirks ultimately attributes the role of the *little king* to the fact that he remained faithful to the social and political structures of the traditional form of government and actually incorporated them.

Dirks considers the fundamental political basis to have been the *little king's* military capacity,[77] with which he could maintain his position in relation to the *great king* above him and, in times of conflict, by which he could defend his status as the *little king* in struggles over power with other rulers. The relation to the *great king* was marked by continual dispute amongst such rulers, which meant that the positions of those involved had to be gauged and regauged continually.[78] On the other hand, the *great king* relied on loyal *little kings* if he had conflicts to settle with other *great kings* or rebellious *little kings*. Dirks argues that in spite of his military might, a *little king* could never raise his status to that of a *great king* since he was confined by his ecological and economic marginality.[79]

Dirks claims that within the *little kingdom* the main focus of the legitimation of rule was ritual, something that represented the king's level of authority and defined his relation to other kings, i.e. which gave expression to the hierarchical grading, or equality, amongst them.[80] The respective *little kings* were placed within a network of relations to other *little kings* and to the *great king*, which continually required restructuring on account of conflicts and alliances. The further away a *little king* was from the *great king*, the less he recognized the territorial supremacy of the *great king* and formed his own small centre on the periphery of the large centre. The *great king* did not have any basis of legitimation to set up or exercise a monopoly of power, but he did occupy the top level in the hierarchy, since he owned the greatest number of legal titles, honours and gifts. Consequently, he was able to distribute the greatest number of prestigious titles and gifts, which meant that the *great king* occupied the highest position in the redistributive system. The difference between a *great* and *little king* had not so much of a qualitative as of a quantitative nature. Due to the lack of any monopoly of power, it was not for the *great king* to control these relations 'from the top' in the direction which he desired. The only way in which he could get involved in this was by carrying out political and ritual actions, which could enable him to influence the *little kings* to suit his purposes.

In the context of a larger, loosely connected state structure, Dirks believes that the *little kingdom* was positioned at the lowest level: 'This region [Putukkōṭṭai] was one of many similar political regions which constituted the lowest level of the late precolonial state, [...].' The large kingdoms loomed over the *little kingdoms*: 'little kingships could not be attained without great kings',[81] i.e. that the *little king* could only be defined in relation to the *great king*, and to other *little kings*.[82] Thus the *little kings* were given two roles within the vertical hierarchy—they had to align themselves upwards and downwards in accordance with their position. In the horizontal hierarchy they played a number of roles in the relationships with their many different neighbours.[83]

Ritual, regarded by Dirks as the '*sine qua non* of kingly activity',[84] consisted of receiving or passing on legal titles, honours, gifts and services. The components of politics and ritual are married here; the ritual became political fact, the politics was imbued with ritual. The *little king's* relationship with his subjects was also symbolized by rituals:

> The acceptance of gifts, which to a very large extent reflected a complicated set of categorizations and gradations of kinship relations, entailed loyalty and service. [...] These gifts linked individuals, and also corporations, symbolically, morally, and politically with the sovereignty of the king and created both a moral unity and a political hierarchy.[85]

Thus great significance was attached to the rituals, according to Dirks; they did not only serve to legitimize rule in the *little kingdom* but also to manifest this rule. They thereby represented an essential part of politics. The British did not recognize the fact that ritual played a decisive role in politics, and consequently split up the two areas. This was thus an area in which conflicts between locals and the British were pre-programmed.

Dirks writes that there was hardly any alteration in the external appearance of the state after the British had taken over power in southern India, although, behind the façade, they were setting up new political, social and administrative institutions. With the introduction of their administration, the British replaced the system of relations and redistribution, which had previously been decisive to political processes, with a Western-style system of bureaucracy. The rājā was deprived of his responsibilities and titles—he continued to function only as a puppet of the British. The honours awarded by the old regime, which played a decisive role in determining relations, actually continued to be given out but they were separated from their infrastructural basis, and were therefore meaningless in any claim to political power struggle. Family relations were banished from politics and were redefined in a separate, autonomous area. Income from taxes was guaranteed by reassessing tax-free land, previously shared among all inhabitants, and attaching this same land to one person.[86] Behind all these changes, the British—as the colonial power—held a wholly disparate view as regards property rights and their implementation:

> The British, with a very different view of property rights, misunderstood all this. When they attempted to sort out who owned the land, they assumed opposition, not complementarity: the owner, they thought, must be either the cultivator or the king, thus creating many of the classificatory problematics of the land systems debates in the late eighteenth and early nineteenth centuries.[87]

According to Dirks, the tearing down of the old structures was manifested most clearly in the separation of religion and politics, which removed the caste system from the political context, thus placing it without any connection in a situation where it appeared to be an end in itself. In this way, the conception of a ruler's sovereignty, which was characterized by relationships and which continually had to be reconfirmed, had been displaced by the Western conception of absolute sovereignty, something which was consolidated by the colonial government's monopoly of power and its laws. To a considerable extent the isolated caste system and many of the 'traditions' which we now consider to be Indian are ultimately a product of colonialism. Only in the nineteenth century did the the structures of the *little kingdom* disappear, writes Dirks.[88]

Dirks' model of the *little kingdom* can be summarized as follows: The state structure is depicted as pyramidal, with the *great king* positioned at the very top. His political and ritual might enables him to exercise supreme power over the *little king*s. The *great king's* range of power, however, continually decreases at the periphery of his 'catchment area'; there, it is the *little king*s who are more important, since they are actually on site. The *little king* legitimizes and manifests his rule through political and ritual actions which express the extent of his participation in power. This pattern is repeated on a smaller scale in the lower levels, right down to the foot of the pyramid to individual person's relations and family relationships.

Having analysed Dirks' model of the *little kingdom* thoroughly I arrive at several points of critique. Dirks' limitation of the theoretical form to the specific situation that prevailed in Putukkōṭṭai in the seventeenth and eighteenth centuries makes it difficult to apply the model to other regions in India. Therefore, he does not do full justice to his own claim that his theoretical approach is generally applicable. His equation of the terms *pāḷaiyakkārar* and *little king*,[89] contradicts his assertion of having presented a general model. *Little king*s were not necessarily *pāḷaiyakkārar*s after all, since they could also play an active role in other functions. This we can see in other Indian regions where research has been done, for example in Orissa. As Georg Berkemer stated in his study of the *little kingdom*s in Kaliṅga, their status was in fact related to the particular social and political context:

> Thus it is also possible for *little kings*—depending on the current political circumstances—to behave as '*tribal chiefs*', '*sāmanta rājās*', '*zamindārs*' and '*inamdārs*', as '*landlords*' in the British sense of the word, or as '*polygars*', and at the same time to fulfil these social, religious and political roles in different cultural contexts.[90]

Dirks essentially considers his depiction of the economic and ecological marginality of the *little kingdoms* as the reason why the *little kings* were faced with no other option than that of sticking to their status.[91] If this assumption was justified then the relationality and dynamics of the interrelationships between *little king*, *great king* and other *little kings*, described by Dirks in exactly the same way, would be limited to such an extent that his model could only be a rigid structure without any scope for development. An inherent textual contradiction can be detected here, which can only be explained by Dirks' failure to include the processuality of events into his model. Instead, he endeavours to form a structural model.[92] Yet if one is to remain faithful to the historical facts, it is imperative to include in the construction of the model the flexibility and mobility which characterized the relations of the *little kings* towards one another and towards the *great king*. Looking for a more dynamic component to complement Dirks' model, we find a suitable approach in Hermann Kulke's work.[93] Although actually designed to fit the medieval state of India, the basic adoption of Kulke's processual model can be used as a supplement to Dirks' model. In the processual model, an analysis is made of the dynamics of the socio-economic, political, and cultural processes which are mutually dependent on each another and which operate in connection with one another. For analytical purposes Kulke assumes that the formation of the state in India occurred in three successive stages: in the initial phase, the kingdom covered an existing core area and, in a second phase, extended into its peripheral areas. In this process, the rulers intensified the political control in its core area and at the same time attempted to gain neighbouring areas under its tributary dependence. At the third stage of the state formation, an imperial kingdom was formed that was linked to the establishment of a regional hegemony. This empire emerged from the continuous process of integrative state formation by local power centres. For the construction of the *little kingdom* model, this aforementioned third stage is generally a situation which is striven for but not actually attained. In this model, one's attention is directed towards the processuality of the development of a state. The inclusion of processes involved in the formation of the state is indispensable to the analysis of historical events. However, the aspects of the dynamic movement and development of a state and its structures are not given sufficient weight in Dirks' construction of the model. Since a *little kingdom* lives by the dynamics of its relations to other states, it is essential to carry this mobility across into the model. And it is precisely in southern India where, in the centuries which preceded British rule, the flexibility of the system is noticeable.[94]

Another problem with Dirks' model lies in his placement of the *little kings* at the lowest level of the state structure. He thereby emphasizes the dichotomy of *great* and *little king*, which he actually seemed to have gotten over with the establishment of relationships between the individual levels. After all, these relationships had to be redefined constantly and could shift in favour of one party or another, i.e. they were in a state of flux, whereas Dirks' dichotomic comparison of *great* and *little king* implies a rigid, static system. In order to avoid this scenario it makes more sense to place the *little kings* at the meso-level, between that of *great king* and minor *chieftains* or persons with corresponding functions, such as e.g. *nāṭuvāḻi*s or *dēśavāḻi*s in Malabar. In this way the *little king* is left with a far greater scope for political, ritual, and military action, the struggle for power is more pronounced and the order of precedence is continually being rearranged. Just how relationships between the *little king* and his respective political partners are determined depends on his status and also on the social, political, and ritual context of those involved.

An additional enhancement to Dirks' concept lies in the introduction of the idea of highly flexible networking activities in which alliances are concluded and dissolved freely. This is done vertically between the *great* and *little king*, and horizontally between the *little kings*. Those alliances were open to change and were based on negotiations that had to be renewed time after time. It was possible for a *little king* to ally himself to the *great* or *little king* who seemed to be the most favourable at the time, but he always kept open the option of breaking off this alliance and entering into a new one, depending on the situation. Consequently, the range of a ruler's power was determined by the shifting alliances with other rulers.

It should be stressed that the alliances entered into were open in principle; they did not end in the establishment of territorially enclosed areas. Taking these considerations into account, this practice is central for the kings' relations, and possible development of relations, to one another—whether between *great* and *little king*, or within the circle of *little kings*. Within this structure of relations, the *little king* effected tributary payments and was only prepared to cooperate if a symbolic or material offering was given in return by the *great king*. However, the ideological, subordinate, political units were often independent de facto.[95] Their relations amongst themselves were always open to change, and constantly required new regulations. The possibility to change alliances enabled them to react flexibly to new situations.

Dirks intends his model to provide an explanation for why the *little kings* were able to react skilfully to new challenges, such as the Europeans' arrival and aspirations of power. This the *little kings* achieved by acting as protectors of the political and social structures exhibited in the old regime, and by putting up opposition to the British. For Dirks they were *little kings* because they seemed to defend and preserve the old system *a priori*. Here he equates traditions with inflexibility and immobility. Yet in this equation Dirks once again fails to recognize the flexibility of the traditional system in southern India, which opened up to the *little kings* a wide range of possibilities for carrying out conflicts with other local élite and rulers, and also for the conflict with the invading British forces. Contrary to Dirks, the traditional organization of political and social structure should thus be seen from a different perspective: '*Little kingdoms* were not *little* because they held more traditional forms of social and political organization, rather they organized matters in a more traditional way because they were *little*.'[96] This means that traditional organization in a *little kingdom* was not synonymous with being trapped in an old-fashioned, immobile structure, but that its deep roots in tradition enabled mobility in the activities undertaken by the different powers within. The fundamental importance of the flexibility inherent in the traditional system in southern India becomes apparent once more in this context.

Taking into account the aforementioned characteristics of the model of a *little king* and bearing in mind the criticism of Dirks' approach, we arrive at the following definition: A *little king* is a ruler who has, within his territory, essential instruments of rule such as financial and military means at his disposal, and who legitimizes his rule through political and ritual acts. Outwardly the *little king* must accept the rule of a *great king* who is superior to him in a ritual and political sense, and who can demonstrate this by military means if necessary. The *little king* also relies on the *great king*, since he can legitimize his rule internally over the *great king* by the system of ritual redistribution, thereby gaining a share of the *great king's* power. Conversely, the *great king* cannot, in the long term, assert his rule over the *little kings* by military means, since he requires the political and ritual support of the *little kings* for the legitimation of his rule. It remains to be said that the individual components of the model are in continual flux, i.e. this is a flexible, processual model. In the following chapter I will examine whether there are any other parameters which must be taken into consideration when applying this, now revised, model of the *little kingdom* to Malabar.

When examining Indian states and their structures, it is absolutely essential to reject outright any preconceptions of a Western-style state. Only if we free ourselves from the Eurocentric concept of the state, which is understood as a firmly defined sphere with political, economic and administrative structures, is it possible to grasp the structures of pre-colonial Indian society. The notion of sovereignty primarily concerns having a share in power, 'i.e. in the legitimate participation in the honour of social standing befitting the élite, and in the distribution of produced goods amongst those who were not producers themselves.'[97] To a large extent the Indian concept of the state, and of state rule, came from proportional exercise of power and not from any attempts to secure a monopoly over power. The aim of every ruler was to occupy the highest position in the state structure, thereby being the head of a hierarchy of 'small' and 'middle-sized' kings, and to hold the title of *mahārājādhirāja*, i.e. king of kings. This title was reserved for a *great king*, who was able to amass for himself the most titles. Even though he occupied the highest position in the hierarchy of the kings the *great king* had no absolute power, since the rulers beneath him commanded a share in his power. A further indispensable element of the Indian concept of the state was that of political and religious acts, which served to determine and illustrate the rulers' relations with one another.

According to traditional state doctrine, which was especially strongly rooted in southern India, the nature of the state was characterized by seven elements: the king (*svāmi*), the minister (*amātya*), the land (*janapada*), the fort (*durga*), state reserves (*kośa*), the army (*daṇḍa*) and the allies (*mitra*).[98] Although the king held the most important position he was a part of, and not outside nor above, the state structure; the king was always linked with the other elements constitutive of this model, and more especially by a structure of relations defined by political and ritual acts. Since the king's power was indebted to the *dharma* which he, as the head of the administration, had to support and implement, he was not able to react alone at his own discretion.[99] In addition, there were advisers and institutionalized committees to which the king was accountable; thus he did not enjoy an absolute status.[100] Dharma can also be regarded as a rule of interdependency, which can be attributed back to natural conditions, and which is necessary in order to maintain social order.[101] In addition to his political and administrative functions, the rājā was also charged with looking after the welfare of the people in his kingdom, i.e. the *rājā-dharma*: 'Therefore with regard to the preservation of dharma the king had two distinct functions, one relating to the conservation of traditions, religion, social organizations and institutions and the other relating to the moulding of society to keep pace with the spirit and tendencies of the age.'[102]

The conception behind rājādharma was multifaceted and involved consequential activities of the rājā.[103] Prosperity and harmony required not only the settlement of conflicts, but also the pleasing of the gods with donations and rituals.[104] Thus, on the one hand, the gods were involved in government whilst, on the other, the king took on a partially divine quality.[105]

The concept of rājādharma allows us to add important elements to our former definition of a *little king* originating in an indigenous concept of rule. In accordance with the earlier mentioned critique, it is unfeasible to apply Dirks' approach of the *little kingdom* to other regions in India without prior modification. This is because, despite intentions to the contrary, he remains too fixed on concrete events in Putukkōṭṭai and partly ties himself up in contradictions with the construction of his model. The result is a loss of the complexity exhibited by the southern Indian structures of power, and the forms in which they appear. When constructing a model one should give close consideration to the wide variety of the forms of power so as to avoid giving too great an emphasis to one particular region. Therefore the elements of processuality, alliance building and rājādharma have to be taken into account for developing a model that is more suitable to the Indian situation. The practice of shifting alliances is seminal to the dynamic and relational structure of relationships. This flexibility and the processuality of a state and its structures should be regarded as essential elements of the model. If these elements are integrated into the model of the *little kingdom* then this model can indeed be applied to different regions in India, provided that the main criteria in the definition of the *little kingdom* are found in the respective regions.

Contact Zone as a Model of Interaction

There are various models that aim to provide a theoretical framework for the phenomena resulting from cultural contacts. A dynamic concept seems most appropriate to the diversity within a culture, and to cultures as a whole. The advocates of such a concept assume that culture is 'constantly constructed and reconstructed in the interrelation between human communities, humans, and nature'.[106] A cultural framework does not develop in complete harmony within a community but from the exchange of different viewpoints. In this context, culture is understood as a series of processes which construct and reconstruct individual components, and consequently create new conditions.[107] With its dynamic notion of culture, this concept transcends differences, since the discussion of differing opinions and the negotiation of compromises belong to the very conception of a community. As a result, conflicts can be resolved verbally, military disputes avoided, and cooperation made possible. Contrary to conceptions like Huntington's *Clash of Civilizations*,[108] a violent confrontation of different interests or cultures does not necessarily ensue.

Instead, it is more sensible to speak of contacts between cultures. This establishment of contacts is generally concerned again and again, and with a varying degree of intensity, with the negotiation of new values in a political, social and economic regard. Processes of negotiation can take place over years and decades, and can prove to be dialogic or confrontational—usually they are a mixture of both forms. The area where these contacts take place may be called the *contact zone*. Originally this approach was developed by Mary Louise Pratt in the field of linguistics; later on she transferred it to the field of literary studies to analyse the genre of travel literature. This genre is characterized by people entering new cultural contexts who have to adapt to their new environment to survive. The emerging linguistic as well as societal shifts find reflection in their travel reports. In this context Pratt defined *contact zone* as follows:

> [...] 'contact zone' is an attempt to invoke the spatial and temporal copresence of subjects previously separated by geographic and historical disjuncture, and whose trajectories now intersect. By using the term 'contact', I aim to foreground the interactive, improvisational dimensions of colonial encounters so easily ignored or suppressed by diffusionist accounts of conquest and domination. A 'contact' perspective emphasizes how subjects are constituted in and by their relations to each other. It treats the relations among colonizers and colonized, or travelers and 'travelees', not in terms of separateness or apartheid, but in terms of copresence, interaction, interlocking understandings and practices, often within radically asymmetrical relations of power.[109]

According to this definition, *contact zones* are to be understood as social spheres in which cultures, previously geographically separated, meet, struggle and fight with each other. However, the contacts between cultures frequently take place in unequally shared power relations of rule and subordination, as was the case throughout colonialism and still is today in the economic relations between the so-called First and Third Worlds. If an attempt is made within a *contact zone* to link and develop longer lasting relations between previously separated cultures, then factors such as language or social context are decisive components of the processes of negotiation, which may lead towards the establishment of an imbalance or the use of force.

The concept of *contact zone* aims to prove that colonial encounters take place in areas in which both colonial and non-colonial social spheres alternate, and in which they meet with varying degrees of intensity. In these overlapping areas, the *contact zones*, the colonizers and colonized must find new ways and means to communicate with each other. Communication can take place at different levels ranging from the peaceful negotiation of different positions to military dispute over supremacy in a certain area. From a higher viewpoint, the overlapping areas that are located between two centres show that the power between these centres presents a continuum of influence. Viewed from the centres, power decreases at the periphery. In the centre—for example in the cities of Calcutta and Madras in colonial India—contact between the cultures in a colonial context was at its most intensive, whilst this was considerably less at the periphery, in some cases nonexistent.

Contact zones are variable areas in which there is a fluid transition from colonial to local culture. The contact between the cultures occurs in accordance with specific patterns of conduct in which dominant patterns of action are strongly influenced by one power. Consequently, British patterns of conduct are predominant in a centre within the European colonial power of India, for example Madras, but they hardly come across on the periphery, the so-called *mofussil*. Instead the indigenous patterns of conduct still apply there, perhaps in a slightly altered fashion due to some contact with the colonial power. Thus varying grades of respective colonial or indigenous conduct patterns are represented in a characteristic 'regional mix' in the area between the centre and the *mofussil*. It follows on from this example that verbal exchanges held in the centres were dominated by the colonial power, whilst those held on the periphery were mostly decided by the local élite. Therefore, the *contact zone* is an area of permanent cultural, political, and economic negotiation for the diverse worlds of European and local forces.[110] Resistance can also be mounted within the *contact zone*, and this can be regarded as a way of opposing the dominant verbal exchange.

The model *contact zone* provides us with a dynamic, processual model. This makes it possible to grasp the diverse nature of meetings held in different regions and the subsequent exchanges between the colonizers and the locals—simultaneously removed from concrete events and yet still appertaining to them. It takes into consideration disputes within the colonial and local exchange of words. The result may be new values or negotiated patterns of conduct. In principle, the 'partners' in this discourse enjoy equal rights, but one must remain aware that in negotiations between colonizers and locals this discourse was often negotiated from unequal positions of power.

An interesting result of the colonial discourse in the *contact zone* is the literature that emerged after the local population's conflict with the colonizers. Here, the locals represented themselves in a way which presupposed interaction with the colonizers, for they used terms characteristic of colonial projections in their descriptions. Pratt refers to this literature as auto-ethnographic and considers it to be a widespread phenomenon of the *contact zone*.[111] In India, official ethnography was an essential part of the British strategy to acquire knowledge of the land and, thus equipped with information, to be able to dominate the discourse in the *contact zone*.[112] Local élites themselves contributed partially to the discourse created by the British.

Two patterns of conduct which are pursued in the *contact zone* and which can determine the discourse will be presented in the following section. One is the discourse in dialogue form, which is fed by a continual process of negotiation between colonizers and locals and which must be reconducted again and again. The other focus of study will be upon resistance as a form of conduct by the locals against the dominant discourse of the colonizers.

Dialogue and Resistance in the *Contact Zone*

Dialogue, as the fundamental condition for communication and negotiation between human beings, is the first mode of conduct to be addressed within a *contact zone*. Eugene F. Irschick emphasizes dialogue as the most important form of discourse between Europeans and Indians. He investigates the acquisition of new knowledge as regards the sphere of agriculture and the cultural identity in Tamil̤nāṭu for the period 1795 to 1895.[113] He concludes that the construction of a new order is based on the British and locals' respective ideas of the past. These ideas functioned as a utopian version not only of the past, but also of the future. The construction was enabled by interaction both heteroglottally and in dialogue form between colonizers and colonized.[114] A motif central to the British argumentation was the view that administration and morals were non-existent in Indian society, the British thereby being obliged to create a new order. Irschick believes that the dialogue which took place between the British and the locals was the result of a long process of negotiation and change, which does not allow an originally indigenous system to be filtered out from existing sources.

For Irschick it follows that the construction of what the British and the local population understood as values belonging to a former time constitutes the attempt at finding answers to current, pressing cultural questions by interactive means. In this he clearly contradicts the argumentation of Said who claims that a stronger body will use deliberate action to manifest knowledge over a weaker one.[115] Instead he considers that altered meanings are the result of a historical situation produced by all parties heteroglottally and in the form of dialogue—even if they are not always involved to the same degree. With 'equal rights' for those involved in the dialogue, Irschick emphasizes the fact that the colonial situation is associated with domination and exploitation, since the colonizers used the wider context of colonialism to secure political, economic and social advantages for themselves.

An example of how certain forms of local culture were adopted may be found in the means of communication which the British copied from local rulers: for example, in order to gain the respect and obedience of the locals they had someone beat the drum when there was news to be announced.[116] Depending on the region, it occurred that the British officials had to rely on local figures—this would have been the case on the periphery of the *contact zone* (as described above) where the local discourse was superior to colonial discourse. During the eighteenth and nineteenth centuries, the British were faced with the problem that in certain areas they had not yet gained the extent of control they were striving for, according to their political claim to sovereignty.

One of the most important measures taken by the British since the 1790s towards creating a centralized state in India was the order and execution of surveys across all the regions in India that were under their control. With this knowledge of regional conditions set down in writing, the British formed a basis for ruling the country.[117] The assessment of taxes, which served to facilitate tax collection, constituted one of the most essential aspects of British administrative control. The aim was to set up a bureaucratic society and its respective institutions, which was based on the idea of order and social irreversibility and in which the state was given a central role.[118] In this way, ran the argument of the British governors, the rule over India could be legitimized to produce a fair system of rule—the slogan was 'just governance'. To them, the rule of law and the right to property were of primary importance; these were the values by which the British defined a 'civilized' people.[119] Accordingly, they felt they were on a 'civilizing mission' of India and its people, as is shown, for example, by Amal Chatterjee in his work on the imagination of colonialism:

> In conclusion, this study demonstrates that an objective reality of India did not exist at all in the British perception at the time. [...] Their perception-representations added up to the fact that the alien nation had to succumb, and in succumbing

proved that which had always been suspected, that the moral crisis among Britons in India and among Indians themselves could only be rectified by the civilizing influence which would be effected by the developing British administration.[120]

In his study, Irschick emphasizes that one cannot trace back the dialogue held between colonizers and colonized, nor the origin of ideas coming from it nor certain results which followed due to exclusively 'Western' or 'indigenous' origins. This is because the discourse was conducted by so many heterogeneous voices. The question may be raised here as to whether Irschick's approach of a dialogue between all those involved may be maintained as one aspect of the *contact zone* on the part of the colonizers and the colonized. In principle, this question can be answered in the affirmative but with certain reservations. More specifically, Irschick refers to the characteristics which show that some parties in the dialogue did not enjoy equal rights fully, but he emphasizes negotiation through dialogue too strongly. Amongst other things, the inferiority which was attributed by the British to non-European societies speaks against the claim that both partners in the dialogue enjoyed equal rights. The conviction that 'Britishness' was something special, namely a 'demarcation of an essential quality of difference', marked out Britain's perception of itself enjoying a position of supremacy as a modern and civilized nation.[121] A division of the processes of negotiation into different areas, and into centre and periphery within the *contact zone*, would assist in the clarification of the varying degrees of each of the dominating patterns of conduct. Most notably, the shift of power which usually took place to the advantage of the colonizers, who did not shy away from using force to assert their power in the negotiation process, is taken up by Irschick only as a marginal theme. The British awareness of their superior military power determined the majority of negotiation processes within a *contact zone*. Within a process based on dialogue, each of the parties should ideally have the possibility of making its own contribution in an atmosphere of equal rights, but this was generally not the case. In the Indian *contact zones* where the most diverse 'regional mix' could be encountered, the British found it difficult to assert themselves and to maintain their position of power in certain places. However, the British were ultimately able to maintain their dominant position—not least through the use of force. The problem with dialogue was also that the British were largely convinced of their superiority, and as a result they took away the chance for the locals to share equal rights in the discourse.

For the *contact zone* India, which includes a whole range of cultures that vary from region to region, it is also essential to consider the dimension of time. This means that the discourse, which took place between European groups and local circles within a particular period of time, also had different shapes that varied according to the respective region. Where a process of negotiation by dialogue failed in the *contact zone*—which could happen, for example, due to overly high demands by the colonial power on the locals in the form of overcalculated tax collections—the locals were left with only one option, viz. to mount political opposition against the colonial power. The move was usually motivated by the local ruler's and population's desire to prevent, or at least restrict, the extent of the colonizer's power. As a result it is difficult to provide a clear definition of resistance. The dividing-lines between political opposition and resistance are blurred.

Resistance against colonial power can take a variety of forms; assuming both the form of passive resistance, such as sabotage, and also active resistance, such as the open disregard for new regulations. James Scott advocates the thesis that certain kinds of rule provoke resistance which does not always become visible but which takes off some pressure within the social spheres of the oppressed people, for example in the adoration of bandit heroes or martyrs of the resistance. Scott calls this kind of 'resistance from the shadows' a *hidden transcript*, in contrast to the *public transcript* which presents the official version of rulers by their way of government. The possible combination of *hidden* and *public transcript* would be, for example, a stratum of rule that would sing its own praises; confronted by a people who had a limited ability to act on their own account but who knew how to use their private spheres.[122]

Another way of defining resistance consists of dividing it up into different categories. The categorizations of resistance against the arrival of Europeans in Africa, as coined by Terence Ranger and continued by Eric Stokes, provide the following division: firstly, *primary resistance*—the hostile reaction of tribes to the invaders; secondly, *secondary resistance*—the measured protest by mass movements, welfare organizations and others; thirdly, the *post-pacification revolt*, which was an act of resistance broader in structure than *primary resistance*; and, fourthly, the emergence of modern political parties as a chronological consequence of the resistance by locals.[123] Looking at the different situations in Indian history, I come to the conclusion, that this categorization can be applied to certain historical events in India, such as the mutiny of 1857, but it does not help in the analysis of the situation in eighteenth-century Malabar. Among other reasons, this is because foreigners had already been part of Malabar society for a long time and it was marked by a correspondingly high level of cultural diversity. Therefore, there was no 'first moment of contact' between locals and Europeans in the fifteenth or eighteenth centuries respectively, as suggested in the model for the example of Africa. Nevertheless, the rulers of India still had to defend their social and political role against the European conception of the state when colonization and land seizure became a real issue in the late eighteenth century.

The fundamental difficulty with the negotiation process and the associated dialogue between colonizers and locals could be put down to the various conceptions of the exercise of power. Because of their posts established in India, initially Bombay, Madras, Calcutta and Surat, the EIC assumed that, as representatives of the British crown, they would have sole sovereignty of the states.[124] During the course of the eighteenth century, the EIC applied this claim to all of their conquered regions on the subcontinent. This was accompanied by the premises that the crown, the representative of which the EIC regarded to be itself, was incontestable, that sovereignty could not be divided up, that the supremacy of the law must be established and that the hierarchy of authorities must be clearly and linearly structured. As a rule, the employees of the EIC already traded in accordance with these maxims during the last twenty-five years of the eighteenth century.[125] Closely linked to sovereignty was tax collection, which was to constitute the basis for establishing 'public tranquillity'.

This British view stood in contrast to the Indian conception of state. The essential features of the Indian concept of rule lay in sovereignty, which was divided up into several rulers, usually at differing levels of the hierarchy; it lay in a redistributive system of the division of honours and land, and also in the social interdependency between ruler and people, as mentioned earlier. Consequently, as their representatives of the state, the British and the EIC provided a sufficient number of areas in which resistance could be sparked off by the indigenous population and its rulers. Within the *contact zone,* resistance was found in those areas in which colonial discourse endeavoured to adopt the dominant position. Resistance was directed, for example, against the tax collections introduced by the British, against their attempts to regulate indigenous kingdoms from the outside, and against their trade and economic policies which were conducted with the aim of gaining a position of monopoly.

Resistance could range from political opposition to evasive action to armed conflict. According to Christopher Bayly, there were three kinds of conflict in India after 1750: firstly, clashes between British and Indian forces which arose from the breakdown of the Moguls' authority; secondly, formations of state at the periphery; and thirdly, very high demands by way of taxes, as well as attempts by the British not only to control local rulers but also trade and economic policies.[126] The first point is only applicable to the states in northern India whilst the second and third points are also relevant to the situation in southern India. A crucial influence here was the deployment of the army, which was to enforce the soaring demands of the British in India during the period around the eighteenth century.

As we have seen, *contact zone* can serve as a suitable model to analyse the situation connected with the British intrusion into India. The processes of negotiation going on between the two groups representing different cultural attitudes could take different shapes. Dialogue would have been the peaceful way for negotiating within the *contact zone*, but in many areas of colonial India the power structure did not allow for an equal standing of the participating parties. In many cases this resulted in passive or even active resistance, as for instance in Malabar where the *hidden transcript* became public. The paramount concern for local élite groups, indeed the chief reason for their resistance, was the EIC's claim to possess sovereignty in India according to the European model. The EIC thus refused to recognize the proportionally exercised sovereignty of local rulers. Sooner or later this situation had to result in the British clashing with those rulers who were not prepared to exchange their rights to sovereignty for a post as tax collector or retired official of the EIC. In such instances there arose a *clash of sovereignty*,[127] which can be understood as a collision of differing conceptions of sovereignty, namely the sovereignty in India which was actually being exerted by local rulers, and the abstract claim to sovereignty of the EIC within the *contact zone*.[128] Chapter Four will offer a closer look at the forms of dialogue that were employed in the negotiation process between the Malabaris and the British from 1790 to 1805.

Notes

1. Cadwell, Sarah L., 'Bhagavati: Ball of fire', in: John Straton Hawley and Donna Marie Wulff (eds.), *Devi: Goddesses of India*, Delhi 1998, pp. 195–226, p. 213.

2. Whilst the concept of a person's idèntity in Western psychology depends on his/her ability to distinguish him/herself from others and to exhibit an individual, unique character, in the Indian context a manifest identity has a different make-up: amongst the goddesses, the ones who are considered strong are often those who bring together contradictory characteristics within one figure. Thus the goddess is strong because she goes beyond the limits of human personalities, and has a character incomprehensible in its complexity. Cf. Michaels, Axel and Sharma, Nutan, 'Goddess of the Secret: Guhyeśvarī in Nepal and Her Festival', in: Axel Michaels, Cornelia Vogelsanger and Annette Wilke, *Wild Goddesses in India and Nepal*, Bern et al., 1996 (Studia Religiosa Helvetica 96), pp. 303–42, p. 333.

3. Cf. Bernier, Ronald M., *Temple Arts of Kerala: A South Indian Tradition*, New Delhi, 1982, p. 65.

4. Cf. Kurup, K.K.N., *The Cult of Teyyam and Hero Worship in Kerala*, Calcutta, 1963, p. 21.

5. MLTMT, Ms. 77, No. 3, in: Mahalingam, *Mackenzie Manuscripts*, p. 294.

6. For the use of the term *dēvī*, cf. Tarabout, Gilles, *Sacrifier et Donner à Voir en Pays Malabar: Les Fêtes de Temple au Kerala (Inde du Sud): Etude*

Anthropologique, Paris, 1986, p. 109. For information on the use of the term *durgga*, cf. Gundert, *Dictionary*, p. 756, col. 1.

7. *Devimahatmyam* (Glory of the Divine Mother), trans. by Swami Jagadiswarananda, Madras s.a., cap. 4, verse 31–34 and cap. 9, verse 31.

8. Cf. Buchanan, *Journey*, vol. 2, p. 512.

9. Caldwell, 'Bhagavati', p. 196.

10. The myth of Bhagavati as Śiva's daughter can be found in Menon, C. Achyuta, 'A Note on Kali or Bhagavati Cult of Kerala,' in: *S. Krishnaswami Aiyangar Commemoration Volume*, Madras, 1936, pp. 234–8, p. 237f.

11. Gundert, *Dictionary*, p. 756, col. 2.

12. *Periyapurāṇam*, Book 33, verse 16, trans. by T.N. Ramachandran, Thanjavur, 1995, p. 4.

13. Parameswaran Pillai, V.R., *Temple Culture of South India*, New Delhi, 1986, p. 157.

14. Coburn, Thomas B., *Devi Māhātmya: The Crystallization of the Goddess Tradition*, Delhi, 1984 (reprint 1997), p. 115. Cf. also *The Śatapatha-Brāhmaṇa*, According to the Text of the Madhyandina School, translated by Julius Eggeling, part 1, Oxford 1882, reprint Delhi, 1963 (Sacred Books of the East 12), p. 219, verse 10.

15. Mani, Vettam, *Purāṇic Encyclopaedia: A Comprehensive Work with Special Reference to the Epic and Purāṇic Literature*, Delhi, 1975, reprint Delhi, 1996, p. 113.

16. Cf. Tarabout, *Sacrifier*, p. 576.

17. Cf. Tarabout, *Sacrifier*, p. 577,. Miller, E., 'Caste and Territory', p. 413.

18. Since any detailed depiction of such a festival would exceed the boundaries of this work, I refer the reader to the following studies: Tarabout, *Sacrifier*; Caldwell, Sarah L., *Oh Terrifying Mother: Sexuality, Violence and Worship of the Goddess Kāli,* New Delhi, 1999; Kurup, *Teyyam*, primarily p. 17; and Freeman, J. Richardson, 'Performing Possession: Ritual and Consciousness in the Teyyam Complex of Northern Kerala', in: Heidrun Brückner, Lothar Lutze, and Aditya Malik (eds.), *Flags of Fame: Studies in South Asian Folk Culture*, Delhi, 1993 (South Asian Studies 27), pp. 109–38.

19. Cf. Gonda, Jan, *Die Religionen Indiens Vol. 2: Der jüngere Hinduismus*, Stuttgart, 1963 (Die Religionen der Menschheit 12), p. 9.

20. Letter by the Senior Kōṭṭayaṃ Rājā to the Commissioners from 20th Karkkaṭagaṃ [= Karkkaṭaṃ] 973/1.8.1798, in SPP, OIOC P/380/72.

21. Report by the *harkārā* Kingayen, who cites therein a speech by Paḷaśśi Rājā, from 30.3.1798, in SPP, OIOC P/380/69.

22. Letter by Paḷaśśi Rājā to Jonathan Duncan from 22. Kuṃbhaṃ 974/2.3.1799, in MCR 1735 (TNSA); Letter by Paḷaśśi Rājā to the government from 20. Mēṭaṃ/ 29.4.1799, in BC, OIOC F/4/62; Letter by Paḷaśśi Rājā to J. Smee from 3. Kuṃbhaṃ 973/12.2.1800, in HMS, OIOC H/471. Subcollector Wilson only mentions Perumāḷ as the protective deity in his report: MCR 2546 (TNSA) (Mr. Wilson's Report, dated 15 February 1801), § 39.

23. Consultation of Sheenoo Patter in Kozhikode on 15. and 17.1.1798, in SPP, OIOC P/380/68.

24. Letter by Paḷaśśi Rājā to John Spencer from 23. Kuṃbhaṃ 974/5.3.1799, in SPP, OIOC P/381/2. Letter by Paḷaśśi Rājā to John Spencer from 27. Mīnaṃ 974/6. or 7.4.1799, in SPP, OIOC P/381/3. Letter by Paḷaśśi Rājā to the government from 20. Mēṭaṃ s.a./29.4.[1799], in BRP, OIOC P/366/25.

25. Vgl. Kieniewicz, Jan, 'Asian Merchants and European Expansion: Malabar Pepper Trade Routes in the Indian Ocean World-System in the Sixteenth Century', in: Karl Reinhold Haellquist (ed.), *Asian Trade Routes*, Kopenhagen, 1991 (Studies on Asian Topics 13), pp. 78–86. p. 86.

26. Miller, E., 'Caste and Territory,' p. 414.

27. Cf. Bernier, *Temple Arts*, pp. 55, 94. There is a brief mention of the Kēraḷite method of contructing temples in Srinivasan, K.R., *Temples of South India*, New Delhi, 1972 (India—the Land and People), pp. 181–90.

28. Oral information from locals, September 1998.

29. According to information given by a descendant from Pindāli-*taṟavāṭu* in an interview on 14.9.1998.

30. These performances take place from 1–3 March. Oral information from Krishna Kumar Marar, 14.9.1998. Raktacāmuṇḍi is used as a synonym for Kāḷi and depicts the 'darker' aspect of Bhagavati here. Coburn, *Devi Māhātmya*, p. 134f.

31. Consultation of Palavīṭṭil Cantu in front of the Commission on 25.5.1798, in SPP, OIOC P/380/70.

32 PR 46 A&B.

33. According to oral information from Krishna Kumar Marar this refers to the goddess Bhagavati. K.K. Marar also makes the assumption that the king portrayed here is a member of the Kōṭṭayaṃ dynasty. Personal communication from September 1998.

34. Cf. Marar, Krishna Kumar, 'Rediscovering a Unique Tradition: Murals of Thodikkalam', *The India Magazine of Her People and Culture*, 12 (1992), pp. 50–9, p. 52.

35. Oral information from the priest during a temple visit in September 1998.

36. According to information given by P. Cantu he must have stayed there in February 1797. Consultation of P. Cantu on 28.12.1798 in BC, OIOC F/4/33.

37. PR 21 B; PR 61 A&B, PR 117 A&B.

38. Extract from the Bombay Political Consultations of 30.5.1797, in BC, OIOC F/4/33.

39. Cf. Marar, 'Rediscovering', p. 52.

40. Oral information by residents. I was not allowed to enter the temple when I visited Maṇattaṇa in September 1998.

41. Sewell, *Lists of Antiquarian Remains*, p. 244.

42. Report by Sheenoo in Kōḷikkōṭu from 15/17.1.1798, in SPP, OIOC P/380/68.

43. Maclean, C.D. (ed.), *Manual of the Administration of the Madras Presidency*, 3 vols., Madras 1885–93, reprint New Delhi and Madras, 1990, vol. 3, p. 1036, col. 2: unit of measure, also known as *macleod seer*(as it was introduced by Macleod

in northern and some parts of southern Malabar). 10 *iṭaṅṅāl*s equal 1 *paṟa*, the nearest real value is 113 3/4 cubic inches. Often called *yadangu*, *yedangaly* or *yidangazhy* in English.

44. Consultation of Paḷavīṭṭil Cantu in Calicut 25.5.1798, in SPP, OIOC P/380/70.

45. Information by P. Cantu, Mayyali 13.12.1798, in BC, OIOC F/4/34.

46. For information on the function of the *harkārā*, cf. Bayly, *Empire and Information*.

47. Report by the *harkārā* Kingayen, Kōṭṭayaṃ 30.3.1798, in SPP, OIOC P/380/69.

48. A British station was the 'usual Anglo-Indian form of settlement' and encompassed 'the requisite official buildings, the fixed camp of the garrison, the living quarters of the officers and officials and all institutions needed to represent and support society'. Pieper, Jan, *Die anglo-indische Station oder die Kolonialisierung des Götterberges: Hindustadtkultur und Kolonialstadtwesen im 19. Jahrhundert als Konfrontation östlicher und westlicher Geisteswelten*, Bonn, 1977 (Antiquitates Orientales series B, 1), p. 129.

49. Letter with instructions to Colonel Dow and the Northern Superintendent by the Commissioners, Calicut 3.6.1796. in SPP, OIOC P/E/10.

50. PR 5 A.

51. Paḷaśśi Rājā to Manjerry Allum from 30. Mēṭaṃ 975/20.4.1800, in HMS, OIOC H/461.

52. Innes and Evans, *Malabar*, p. 424.

53. *Census of India 1961*, vol. 7: Kerala, part 6 H: Village Survey Monographs Tribal Areas, Trivandrum and Kottayam, 1974, p. 226, col. 1.

54. Cf. *Census of India 1961*, Kerala State, Distict Census Handbook 1 Cannanore, s.l. 1965, p. 77. Oral information on site in September 1998. Regarding the myth about the foundation of the temple cf. Nair, C. Gopalan, *Malabar Series. Wynad: Its Peoples and Traditions*, Madras, 1911, p. 116.

55. *Census of India 1961*, vol. 7: Kerala, part 6 H, p. 227, col. 2.

56. Nair, C.G., *Malabar Series*, p. 120.

57. Information received during a visit of the temple on 26.9.1998.

58. Letter by Paḷaśśi Rājā to Alexander Dow from 11. Mīnaṃ 973/21.3.1798, in BC, OIOC F/4/68.

59. Information given by local residents during visit of the temple on 26.9.1998.

60. The temple of Kōṭuṅṅallūr was dedicated to Bhagavati. Cf. MLTMT, Ms. 79, No. 11, in: Mahalingam, *Mackenzie Manuscripts*, p. 320.

61. Nair, C.G., *Malabar Series*, pp. 123–6. Pillai also speaks of the Vaḷḷiyūramma as the Koṭuṅṅallūr Bhagavati. Pillai, *Temple Culture*, p. 177.

62. Whilst visiting the temple on 27.9.1998.

63. According to information given by the principal of the Paḷaśśi Rājā College in Pulpaḷḷi, 28.9.1998. The inscription stone, on which the land donor's documentation is carved in Vaṭṭeḻuttu script, was found by the principal and handed over to the University of Calicut, Kōḻikkōṭu, Kēraḷa. Unfortunately, on request the stone

could not be found there anymore. This stone is also mentioned in Sewell. Cf. Sewell, *Lists of Antiquarian Remains*, p. 245.

64. These are described in detail in Vaidyanathan, K.R., *Temples and Legends of Kerala*, Bombay, 3rd edn., 1994, p. 179f.

65. Moorthy, K.K., *The Kovils of Kerala: An 18-Petal Fragrant Rose*, Tirupati, 2nd edn., 1997, p. 170f.; Vaidyanathan, *Temples and Legends*, p. 181f.

66. Vaidyanathan, *Temples and Legends*, p. 184.

67. Innes and Evans, *Malabar*, p. 429.

68. Cf. Dirks, *The Hollow Crown*, p. 10f. The supporters of *ethnohistory*, contrary to traditional Western historiography, firstly lay great store by the study of non-material culture, which is manifest in honours or titles, for example. Secondly they consider social structuring, defined as dynamic, to be a tool for analysis. Thirdly they challenge inventive contact with the existing data instead of a quantification of the historical material, which often no longer exists in the case of South Asia anyway. Fourthly they demand that historical facts be depicted with as little interpretation as possible, i.e. just as facts. Copland, Ian, 'The Historian as Anthropologist: "Ethnohistory" and the Study of South Asia', *South Asia* 11 (1988), pp. 101–16, p. 107f.

69. Legitimation and manifestation are used here as technical terms. They were coined by Dietmar Rothermund. Cf. unpublished script of his lecture at Heidelberg University in Winter Semester, 1993/94.

70. Clearer than in *The Hollow Crown*, this can be found in: Dirks, Nicholas, 'The Pasts of a *Pālaiyakkārar*. The Ethnohistory of a South Indian Little Kingdom', *JAS* 41 (1982), pp. 655–83, p. 659.

71. Cohn, Bernard, 'Some Notes on Law and Change in North India', in: idem, *An Anthropologist Among the Historians and Other Essays*, New Delhi, 1990, pp. 554–74.

72. Cohn, Bernard, 'Political Systems in Eighteenth-Century India: The Banaras Region', in: idem, *An Anthropologist Among the Historians and Other Essays*, New Delhi, 1990, pp. 483–99. First published in *The Journal of the American Oriental Society* 82,3 (1962).

73. Dirks, *The Hollow Crown*, p. 5. Cf. also Dirks, 'The Pasts', p. 681.

74. Cf. Dirks, Nicholas, 'The Structure and Meaning of Political Relations in a South Indian Little Kingdom', in: *CIS*, 13 (1979), pp. 169–206, p. 169.

75. Dirks, *The Hollow Crown*, p. 123f., cf. also p. 53.

76. Dirks, *The Hollow Crown*, p. 246, cf. also p. 28.

77. Cf. Dirks, *The Hollow Crown*, p. 53f., 123; idem, 'The Structure', p. 203.

78. The necessity of conflict is also underlined by Shulman, who describes the king's power as vague: the king was not so much the centre of power but more the focus of balance and the embodiment of society's consensus—whereby the consensus was primarily reached by conflict, both internally and externally. Thus the king had to make his position clear time and time again, if necessary through conflict. Shulman, David D., 'On South Indian Bandits and Kings', *IESHR* 17,3 (1980), pp. 283–306, p. 305f.

79. Cf. Dirks, *The Hollow Crown*, p. 95.

80. Cf. ibid., p. 29.

81. Ibid., p. 5 resp. 70.

82. Cf. Dirks, 'The Pasts', p. 659.

83. Cf. Dirks, *The Hollow Crown*, p. 95f.

84. Ibid., p. 29; cf. also p. 129: 'No gift was given without reason, intention, and interest.'; p. 130: 'The gift was thus a principal element of statecraft.' and 'The political economy was thereby predicated on a set of moral principles and understandings.'

85. Dirks, Nicholas, 'From Little King to Landlord', in: idem (ed.), *Colonialism and Culture*, Ann Arbor, 1992, pp. 175–208, pp. 179, 180.

86. Cf. Dirks, 'The Structure', p. 204.

87. Dirks, *The Hollow Crown*, p. 126.

88. Cf. ibid., p. 8; p. 53f.

89. Cf. ibid., p. 19; Dirks, 'From Little King', p. 180.

90. Berkemer, *Little Kingdoms,* p. 14.

91. Cf. Dirks, *The Hollow Crown*, p. 95.

92. Cf. ibid., p. 11.

93. Cf. Kulke, Hermann, 'The Early and the Imperial Kingdom: A Processural Model of Integrative State Formation in Early Medieval India', in: idem (ed.), *The State in India 1000–1700*, Delhi, 1997, pp. 233–62.

94. Cf. Appadurai, Arjun, 'Kings, Sects and Temples in South India, 1350–1700 A.D.', *IESHR* 14,1 (1977), pp. 47–73.

95. Cf. Berkemer, *Little Kingdoms*, p. 14.

96. Schnepel, *Die Dschungelkönige*, p. 54. Additionally Schnepel points out in his definition of a *little king*: 'A king can also be a person who proclaims royal authority for himself—but who does so in accord with generally accepted collective conceptions about the nature of royal authority and about the requirements for its appropriation and ownership, which are commonly expressed through ideology and ritual. *And* this person requires recognition by (a sizeable proportion) of the local population, which is subordinate to such a kind of demanded authority.' Ibid., p. 72.

97. Berkemer, *Little Kingdoms*, p. 10.

98. Cf. Kautilya, *The Arthashastra*, ed. by L.N. Rangarajan, New Delhi, 1992, book VI, chapter 1, verse 1.

99. Cf. Mahalingam, T.V., *South Indian Polity*, Madras, 2nd edn., 1967, p. 18.

100. Cf. Price, Pamela G., *Kingship and Political Practice in Colonial India*, Cambridge, 1996 (University of Cambridge Oriental Publications 51), p. 17.

101. Cf. Lingat, Robert, *The Classical Law of India*, California, 1973, reprint Delhi et al., 1998, p. 211; Inden, Ronald, 'Ritual, Authority, and Cyclic Time in Hindu Kingship', in: John F. Richards (ed.), *Kingship and Authority in South Asia*, Delhi et al., 1998, pp. 41–91, p. 50f.

102. Mahalingam, *South Indian Polity*, p. 30.

103. These activities are specified in Kautilya, *Arthashastra*, book II, chapter 1.

104. Cf. Price, Pamela G., 'Raja-dharma in 19th Century South India: Land,

Litigation and Largess in Ramnad Zamindari', *CIS* 13,2 (1979), pp. 207–39, p. 209. Fuller stresses that the protection of a kingdom required the king to have had a respective relationship with the gods and to have taken responsibility for the correct adherence to the rituals. The role of the king in the temple was a constitutive element of his rule. Fuller, Christopher J., 'The Hindu Temple and Indian Society', in: Michael V. Fox, (ed.), *Temple in Society*, Winona Lake, 1988, pp. 49–66, pp. 57, 59.

105. Price, *Kingship*, p. 15f. Appadurai and Breckenridge go so far as to describe the deity as a sovereign ruler—not one that rules over a territory, but rather one that governs over the whole redistributive process. Appadurai, Arjun and Breckenridge, Carol A., 'The South Indian Temple: Authority, Honour and Redistribution', *CIS* 10,2 (1976), pp. 187–211, p. 195.

106. Jahn, Beate, 'Globale Kulturkämpfe oder einheitliche Weltkultur? Zur Relevanz von Kultur in den Internationalen Beziehungen', *Zeitschrift für internationale Beziehungen* 2 (1995), pp. 213–36, pp. 230, 218.

107. Cf. Wolf, Eric R., *Europe and the People Without History*, Berkeley, Los Angeles and London, 1982, p. 387.

108. Huntington, Samuel P., *The Clash of Civilizations and the Remaking of World Order*, New York, 1996. This work is an enlarged version of his article that appeared three years earlier, in which he stamps the clash of civilizations with a question mark. Huntigton, Samuel P., 'Clash of Civilizations?', *Foreign Affairs* 72,3 (1993), pp. 22–49.

109. Pratt, *Imperial Eyes*, p. 6f.

110. Christopher Bayly speaks of Indian society in the eighteenth century as a typical 'frontier society', whose internal influence over the state was in constant flux. Bayly, Christopher A., *Indian Society and the Making of the British Empire*, Cambridge, 1988, reprint Cambridge, 1997 (The New Cambridge History of India II, 1), p. 31. Sivaramakrishnan labels the periphery zones of Bengal in the eighteenth and nineteenth centuries as 'zones of anomaly', since they evaded British attempts to meddle with the state and thus showed the limits of colonial means of intervention. Sivaramakrishnan, K., 'British Imperium and Forested Zones of Anomaly in Bengal, 1767–1833', *IESHR* 33,3 (1996), pp. 243–82, pp. 245, 281.

111. Cf. Pratt, *Imperial Eyes*, p. 7.

112. Cf. Cohn, Bernard S., 'The Past in the Present: India as Museum of Mankind', *History and Anthropology* 11,1 (1998), pp. 1–38, p. 29. See also Frykenberg, Robert E., 'The Emergence of Modern "Hinduism" as a Concept and as an Institution: A Reappraisal with Special Reference to South India', in: Günther-Dietz Sontheimer and Hermann Kulke (eds.), *Hinduism Reconsidered*, 2., ext. ed., New Delhi, 1997 (South Asian Studies 24), pp. 82–107, p. 92. The founding of the Asiatic Society of Bengal on 15.1.1784 also acted to survey Indian traditions. For this cf. Kejariwal, O.P., *The Asiatic Society of Bengal and the Discovery of India's Past, 1784–1838*, Delhi et al., 1988.

113. Irschick, *Dialogue*.

114. Ibid., pp. 4, 70.

115. Said defines the East as the weaker unit and the West as the stronger one. Cf. Said, *Orientalism*, p. 204. Irschick's critique on Said can be found in Irschick, *Dialogue*, p. 8.

116. Cf. Irschick, *Dialogue*, p. 22.

117. In Maisūr, Kanara and Malabar, Francis Buchanan was the one who compiled the first report—unfortunately it was far from comprehensive. Cf. Buchanan, *Journey*.

118. Cf. Irschick, *Dialogue*, p. 68f.

119. Cf. Metcalf, Thomas R., *Ideologies of the Raj*, Cambridge, 1995 (The New Cambridge History of India III, 4), p. 1.

120. Chatterjee, Amal, *Representations of India, 1740–1840: The Creation of India in the Colonial Imagination*, London and New York, 1998, p. 202.

121. Metcalf, *Ideologies*, p. 4. Bitterli also refers to the inequality of the partners. Cf. Bitterli, Urs, *Die 'Wilden' und 'Zivilisierten': Grundzüge einer Geistes- und Kulturgeschichte der europäisch-überseeischen Begegnung*, 2., ext. edn., München, 1991, pp. 173–9.

122. Scott, James, *Domination and the Arts of Resistance: Hidden Transcripts*, New Haven and London, 1990, pp. xi, xii, 18. Elsewhere Scott describes this kind of resistance as a form of Brechtian class struggle, which can be understood as self-help. Individual actions are thus linked through loose coordination. Scott, James, 'Resistance Without Protest and Without Organization: Peasant Opposition to the Islamic *Zakat* and Christian Tithe', *Comparative Studies in Society and History* 19,3 (1987), pp. 416–52, pp. 419, 452.

123. Stokes, Eric, 'Traditional Resistance Movements and Afro-Asian Nationalism: The Context of the 1857 Mutiny Rebellion in India', in: idem, *The Peasant and the Raj*, Cambridge, 1978 (Cambridge South Asian Studies 23), pp. 120–39.

124. The documentation with the authorization for free trade within Bengal and the regions which belonged to it was often cited as proof, as was an exemption from certain taxes dating to 1717, which did not entitle the British to any rights of sovereignty whatsoever, but the British interpreted this differently. Cf. Bayly, Christopher A., 'The British Military-Fiscal State and Indigenous Resistance, India 1750–1820', in: Lawrence Stone (ed.), *An Imperial State at War: Britain from 1689 to 1815*, London and New York, 1994, pp. 322–54, p. 329.

125. Cf. Bayly, C., 'British Military-Fiscal State,' p. 332f.

126. Cf. Bayly, C., 'British Military-Fiscal State,' p. 334.

127. Bayly talks of a 'clash of authority'. Bayly, C., 'British Military-Fiscal State', p. 347.

128. The European term sovereignty encompasses, on the one hand, the state autonomy over external forces and, on the other hand, the internal autonomy of the people of the state in matters of the community. Cf. Kühnhardt, Ludger, *Stufen der Souveränität: Staatsverständnis und Selbstbestimmung in der 'Dritten Welt'*, Bonn, 1992, p. 9f. For information on the history of the term, cf. Quaritsch, Helmut, *Souveränität: Entstehung und Entwicklung des Begriffs in Frankreich und Deutschland vom 13. Jh. bis 1806*, Berlin, 1986.

Three

In Search of Black Gold

Since ancient times trade had been one of the most important factors for Malabar in its contact with other powers. The trade between Europe and Malabar is relatively well documented for pre-modern times.[1] However, markedly scant sources on Malabar's relationships with other Indian powers make it hard to form any adequate impression of Malabar's position within Indian trade networks before the sixteenth century. It is only possible to present here a brief outline of the historical context in which the British pursued their expansionist policy in the second half of the eighteenth century.

From the sixteenth century onwards, Malabar's relations with European powers came increasingly to the fore. This contact with the Europeans also brought a change to the quality and intensity of Malabar's external relations: enduring contacts were created, replacing the trade contacts that had previously occurred only from time to time. Starting with the early trade contacts between Malabar and merchants of different origins, this chapter will then discuss, in chronological order, the contact between Malabar merchants and rulers and the Portuguese, the Dutch, the French, and the British, who had been coming to Malabar since the sixteenth century. Each power tried to control the trade in a different way and, in the long term, deprived the Malabar rulers of their sovereignty. Another subsection is devoted to the relationships of the Malabar rulers with their most powerful neighbours in the north, Maisūr, and to the period of the Maisūrian hegemony in Malabar during the eighteenth century.

Economic Attractiveness of Malabar

It was the economic importance of the so-called genuine pepper, *piper nigrum,* a plant native to Malabar and considered so valuable that it was known as 'black gold', that led the European powers to seek a sea route to India. In fact, pepper constituted one of the most important trading goods from classical times—the Greek and the Romans amassed exceptionally high profits by trading in Malabar pepper.[2] In subsequent centuries, pepper also made up approximately three-quarters of the cargo which was shipped westwards from

India.[3] One reason for this was the importance of pepper in Europe for conserving meat, and another was its purported medicinal effect.[4] The cultivable areas for pepper are spread out acoss the whole of Malabar, but it was the pepper gardens in Kottayam and north-west Cirakkal that held special attraction for merchants.[5] Here the pepper lianae grew in the shade of other trees and lived up to fourteen to twenty years.[6] Two types of produce are harvested from the pepper gardens of this region. The first is black pepper, which is the end product from unripened and unpeeled dried fruits and the second is white pepper, which is harvested from ripe, peeled fruits.

Besides pepper, cardamom and cinnamon were also important goods of trade for merchants of Malabar and abroad. Cardamom, *elettaria cardamomum*, also known as genuine cardamom and belonging to the ginger family, is a plant native to south India[7] and was especially cultivated in Vāyanāṭu. The cardamom from Vāyanāṭu was of a higher quality than that from the lowlands and could be sold for up to 100 rupees more per *kaṇṭi*[8] than the cardamom from other spice-growing areas. The annual cardamom harvest in Vāyanāṭu amounted to between 50 and 100 kaṇṭis in the eighteenth century.[9]

Cinnamon also played a crucial role in the trade of ancient times. One of the Roman and Greek uses for cinnamon was in the manufacture of perfumes.[10] The Dutch held the monopoly on cinnamon from 1636, the English from 1796 to 1832. Yet this monopoly became less important on account of the spread of cinnamon trees to other tropical areas. From among the different kinds, Ceylonese cinnamon (*cinnamomum zeylanicum*), which the Romans called *malabathrum*, is still grown in Malabar today.[11] During the sixteenth century, there was also an increasing demand for ginger, *zingiber officinale*, and it was consequently cultivated to a greater extent.[12]

The products of the coconut tree (*cocos nucifera*) can be used in a variety of ways. In Kēraḷa, where the fruits are counted amongst the most important foodstuffs, the palm branches are also useful in the construction of huts or for covering roofs. The fibrous bark of the coconut tree is made into *kāyar*, the uses of which include the manufacture of ropes—which is still an important product for sea travel.[13]

The basic function of trade is to exchange goods which either do not exist, or do not exist in sufficient quantity in the respective partner region. A decisive factor which marked the economy of Malabar in the eighteenth century, and continues to do so today, is the constant rice deficit and the desire to make up this deficit through imports from neighbouring regions. From the sixteenth to the eighteenth centuries, the other regions' demand for pepper thus proved advantageous to the trade of the Malabar merchants.[14] Through the import of rice and export of pepper, both basic constants for trade were laid down—the economy of Malabar thus gained stability. Trade was an important source of income not only for the merchants but for the local ruler(s) as well.[15] This again had its impact on the kind of governance exerted in Malabar, which we earlier depicted as ecology of rule.

The network of water-routes was highly significant to the trade of this epoch, since it provided an ideal transport route for goods. At the same time, the use of water-routes reduced transport costs considerably and enabled the pepper producers themselves to be present at the coast to sell their goods.[16] Steep mountainsides, jungles and rivers made conditions difficult for transporting goods over land, which is why such transports were undertaken either by caravans of oxen or by porters. The use of land-routes was indispensable, however, since they connected different water-routes with one another. Of particular importance were the land-routes between Malabar and the area of today's Tamiḻnāṭu: Tamiḻ merchants brought goods including rice and different kinds of fabric to Kēraḷa and, on their return to the Coromandel coast, took back highly sought-after pepper, which financed the costs incurred by the land-based trade. Weekly bazaars, *aṅṅāṭi*s, functioned as the focal points of this trade.[17]

Trade in Malabar fitted into the larger trade network of the Indian Ocean. According to K.N. Chaudhuri, it is possible to determine two kinds of trade pattern within the area of the Indian Ocean from the seventh to the fifteenth century: firstly, transcontinental trade and secondly, trade by shorter routes, i.e. the flow of goods to regional markets.[18] The latter can be subdivided further into local trade on the spot and regional trade with villages further away. These villages were usually located on the same continent and could be reached either by land or sea-routes. The following regions were important for Malabar's regional trade: firstly, Kanara with its principal ports of Bhatkal and Honavar. Kanara exported rice to Malabar and imported pepper. The important horse trade also connected the ports of Bhatkal and Honavar with Kannūr. Secondly, Gujarat and in particular the port of Surat which imported pepper, coconut, areca nut, palm sugar and copper, and exported rice, indigo, sealing-wax, and gold and silver coins. The Gujarati merchants constituted one of the most important groups for Malabar trade. Their posts were located in Kannūr, Kocci and Kōḻikkōṭu.[19] Thirdly, the Coromandel coast, which delivered mainly rice and cotton textiles to Malabar and to which was brought in return pepper, palm sugar, areca nut and kāyar. Fourthly, Bengal, which supplied Malabar with textiles, cereals, sealing-wax, sugar and rice, and to which the Malabar merchants exported spices. These few examples of regional trade within India show that Malabar played an important role within the inner Indian trade. This importance also applies for Malabar's trade with other Asian countries; the Malabar merchants delivered pepper, ginger, cinnamon, cloves, nutmeg, cardamom, kāyar, sandalwood and coconut to South-East Asia. They imported sealing-wax, textiles and sugar in return. Although this trade was restricted by the commercial activity of the different European powers, it still continued to function throughout the whole of the eighteenth century.[20] The intra-Indian trading routes, of which Malabar was the centre, contributed to the formation of a 'world system' of the Indian Ocean.[21]

Attention can now be turned towards transcontinental trade. In ancient times, trade between the Malabar coast and western countries was effected primarily from the central ports of Muziri, present-day Koṭuṅṅalūr,[22] and Patale (probably present-day Pantalāyini Koḷḷaṃ). Very little is known about the subsequent centuries: Trading activity between East and West can be assumed but not proven. Islamic merchants from West Asia had been forming trading relations in the Indian Ocean since the ninth century and had partly established themselves on the Malabar coast as well. Through the influence of the Muslims, an exchange of ideas, economic systems, social requirements, political institutions, and artistic traditions took place between Islamic merchants and the Indian population, which was predominantly characterized by Hinduism and Buddhism.[23]

Since the tenth century, transcontinental trade had been divided up into several small routes: instead of making a trade voyage from West Asia to East Asia and back in one go, as had been customary in previous centuries, merchants now preferred to divide up this route into successive, smaller segments by setting up intermediate stops and goods transfer stations in the ports situated on the west coast of India, above all in the ports of Malabar. These emporia extended along the west coast of India from Malabar to Gujarat; some of them were also trade emporia at which ships were put in at port directly from West Asia. Kōḻikkōṭu counted among the emporia on the Malabar coast[24]—it was also known as 'the pivot in the exchange between Eastern and Western Asia'.[25] Regional coastal shipping and overseas trade overlapped in these emporia an̦d, as a result, up until approximately 1350, the entire Indian Ocean formed a sphere for trade and economics. Trade could be pursued here regularly and without interruption up until the sixteenth century.[26]

In the seventeenth century the demand for products from the Malabar coast was stimulated by the increasingly competitive European powers, most notably the British and the Dutch, although Indian and Asian merchants continued to dominate the trade of the Indian Ocean. Yet by the end of the seventeenth century, the influence of the Indian merchants was in continual decline due to political and administrative problems, which proved to be an obstacle to trade in the majority of Indian regions.[27] They only became visible on the Malabar coast during the eighteenth century, when the sphere of domestic policy lost its equilibrium due to the invasions of Haidar Ali and Ṭippu Sulttān. The aggressive practice of European merchants, who wanted to gain control of trade by force of arms also contributed to these problems. Just how the effects of these developments appeared in detail is subject to controversial debate. Arasaratnam's opinion is that the use of force by the Europeans was no reason for the decline of Asian dominance at the end of the seventeenth century—he argues that only the European private merchants brought about the decline of Asian trade.[28] Opposed to Arasaratnam, however, is the view that necessary space was taken away from Indian merchants by the—mostly forcible—seizure of different ports and trading places, and that they were thus no longer able to transact their business in the usual manner. As a result, the Europeans grew in importance and were gradually able to take hold of and determine the structure of trading and later also of production in the hinterland.

An essential aspect of the trading structure was the establishment of direct merchants' relations between producers of goods and the tradesmen. The traffic of trade lay in the hands of highly qualified merchants: Firstly, trade was run privately, i.e. with little support from the rulers. Secondly, the merchants enjoyed a considerable degree of political freedom and thirdly, the ports were politically neutral.[29] This meant that the merchants had a relatively free hand while pursuing their trading activity, and that they were not placed under any state control. Due to political fragmentation and the emergence of numerous subdivisions in Malabar, neither the merchants nor the local élite were able to control or dominate the production of goods. Nevertheless, trade still supplied the rājās in Malabar with an important source of income: the route duty on goods, *cuṅkaṃ,* was charged at the borders for transporting goods. However, no direct land taxes were taken from the population.[30] According to Ashin Das Gupta, the rulers joined together with the merchants in order to keep out the Europeans from trade. In accordance with traditional customs, if the merchants exported their goods—above all pepper—to neighbouring regions, then the rulers received cuṅkaṃ, which would have been lost had the purchase of goods been made by Europeans.[31]

The most striking difference between pre-modern and modern trade can be found in the differing time cycles of trade and in the various degrees of dependency upon goods. Pre-modern trade was essentially less centralized than the trade of today. This can be put down to the fact that pre-industrial societies enjoyed a greater degree of self-sufficiency. Consequently, less importance was attached to long-distance trade. As mentioned previously, the main purpose of pre-modern trade was to make up for deficits of certain goods in certain areas by using the overproduction of these same goods from other areas. Since the economic situation of Kēraḷa was characterized by a rice deficit and an overproduction of essential cash crops, including pepper and coconut, greater importance was attached to trade in these goods.

The Portuguese, the Dutch and the French

As mentioned previously, India—and in particular the Malabar coast—was attractive to European merchants because it offered an abundance of goods that were not available in Europe. In the 'age of discovery', the sea-route to India around the Cape of Good Hope was also rediscovered. Trade structures in the Indian Ocean were to change drastically as a result of the Europeans' trade and their attempts to control trade by monopolies. Within the course of the century, the British converted their economic supremacy in India into a territorial supremacy, preparing the ground for the conflict that arose between the Europeans and the local people on the Malabar coast.

The Portuguese

The arrival of Vasco da Gama (1469–1524) on the Malabar coast in May 1498 marked a new 'era' for the population and especially the merchants of Malabar.[32] It seems most likely that the Portuguese first headed for the Malabar coast, and not for Gujarat or the Coromandel coast because Kōḻikkōṭu was known as the Indian Ocean's largest spice market, and also because Muslim merchants who had settled there had cultivated good relations with the Tāmūtiri, the ruler of Kōḻikkōṭu.[33] Trading towns such as Kōḻikkōṭu were centres that acted as focal points through which the exchange of economic products and all manner of information was quickened.[34]

The Portuguese arrival in India signalled the end for the previously self-determined trade within the Indian Ocean.[35] As is well known, there were two methods by which the Portuguese sought to control trade: one method was the *cartaz* system, which was introduced by Vasco da Gama in 1502[36] and allowed trade only for those in possession of a cartaz. The aim of issuing cartazes was to secure Portuguese control over all trade within their sphere of influence. The introduction of cartazes not only aroused the contempt of Indian merchants, but has also provoked controversial debates within the research on this period. Dietmar Rothermund explains the introduction of the cartazes with the fact that the Portuguese, on the basis of their superiority at sea, wanted to force local merchants to start manning the toll stations which they, the Portuguese, had constructed in certain ports. In this way the cartazes were used by the Portuguese to charge tolls, which was actually their economic motive.[37] In following years, it was not only the rājās of the Malabar coast, but also the Mogul and other rulers who were forced to acquire cartazes in order to permit their merchants to continue trading. Nevertheless, Indian merchants did still try to avoid purchasing cartazes—this occurred in Kēraḷa, for example, through the use of land-routes to the Tamil land. Thus large quantities of pepper escaped the notice of the Portuguese, since they were only in control of sea-routes. In other instances ships were simply sent on their route without a cartaz because the merchants received higher prices for their goods, especially pepper, from other trade partners. Consequently, the Portuguese managed to get only about one-fourth of the entire pepper production, although they had aimed at controlling the market by establishing a monopoly through the cartazes. As a second measure in the attempt to gain complete control of the spice trade, the Portuguese entered into agreements with Indian rulers which allowed for pepper to be bought at lower prices; such a business corresponded to a royal monopoly. They then sold the pepper in Europe at higher prices, which meant, even after the deduction of expenditure for forts and controls, that a considerable profit margin was achieved.[38]

In spite of every attempt to control trade on the Malabar coast the Portuguese had to rely on the cooperation of local merchants in Malabar, at least in the sixteenth century:

> The Portuguese tried to persuade the local rulers to participate in the organization of deliveries to their factories, but without great success. Thus the Portuguese were for the whole of the sixteenth century dependent upon the local merchants. In any event, they did not manage to carry out their plans to effect control of the routes or to subordinate the cultivators.[39]

Yet the Portuguese were still able to establish trading-posts in Kannūr, Koṭuṅṅalūr, Kocci and Koḷḷaṃ. It was in Kocci in 1503 that the first European fort was built on Indian soil, the one in Kannūr soon followed around 1505.[40] The forts had been built to safeguard the trading-posts and were located at strategic points along the coast. They did, however, restrict Portuguese control to only those places where they had built forts—excluding the hinterland.[41] To conduct sea trade it was necessary for the respective rājās to purchase cartazes; Kannūr occasionally received permission to take part in the horse trade.[42] Kōḻikkōṭu suffered a severe blow at the start of Portuguese rule: Vasco da Gama pillaged the town and demanded the expulsion of all Muslim merchants. However, the Tāmūtiri of Kōḻikkōṭu did not obey this demand, because Muslim merchants had been settled for centuries and were indispensable to trade. In retribution the Portuguese carried out frequent attacks on Kōḻikkōṭu; as a result and despite the protection offered by the Tāmūtiri, many of the Muslim merchants left the town and this led to the decline of a once flourishing trade.[43] The politics employed by the Portuguese were characterized also in the following centuries by the attempt to gain political and economic control of the Indian Ocean merchants. The Portuguese set up the headquarters of the *Estado da India* in Goa, which, with the aid of a newly created administrative structure, was charged with the day-to-day control of the remaining Portuguese bases.[44] All Portuguese efforts were aimed towards gaining monopoly over all spices, and yet they were only able to achieve partial success in the case of the pepper trade.

Clearly then, the main reason why a nation as small as Portugal succeeded in dominating the trade system in the Indian Ocean for such a long time[45] was the cartaz system, which resulted in their control of considerable sections of the Indian Ocean. The many Portuguese operations were financially supported by German and Italian sponsors. However, the Portuguese did not command sufficient power to exercise complete control over an area; they therefore stuck to controlling ports by building forts and foreign trading-posts.[46]

The arrival of the Dutch and the British in Asia presented a new challenge for the Portuguese, to which they had to pay attention. The British and the Dutch were in a position to break the Portuguese control over trade in the Indian Ocean: the cartaz system had no role to play in the new, structurally capitalist system of the British and Dutch trading companies.[47] The establishment of a liberal trade policy[48] by the North European powers went hand in hand with the gradual decline of Portuguese power and its economic prosperity.

The Dutch

The Dutch had already sealed a treaty with an Indian prince in 1604,[49] but up until approximately the mid-seventeenth century, they remained insignificant in the grand scheme of securing the largest profits from trade in the Indian Ocean. Heavy battles first broke out with the Portuguese over supremacy of the Indian Ocean in the second half of the seventeenth century. The Dutch laid the foundation, for the territorial control of India by European powers, partly through the use of violence. In order to usurp the exclusive position of the Portuguese in India, the Dutch Verenigde Oostindische Compagnie (VOC) also tried to gain control over the various Portuguese trade routes. Additionally the Dutch developed the art of diverting the Asian goods of the Portuguese into their own routes.[50]

For Portuguese merchants, the Dutch conquest of Kocci in 1663 marked the end of their dominance.[51] Thanks to the structures in Malabar that the Portuguese had established, such as trading-ports and forts as well as numerous trade conventions, the Dutch inherited a solid foundation to control trade in Malabar.[52] Yet in taking on Portuguese estates the Dutch also inherited the problems of the Portuguese.[53] The VOC's tactics—oriented towards the Portuguese model—were to seal exclusive treaties with Asian rulers in order to secure Dutch economic advantages within the area over which the respective prince ruled. On many occasions such treaties were signed under duress. Thus it took the Dutch just a short century to establish a number of fixed bases in Malabar, including the trading ports in Taṅṅaśśēri, Kocci, Koṭuṅṅalūr and Kannūr.

Hardly any sources exist on the Dutch position in Malabar for the decades at the turn of the eighteenth century, but one can presume that the Dutch, besides their problems with local rulers, also had to fight out conflicts with other European powers, especially the British. Some of the Dutch estates were located within Tiruvitāṃkūr, with whose rājā the Dutch had been disputing over a free passage through his territory since the 1730s. The resulting military clash lasted five years—in 1753, the Dutch had to admit defeat in Tiruvitāṃkūr. Consequently, Tiruvitāṃkūr had moved its northern border up to Kocci. The Dutch were thus denied thē chance of purchasing pepper at relatively cheap prices in Tiruvitāṃkūr, and transferring it to their main base Kocci. Also, the Rājā of Tiruvitāṃkūr stripped the Dutch supervisors of their sovereign status in Kocci, which meant that they then had to buy pepper at the usual market rates.[54] This was the beginning of the end of Dutch colonial rule in Malabar, since Kocci was the central key element of Dutch trade in India.[55] The Dutch power in Malabar dwindled once Rājā Martanda Varmma deprived them of their trade privileges, most importantly of the price-fixing of pepper in their favour. From the time of this treaty onwards the Dutch were no longer the dominant European power in southwest India.[56] In the following years the Dutch gave up more bases on the Malabar coast; for example, they sold fort St. Angelo in Kannūr to Ali Rājā in 1771.[57] Dutch supremacy in Malabar came to an end in 1795, when they abandoned Kocci. According to Ashin Das Gupta, this end actually brought more relief than regret for the Dutch, firstly because the pepper trade had not flourished to the degree they expected, and secondly because domestic Asian trade was not going as well as it had been in the 1770s.[58] A reason for the stagnation of Dutch trade with Asia was that having accumulated a relatively large amount of capital through trade in the seventeenth century, in the eighteenth century, the Dutch increasingly specialized in investing capital. They then gave higher priority to financial transactions, and this is one of the explanations for why Dutch capital investors held approximately a one-third share of the English EIC.[59]

A new aspect concerning the Dutch (and the British, see below) lay in their merchants coming together under trading organizations. In principle, these organizations separated those owning capital from skilled workers, here the merchants and employed paid administrators. Consequently, bureaucratic economic organizations (VOC, EIC) took over parts of the previously monopolized or private trade. The result was a fundamental change to previous trade structures: in ancient times, trade relations between Western and Asian merchants were isolated in nature, whereas the Europeans strove for long-lasting exchanges of goods at fixed prices. Associated with this was their desire to maximize profits, the realization of which meant added costs for Asian merchants. The result was a considerably closer contact between members of different cultures than ever before.

The influence of the British and Dutch companies can be put down to several points according to K.N. Chaudhuri: firstly, the new way of organizing capital into joint stock, secondly, the introduction of national monopolies and thirdly, the integrated organization of the merchants. These three aspects exhibited innovative features: the investment of capital into joint stock guaranteed the merchants long-term security over financial matters. The monopolies—even if they were not always exercised to their full extent—guaranteed the respective trading nations a partial exclusivity over their trading goods, and a better organization of the merchants in Asia resulted in more efficient teamwork. The pinnacle of economic activity for the VOC and EIC was attained in the early years of the eighteenth century. Amsterdam and London, the principal trading cities in Europe, were the leading emporia for re-export. Large trading regions of the Indian Ocean (India, China, South-East Asia) had to cooperate within a system of dependent economic relations; within their respective internal economic system, however, they pursued autonomous activities as they had done previously.

Both the British and the Dutch had a declared goal: dominance in the trade with India. They sanctioned their actions with weapons and did not shy away from attacking Asian countries even without prior provocation. The use of force remained a part of the Europeans' policy in Asia for the following reasons: firstly, they required military and political security in order to protect their relatively large accumulation of capital and goods; secondly, force was considered to be a legitimate means to achieve certain goals; and thirdly, they attempted to gain and maintain tolls, for example as income payments for political authority, in order to be able to cover the high costs of sustaining a merchant fleet.[60] With these motivations in mind the Europeans pursued a different trading policy than was applied in the Indian Ocean before their arrival. Not only did trade routes change, but so did the manner of conduct between the different merchant groups and merchants: a colder breeze began to blow.

The French

On various occasions throughout the seventeenth century, attempts were made to found a French East India Company. These attempts, however, either died from the outset or the expeditions towards Asia came to nothing. This was mainly due to the fact that the French companies were set up by the state and thus functioned without private capital and its attendant flexibility.[61] Finally, minister Colbert established the Compagnie des Indes Orientales in 1664, which was set up in Putuccēri in 1674.[62]

In 1725, on the Malabar coast, the French captured Mayyaḻi, which was renamed Mahé after the French general who was victorious there. The French ambition to establish themselves in India gave rise to the formation of another front for clashes with the British besides those in Europe. The British and the French, however, made peace in 1728 so that they could unite in keeping down the price of pepper: 'We, for the benefit of each other, do agree, from time to time, to settle the price of pepper, as often as is necessary, and neither can break the price without advising the other, nor yet raise it without the other's knowledge.'[63] Yet this peace did not last for long. The subsequent clash with the British took place in 1751; after the siege of Talaśśēri the French flag flew over the town and a peace treaty was concluded in 1752. By 1756, however, military skirmishes occurred in India as a result of the Seven Years War in Europe. The French occupation of Fort St. George in Madras in 1759 ended in a fiasco; shortly before being captured, Putuccēri was razed to the ground by the British in 1760. The French began to forge links with Haidar Ali from 1766. This was also the reason for retaining Mayyaḻi as the French base on the west coast, since Mayyaḻi was the closest French town to Śrīraṅgapaṭṭaṇam. Even after the death of Haidar Ali in 1782, the connection to Maisūr's new ruler, Ṭippu Sulttān, was maintained. Both Putuccēri and Mayyaḻi remained bones of contention between the two European powers well into the nineteenth century, when they finally came under French control. However, the French were unable to achieve any further territorial gains in India, making the British the only European power with territorial dominion.

In view of the century-long attempts by different European powers to achieve supremacy in the Indian Ocean, the question arises as to which motives led them in this pursuit. One reason was the desire to make the most profitable trade possible in spices and other exotic goods, a second reason was the subsequent intention to largely monopolize this trade in order to turn out an even higher profit for themselves. In this endeavour the European merchants were generally not concerned so much with the quality of the goods, but with the quantity and the profit which was to be made as a result.[64]

In principle, trade was an attractive business for Indian merchants as well as rulers, for whom tolls on routes constituted a part of their income. Thus, they initially looked upon trade with Europeans favourably. Only when the demands by the Europeans for trade monopolies and, later on, for territorial control of the land emerged, did relations between Indians and Europeans become more tense. However, the question remains as to why the Indian rulers were not able to repudiate and prevent the territorial claims of the Europeans, which resulted from their trading power. A cluster of factors can be called upon here, ones which relate partly to the military and naval weaknesses of the local states of the Indian Ocean in their international relations, and partly to a fundamentally different understanding of trading and state interests. The Asian rulers were unable to maintain the neutrality of their trading ports since they generally lacked the requisite naval power to do so. Furthermore, political and economic concepts of European companies were alien to Asian rulers (the system of passes, mercantilism)—they had nothing with which to resist them other than their handed-down traditions.[65] A phenomenon which allowed the European domination of trade, and later of politics, particularly in southern India was the prevailing political fragmentation: there was no central power that could have opposed the strong grip on the country by the Europeans. Moreover, local élite did not regard trade at sea as a problem of power—anybody could sail and trade on the ocean.[66] Accordingly, Indian merchants traded with European just as with Arab and Chinese merchants during earlier centuries. And consequently, Indian rulers did not recognize the danger coming over the sea—the claim to territorial power by the Europeans.

Initial Contacts with the British

The economic factor was and continued to be the motive behind the British establishment in India. Thus the particular officials who pursued their own private trading interests were crucial to policy on site, whilst the guidelines of the EIC Court of Directors in London were usually not put into practice. The aim of the EIC was to gain political concessions from the local rulers so that the British could trade profitably.[67] In the long run they succeeded with their policy of manipulating Asian trade according to their own rules. When Asian merchants reduced their share in this trade, the British could step in and eventually fill the existing trade vacuum.[68]

The rivalry among the Europeans caused the British to build up an army in Asia, which was also deployed against the local population later on. From the eighteenth century onwards they also took on Indian soldiers, the so-called *sepoys*.[69] Since the foundation of the EIC, Malabar had been one of the most important destinations for British traders, primarily because of spices.

Pepper was exported on a direct route from Kocci to England for the very first time in 1635. During the seventeenth century the British were also able to establish a permanent bridgehead in Malabar in Añcuteṅṅa. They had received this permission in 1684 from the Āṟṟiṅṅal Rāṇi. Pepper was available there in abundance; the calicos from the region around Añcuteṅṅa were of high quality. These advantages made up for the disadvantage that the coast there was not well suited for landing of ships. Six years later the British were granted permission by the Rāṇi to build a fort in Añcuteṅṅa, from which both the road and the sea could be observed. This fort could also be used for other strategic purposes. At the end of the seventeenth century, the British established another trading-post in Talaśśēri—their second permanent base on the Malabar coast. One reason for this choice was its 'proximity to the finest pepper and cardamom lands in Malabar',[70] which were located in the hinterland of Talaśśēri. The most productive pepper gardens were situated in the prinicipality of Kōṭṭayaṃ, which comprised Talaśśēri. In the early years of its existence the British factory was simply a trading-post. In 1704/5, the British started to build a fort in Talaśśēri on the rock jutting out of the harbour bay. The fort was completed in 1708, and was intended to protect the port in the event of surprise attacks.[71]

According to Buchanan's report, 15,000 kaṇṭis of pepper were produced in Malabar in the years 1764/5. At the beginning of the nineteenth century, 8,000 kaṇṭis of pepper p.a. were harvested in Malabar, of which 4,000 kaṇṭis were from Kōṭṭayaṃ. During the time of Paḷaśśi Rājā's rebellion, only 2,500 kaṇṭis of pepper were produced in Kōṭṭayaṃ.[72] In 1772, the British carried out the first 'regular revenue assessment' in Talaśśēri, which projected a tax of 40 per cent of the harvest for the rice fields owned by the EIC.[73] From the years 1776 to 1784, Talaśśēri had the status of a British residence, which meant that the troops protecting the fort were withdrawn. Only from 1784 was Talaśśēri rewarded the status of a fort and built up into a defensive base.[74] Talaśśēri remained one of the principal British ports in Malabar up until 1792. In the subsequent years until 1805, it was the bridgehead for the territorial conquest of Malabar. Both the port and the fort of Talaśśeri were strategic points and thus a stronghold for the British against the invasions from Maisūr.

In order to give an official framing to the trade with Kōṭṭayaṃ, the British sealed an initial peace treaty with local rulers in 1736. The treaty included such promises as that of the Rājā of Kōṭṭayaṃ to regard all enemies of the EIC as his enemies too, and to deal with them accordingly.[75] The first treaty containing mutual obligations followed fifteen years later, and provided a payment of 40 rupees per day for the Rājā, payable every fifteen days. On the other hand, the treaty obliged the Rājā to provide the EIC with a thousand men if so required and not to put any obstacles in the way of the British trade from and to Talaśśēri, which ran through his land.[76] If we examine these agreements it becomes evident that the British consistently strove to link treaties formed on economics with their own political and military advantages—a tactic which gradually brought them political influence in India.

The British settlement on the Malabar coast marked the beginning of the gradual subjugation of the country, initially by Western ideas of trade and economy but increasingly also in political and administrative regard, which ended in the territorial appropriation of the country by the British.[77] Furthermore, the British were largely able to drive back the influence of other European powers, above all the Dutch and French.

Yet it was not only with European competitors that the British came into conflict; they came increasingly under fire from Indian rulers, within and outside of Malabar. At the end of December 1789, the ruler of Maisūr, Ṭippu Sulttān, attacked the Travancore lines, the fortified border between Kocci and Tiruvitāṃkūr. This provided the British with a welcome opportunity to declare war. In accordance with a decree that Lord Cornwallis[78] had drawn up on 13 November 1789, the British understood this as *casus belli*:[79] they perceived it as occasion and fair reason to start a war against Ṭippu Sulttān. The result was the start of the third Anglo–Maisūr war. Lord Cornwallis decided to travel southwards himself and set things right there, as well as to ask the Marāṭhās and the Nisām of Haidarabād for help against the Maisūrians. At the same time, the British called for the support of the Malabar rājās with 'general assurances of protection'[80] under which they were guaranteed their independence after the end of the war. Cornwallis presumably held the view that the taxes of the Malabar rājās, regarding planned cargoes of spices to Europe, could also be handed over to the British even if these rājās did not come under British administration. In a proclamation in April 1790, it was announced that all those who were subordinate to the EIC would be guaranteed protection, whereas those who refrained from it would be considered enemies of the EIC in future.[81] This proclamation resulted in a change of direction regarding the rājās' actions towards the British.[82] On the one hand, this meant 'carrot and stick' tactics by the British, who held out only the prospect of peace for the Malabaris in exchange for their involvement in the war, but on the other hand, the rulers were left with no other choice than making a deal with the British if they wanted to shake off the burden of the occupying forces and taxation by Maisūr.

On 4 May 1790, the Kōṭṭayaṃ Rājā, along with the other northern rājās, accepted the conditions of the British. In return, the British assured the rājās of the following:

In the name of the English East India Company and the Governor-General of Bengal I [...] do hereby assure you [...] to render you independent of Tippoo Sultan, and as you have agreed to enter into an alliance with the Honourable Company on the same basis of friendship that formerly subsisted between both parties, [...] I do hereby further assure you that, in any future treaty that may take place between the Company and Tippoo Sultan you shall be included and considered as an ally of the Honourable Company.[83]

At the end of May 1790, Lord Cornwallis once again confirmed that he would do everything possible for the independence of the Malabar rājās, whilst at the same time sealing their dependence on the EIC; he did this by fixing 'moderate tributes' to and trade privileges for the EIC.[84] In the government in Bombay, however, the sovereignty and rule of the rājās of Malabar did not appear to be questioned.[85]

In August of the same year, the British forced the Bibi of Kannūr to enter into a provisional treaty under which she had to grant the British entitlement to access her fort at any time. From then on it served as a garrison for British soldiers in Kannūr. As a result the Bibi traded as an ally of the British, just like other Malabar rājās.[86] The hesitant acceptance of treaties by local rulers can be taken to show that they saw through the British game. This is evident, for example, in the delayed fulfilment of the treaty by the Bibi of Kannūr: only in November 1790 did she send the Maisūrian troops stationed in Kannūr back to Maisūr. In December 1790 she then signed the final capitulation and submitted to the British: 'Thus Cannanore, the first place in India to welcome Europeans to Indian shores, was the last of the important places in Malabar to pass into the conquering hands of the British.'[87] The Bibi of Kannūr was the last amongst the local rulers to enter into a treaty with the British. Yet as far as resistance by the rājās is concerned, Kōṭṭayaṃ was the principality that became British property last of all; and this happened only after the death of Paḷaśśi Rājā in November 1805.

In February 1792, the British won the war against Ṭippu Sulttān, thanks to the active support they had received from the Malabar rājās.[88] The British dictated a peace treaty on 18 March 1792 in Śrīraṅgapaṭṭaṇaṃ, which provided for the handing over of Malabar from Ṭippu to the British.[89] Shortly before the conclusion of the treaty Cornwallis had decided not to grant independence to the rājās in Malabar contrary to the agreement of 1790, but to place them under the direct administration of the British.[90] This action may be interpreted as a strategy to achieve economic monopoly over the products of Malabar with the aid of political control. In addition, the annexation of Malabar and the economic gain which was expected to follow would relieve the financial problems of the EIC in the Bombay Presidency.[91]

Such was the situation in 1792 from the point of view of the local rulers:

actually the temporary hegemony of Ṭippu Sulttān over Malabar had caused serious problems,[92] and yet the end of the Maisūr rule, which was brought about by the British in 1792, did not bring the peace that was longed for. Instead foreign rule was in store once again: this time that of the British. The guarantee of independence for the Malabar rājās which had always been emphasized and confirmed on several occasions by the British, now appeared, after the victory over Ṭippu, to have passed into oblivion in the eyes of the British.

> [...] yet neither common sense, or common justice could give any ground to suppose it was meant that they should retain their countries, and all the revenues of them, free and independent of us and of our interior control. [...] that their protection and security under some reasonable participation of the revenue is the utmost they could expect.[93]

Subsequently, conflict broke out between the Malabar rulers and the British. For with this breach of the treaty of 1790, the British denied the rājās their sovereignty and relieved them de facto of the administration of their territories—contrary to the earlier concluded treaties. Particularly humiliating for the ruler of Kōṭṭayaṃ, Kēraḷa Varmma Paḷaśśi Rājā, was the British agreement with Vira Varmma Rājā of Kurumpranāṭu over tax collections in Kōṭṭayaṃ. In this, the British suppressed the authority of Kēraḷa Varmma in Kōṭṭayaṃ; they no longer recognized him as a partner in negotiations. The British change of mind over their policy in Malabar was unexpected but could be explained by their economic ambitions.[94] After Paḷaśśi Rājā had been denied the peace that was promised in 1790, and the British had undermined his authority with their treaty with Vira Varmma, he began to doubt their integrity.

By the treaty of Śrīraṅgapaṭṭaṇaṃ in 1792, the British pursued additional measures designed to incorporate the individual principalities of Malabar into the British Bombay Presidency. This resulted in changed relations between the British and the Malabar rājās: If the British had been concerned up until that point with the extension of their economic and political control over the rulers and merchants, then their interest was now focused on establishing an efficient administrative structure in the new province, which was to support itself financially through tax payments and which was ideally to aspire to yielding profit. Henceforth, the British regarded themselves as masters of the land and people, something which certain rājās did not care to accept without resistance. Furthermore, the Malabar rājās were caught between the Maisūrian-British front; they found themselves 'between the devil and the deep sea'. This was most evident in the clash over Vāyanāṭu, which Ṭippu and the British fought out at the cost of Paḷaśśi Rājā.[95] The consequences of this situation will be looked into in the following chapter.

The Invasions of Haidar Ali and Tippu Sulttān

This section will focus on the events that shook Malabar from the mid-eighteenth century onwards and exerted a lasting influence on internal structures in Malabar. At that time, Maisūr, which was situated north of Malabar, was one of the most powerful Indian kingdoms, and it was the most sizeable opponent of the British in the conflict over supremacy in Malabar. Due to the lack of sources, however, it is only possible to look at the most prominent events and provide a highlighted account of Maisūrian policy in respect to Malabar.

With Haidar Ali's usurpation of the throne of Maisūr in 1761, and his subsequent expansionist actions, a new political situation was emerging in southern India. Only a short while after he had secured his position, Haidar Ali carried out campaigns of conquest into the lands to the south and north of his kingdom. The series of Maisūrian invasions caused devastation to a degree hitherto unknown and also brought about fundamental long-term changes to the social and economic structure of Malabar. This period was a milestone in history for Kōṭṭayaṃ, too.[96] Haidar Ali's policy of expansionism and conquest can be explained primarily through his interests relating to foreign policy; on the one hand he was concerned with creating a large kingdom in southern India and, on the other hand, with shutting out the growing British power as much as possible.[97] After his death in 1782, his son Ṭippu Sulttān assumed power in Maisūr, and took on his expansionist and anti-British policy as well.[98]

In the spring of 1766 Haidar Ali moved up with his troops to Malabar for the very first time. Initially he made good headway, appointed Ali Rājā of Kannūr as his governor in Malabar, and left Malabar eastwards in the direction of Kōyamputtūr.[99] Yet in June of the same year the Nāyars of Kōṭṭayaṃ began to put up resistance against Haider Ali's plans for conquest.[100] They were able to capture the fort of Niṭṭūr near Talaśśēri in September, thereby giving the signal to rebel not only in Kōṭṭayaṃ, but in the whole of Malabar. Even if the Maisūrian troops seemed to be overwhelmingly numerous in comparison to the population of Malabar, the invasions met with resistance. Though Malabar was divided in numerous parts, most of the local rulers united in their action against the invaders.

Even where the land appeared to have been conquered in military terms, none of the rājās were ready to give up their sovereignty. They tried using their own methods to avoid Maisūr's hegemony over Malabar. The Rājā of Tiruvitāṃkūr supported the Malabar rājās in their rebellion against Haidar Ali in order to keep him busy in Malabar, and thus stall his planned attack of Tiruvitāṃkūr.[101]

The rebellion caused Haidar Ali to head back to Malabar where he was able to crush it with his troops. Haidar Ali's advantage over the Malabar people lay in his well-drilled army, which had been partially trained by Europeans. Contrarily, the Nāyars were not coordinated as a concerted unit, which meant that neither their military training nor their knowledge of the partly impassable terrain helped them to victory when fighting the superior strength of the Maisūrians.[102] Haidar Ali's reaction to the rebellion was severe: his troops devastated the land and treated the civilian population roughly. Several men were hanged, numerous women and children enslaved. Furthermore, Haidar Ali had an edict enacted which declared the following: firstly, the Nāyars were deprived of their privileges; secondly, their caste status was to take the lowest standing in the order of caste; and thirdly, it was forbidden for the Nāyars to carry weapons (any Nāyar who carried a weapon was considered to be an outlaw). Haidar Ali's intention behind the edict, presumably, was to alienate Nāyars from the rest of the population. Their influence, unchallenged to date, needed to be broken. When it proved impossible to implement this edict, however, it was toned down by an additional edict, which promised the retention of privileges to those Nāyars who turned to Islam.[103] This measure signalled a forced conversion to Islam of the Nāyars and triggered their mass flight from Malabar to Tiruvitāṃkūr. A few of them, however, did remain in the country after having given in to the pressure and having converted to Islam. After Haidar Ali departed from Malabar, leaving behind troops in all of the strategically important places in the country, and having ordered the construction of a fort in Pālakkāṭu, it appeared that the land was at peace. Yet the rājās of Malabar, the Kōṭṭayaṃ Rājā included, were determined to free their land from Haidar's rule and asked the British in Talaśśēri for help against the occupation of Haidar Ali, finally sealing a treaty with the British.[104]

Threatened in the north and north-east by the Marāṭhās and by the Nisām of Haidarabād, Haidar Ali decided in November 1766 to leave the entire pepper harvest as well as other products of Malabar to the British trading-post in Talaśśēri. This generous gesture was designed to pacify at least one of his opponents for some time.[105] His actual aim was to attack Tiruvitāṃkūr because its rājā had steadfastly resisted the status of a tributary state of Maisūr. Haidar Ali required free passage through Malabar in order to do this. Yet the Nāyars in Kōṭṭayaṃ succeeded in inflicting a defeat on one of his troops which was stationed on the route to Tiruvitāṃkūr in 1767. This victory gave the signal for further general rebellion in Malabar and shook the Maisūrian position for a short while. August of the same year marked the outbreak of the first British war against Haidar Ali. The Rājā of Kōṭṭayaṃ remained true to the alliance with the British because he saw in them a reliable ally. Thus in March 1769 the British and 1,700 Nāyars from Kōlattunāṭu and Kōṭṭayaṃ fought together under the command of a British officer against Haidar Ali, and yet they remained unsuccessful. On 3 April 1769 Haidar Ali dictated the conditions for a peace treaty in Madras, which declared amongst other things that the British had to return the fort of Niṭṭūr (near Talaśśēri) to the Rājā of Kōṭṭayaṃ. This peace treaty marked the end of the first Anglo–Maisūrian war and peace appeared to have returned again to Malabar.[106]

Twelve years later, in 1778, Haidar Ali took the opportunity of using the military clash between the French and the British, which broke out on account of the French recognition of the American declaration of independence, for his own military operations.[107] With a large army he moved southwards against the British; he supported the French because he was reliant on French deliveries of horses and weapons and European reinforcement over Mayyaḻi—his 'window to Europe'.[108] The rājās of Kōṭṭayaṃ, Kaṭattanāṭu and the Tāmūtiri of Kōḻikkōṭu remained loyal to the British.[109] The French capitulated on 19 March 1779, and one day later the Union Jack was flying over Mayyaḻi. As a reward for their loyalty to the British, the Rājā of Kōṭṭayaṃ and the Tāmūtiri of Kōḻikkōṭu were temporarily returned those areas that they had lost to Haidar Ali.[110] However, the hostilities were not over yet. By the following year (1780) the Maisūrians had subjugated southern Malabar. In addition to military conquest, Haidar Ali attempted to establish his supremacy through negotiations with as many of the rājās of Malabar as possible. A meeting was finally held in February 1780 in Tamaraśśēri between Sirdār Khān, the representative of Haidar Ali in Malabar, and the Kōṭṭayaṃ Rājā, in which a tributary payment of two lakh rupees from Kōṭṭayaṃ to Maisūr was agreed. However, since Kōṭṭayaṃ was only able to pay a maximum of one lakh rupees by itself, and since it did not receive any support from the EIC despite being its ally, a presumed total of 60,000 rupees was actually paid to Sirdār Khān. It is not clear from existing sources as to whether the remaining 140,000 rupees were paid at a later date. In addition, Talaśśēri was occupied by Maisūrian troops for eighteen months from the middle of 1780.[111] During these conflicts Kōṭṭayaṃ was a reliable ally to the British, one reason for this being that Talaśśēri—ruled by the British—was a safe place for all those who had to fear losing property to Maisūr. Additionally, all those who had to pay taxes to Maisūr tried to avoid doing so by moving to Talaśśēri. This was possible at least as long as the British did not levy any direct taxes. On the other hand, Talaśśēri was situated in the area of Kōṭṭayaṃ, which meant that the British were in some ways dependent on the Rājā of

Kōṭṭayaṃ.[112] Had the Kōṭṭayaṃ Rājā broken the alliance at this stage, the days of the British in Malabar would have been numbered. Yet they did not seem to have been aware of the explosiveness of the situation and refrained from making any payments to the Kōṭṭayaṃ Rājā to reward his support.[113]

At the end of 1781, the fortune in war was favouring the British: After the government in Bombay had provided a further supply of troops, they were able to notch up a victory against the Maisūrian troops in Malabar. The commanding officer of the Maisūrian army, Sirdār Khān, committed suicide, presumably because of the defeat. These events triggered rebellions in the whole of Malabar; an end to the skirmishes was not in sight. As a result, Ṭippu Sulttān moved southwards and occupied southern Malabar, whilst northern Malabar continued to remain in the hands of the local rājās and the British.[114] The news of Haidar Ali's death in December 1782 caused Ṭippu Sulttān to suddenly leave Malabar in order to safeguard his own assumption of power. Contrary to all expectations he managed to do this by peaceful means, which meant that he could continue fighting in Malabar.[115] Finally, the second Anglo–Maisūrian war came to an end in March 1784 with the peace settlement of Maṅgalūr in favour of Ṭippu. The peace agreements involved Malabar coming under the occupation of Ṭippu even though the rājās of Malabar had fought on the side of the British for their liberation from Maisūr. In spite of their loyalty to the British, they were now once again at the mercy of Ṭippu's occupation.[116] Thus the rājās of Malabar were the real losers in the hostilities between Ṭippu Sulttān and the British.

In April 1788, Ṭippu Sulttān stayed in northern Malabar to settle the differences between his commanding officers stationed in Malabar and to build a fort at the Bēppūr river.[117] From there he held several audiences with English residents in Kōḻikkōṭu, but these ended without any agreements. Ṭippu's rule over Malabar had the result that the messengers of the rājās, who were generally Brahmins, were no longer safe. Consequently, the rājās of Kōṭṭayaṃ and Kaṭattanāṭu asked the British for protection.[118] Ṭippu Sulttān reacted to this with the order to carry out forced conversions of the Brahmins to Islam.

> [...] to begin the so much desired work of the conversion of the Hindoos and to seize on the Brahmins, (whether Namboories or others,) and make them examples to the other inferior casts, in becoming Mussulmans, by suffering circumcision and being compelled to eat beef: accordingly many Brahmins were seized in or about the month of July 1788, and were thus forcibly deprived of their casts, whilst others sought for shelter with the Raja's of the Samoory's family [...][119]

The forced conversions from July to November 1788 resulted once again in a rebellion which was led by Ravi Varmma from the House of the Tāmūtiri.

This uprising is regarded as the most dangerous rebellion against Maisūrian rule.[120] Ravi Varmma was successful against the Maisūrians and moved towards Kōḻikkōṭu. Ṭippu's troops drove him out from there, however, and pursued him into the interior of the country. Yet Ṭippu was unable to defeat Ravi Varmma in the hinterland. The rebellion spread to northern Malabar,[121] something which approximately 30,000 Brahmins, with their families, took advantage of in order to flee to Tiruvitāṃkūr. On 15 February 1789, Ṭippu Sulttān called upon the British in Talaśśēri not to guarantee protection to any Nāyars. His march from the Tamaraśśēri pass in the direction of northern Malabar caused a general exodus of northern Malabar Nāyars and rulers.[122] Among the fleeing people was also the senior rājā of Kōṭṭayaṃ who, prior to his flight to Tiruvitāṃkūr in 1788/9, had handed over responsibility for his people to Kēraḷa Varmma Paḻaśśi Rājā of Kōṭṭayaṃ, presumably one of his nephews.[123] Memories of Ṭippu Sulttān's forced conversions are still alive today within the population of Malabar.[124]

Ṭippu Sulttān not only applied military strategies to consolidate his rule in Malabar; he also established a marriage alliance between his own and one of the Malabar royal families, which he hoped would guarantee friendly relations between the ruling families, and acceptance by the people. Accordingly, in April 1789, one of Ṭippu's sons (Abd-ul-Khalic) and one of the daughters of the Bibi of Kannūr were married. Ṭippu gave the Bibi a part of Cirakkal as a wedding present. Presumably, this was a strategy used by Ṭippu to keep the Bibi in a peaceful state of mind, and also to put an end to the rebellions by the population in Kannūr, primarily made up of Māppiḷḷas who supported their rulers. This was thus a politically important marriage, planned by Ṭippu for strategic reasons. Nevertheless, the Bibi appeared as amicable as ever towards the EIC, even if she secretly did not always behave according to the rules; trade, for example, was more profitable if it was not carried out using the intermediate stages of the EIC.[125]

Still Ṭippu Sulttān did not seem to be satisfied with the extent of his territory: he planned to subdue Tiruvitāṃkūr as well. The third Anglo–Maisūrian war started at the end of December 1789 with Ṭippu Sulttān's attack on the Travancore lines, the northern border fortification of Tiruvitāṃkūr. Among their allies the British engaged some of the rājās of Malabar. In the south Indian power struggle, that characterized the third Anglo–Maisūrian war, the tides had shifted: For the first time during his reign Ṭippu Sulttān had to fight against the British without any allies, whilst they could rely on the support of several allies, including the Nisām of Haidarabād.[126] One of the main reasons for Ṭippu's isolation in Malabar was the forced conversions that he had carried out, which had done great damage to his reputation.[127] In addition, the enormous tax levels that Ṭippu Sulttān had imposed on the Malabar rulers burdened the whole country to an extent hitherto unknown, something which was carried over to the population in the form of dissatisfaction and unrest. At the start of the war Ṭippu Sulttān was able to notch up some successes in spite of his difficult situation. One of the battlefields between the British and the Maisūrians was Kōḻikkōṭu, which Ṭippu Sulttān attacked in 1790; this endeavour was animatedly described as follows:

> [...] [Ṭippu Sulttān] appointed a detachment of his troops to ravage the country of his enemies, and they accordingly lighted up the fire of oppression in all the towns and villages in that neighbourhood. [...] After the whole country had been swept by the besom of devastation, and when a host of the refractory and rebellious had been carried away by the whirlwind of desolation, those who remained being subdued, placed the ring of servitude in the ear of their lives, and with their hands tied together submitted.[128]

But Ṭippu's success did not last. Over the course of 1791, Malabar largely came into the hands of the British.[129] Ultimately, the British were able to secure victory in the third Anglo–Maisūrian war. The peace treaty of Śrīraṅgapaṭṭaṇaṃ was sealed in March 1792—a humiliation for Ṭippu Sulttān, who had to cede half his kingdom; amongst other spoils, the British received large parts of the Malabar coast, including the ports of Kannūr and Kōḻikkōṭu. It was especially painful for Ṭippu that the British gained completely new territories on top of their previous estates. On the other hand, other Indian rulers, such as the Nisām of Haidarabād, were simply returned their old areas. Furthermore, Ṭippu had to pay large sums as reparations, which were used to give special gifts of money to British officers and soldiers.[130] As a consequence, the year 1792 can be considered a turning-point in Ṭippu's career as a ruler: while he was occupied until 1792 with extending and restructuring his kingdom, he was forced after the first peace settlement of Śrīraṅgapaṭṭaṇaṃ to make payments as reparations in order to free his son who had been taken hostage by the British. He also increasingly turned to religion, and he even tried to recruit allies to help expel the British from India.[131] However, Ṭippu Sulttān's attempts to get rid of the British were all in vain. In the fourth Anglo–Maisūrian war, Maisūr suffered its final defeat[132] and Ṭippu Sulttān died defending Śrīraṅgapaṭṭaṇaṃ. The second peace settlement of Śrīraṅgapaṭṭaṇaṃ was signed in May 1799, under which the British annexed large parts of Maisūr. This brought the British one large step closer to territorial supremacy in southern India.[133]

The invasions of Haidar Ali and Ṭippu Sulttān brought about great upheavals in the socio-economic and political structure of Malabar, which will be considered in closer detail in the following chapters. At the same time, the British had been trying since the 1790s to gain territorial supremacy over Malabar. As a result, the Malabar rājās found themselves in the uncomfortable situation whereby two different powers were demanding rulership over their land, and they had to assert their sovereignty to completely different opponents often at the same time. After the death of Ṭippu Sulttān and the British victory of 1799, there was an even slimmer prospect of independent rule for the rājās than there had been at the time of the Maisūrian hegemony.

NOTES

1. For example Schoff, *Periplus* and Majumdar, Ramesh Chandra, *The Classical Accounts of India: Being a Compilation of the English Translations of the Accounts Left by Herodotus, Megasthenes, Arrian etc.*, Calcutta, 1960. Cf. also Sridharan, K., *A Maritime History of India*, New Delhi, 1965.

2. In pre-Christian times, it was mainly Egyptian, Indian and South Arabian merchants who carried out the East–West trade. This trade boomed after Egypt was conquered by Rome in 30 B.C., because luxury goods such as spices, particularly pepper, perfumes, jewels and pearls, were highly sought after goods in the Roman Empire. The trade in classical antiquities with India is illustrated in greater detail in Wiesehöfer, Josef, '*Mare Erythraeum, Sinus Persicus* und *Fines India*: Der Indische Ozean in hellenistischer und römischer Zeit', in: Stephan Conermann (ed.), *Der Indische Ozean in historischer Perspektive*, Hamburg, 1998 (Asien und Afrika. Beiträge des Zentrums für Asiatische und Afrikanische Studien (ZAAS) der Christian-Albrechts-Universität zu Kiel 1), pp. 9–36, passim.

3. Schoff, *Periplus*, p. 214. Schoff does not give figures for the profit margin, but stresses that the pepper trade brought the merchants 'unheard-of profits'.

4. Cf. Mathews, Johnsy, *Economy and Society in Medieval Malabar (A.D. 1500–1600)*, Changanacherry, 1996, p. 81; Thomas, P.J., 'The Pepper Trade of India in Early Times', in: *S. Krishnaswami Aiyangar Commemoration Volume*, Madras, 1936, pp. 226–33, p. 232.

5. Cf. Logan, *Malabar*, vol. 1, map 11 facing p. 182; Buchanan, *Journey*, vol. 2, p. 520; Kieniewicz, 'Asian Merchants', p. 80.

6. Cf. Buchanan, *Journey*, vol. 2, pp. 463–5 and 521–3. It is not known how reliable these entries are. Das Gupta speaks of a life expectancy of the pepper plant as twenty-five years, whereby the best yield could be kept up for six to seven years. Cf. Das Gupta, Ashin, 'Malabar in 1740,' *Bengal Past and Present* 80 (1960), pp. 90–117, p. 106.

7. Cf. Mathews, *Economy and Society*, p. 83.

8. Gundert, *Dictionary*, p. 199, col. 2: a weight of 500 lbs, in Bombay of 560 lbs. Yule, Henry and Burnell, A.C., *Hobson-Jobson: A Glossary of Colloquial Anglo-Indian Words and Phrases, and of Kindred Terms, Etymological, Historical, Geographical, and Discursive*, London, 1903, reprint New Delhi and Madras, 1995,

p. 155: a weight which varied according to the region, generally 500 lb; known in English as *candy*.

9. Cf. Buchanan, *Journey*, vol. 2, p. 512.

10. The Greeks and Romans considered cinnamon to be an Indian plant but it actually originates from south China and South-East Asia. Casson, Lionel, *The Periplus Maris Erythraei: Text with Introduction, Translation, and Commentary*, Princeton, 1989, p. 123.

11. Cf. Schoff, *Periplus*, p. 82.

12. Cf. Bouchon, Geneviève, 'Sixteenth Century Malabar and the Indian Ocean', in: Ashin Das Gupta and M.N. Pearson (eds.), *India and the Indian Ocean 1500–1800*, Calcutta, 1987, pp. 162–84, p. 166.

13. Cf. Logan, *Malabar*, vol. 1, map 7 facing p. 182.

14. Cf. *Reports of a Joint Commission*, § CCCCXII; Kieniewicz, 'Asian Merchants', p. 81.

15. Cf. Kieniewicz, 'Asian Merchants', p. 84; Verghese, *Agrarian Change*, p. 16.

16. Cf. also Kieniewicz, 'Asian Merchants', p. 81.

17. Cf. Malekandathil, Pius M.C., *Portuguese Cochin and the Maritime Trade of India: 1500–1663*, New Delhi, 2001 (South Asian Studies 39), p. 80f. See also Kieniewicz, 'Pepper Gardens', p. 22.

18. Cf. Chaudhuri, *Trade and Civilisation*, p. 37.

19. Barbosa, Duarte, *An Account of the Countries Bordering on the Indian Ocean and Their Inhabitants*, translated from the Portuguese, 2 vols., reprint New Delhi and Madras, 1989, vol. 1, p. 128f. vol. 2, p. 73.

20. Cf. Das Gupta, 'Malabar in 1740', p. 103.

21. Cf. Kieniewicz, 'Asian Merchants', p. 86.

22. Pliny the Elder (Gaius Plinius Secundus, 23/24–79) cites Muziris as the nearest port in India, which could be reached, with the right wind, within 40 days; Claudius Ptolemy (~100–160) mentions Muziris as an emporium. Majumdar, *The Classical Accounts of India*, p. 339 or 365. Cf. also Casson, *Periplus Maris*, p. 296.

23. Chaudhuri, *Trade and Civilisation*, pp. 35–7.

24. Cf. Chaudhuri, *Trade and Civilisation*, pp. 39, 49, 102. Conermann explains the prominent position of Kōḷikkōṭu, which Ibn Batuta compared with the port of Alexandria. Conermann, Stephan, 'Muslimische Seefahrt auf dem Indischen Ozean vom 14. bis zum 16. Jahrhundert', in: idem (ed.), *Der Indische Ozean in historischer Perspektive*, Hamburg, 1998 (Asien und Afrika: Beiträge des Zentrums für Asiatische und Afrikanische Studien (ZAAS) der Christian-Albrechts-Universitat zu Kiel 1), pp. 143–80, p. 149.

25. Das Gupta, 'Malabar in 1740', p. 92; cf. also p. 90.

26. Cf. Conermann, 'Muslimische Seefahrt', p. 148.

27. Cf. Arasaratnam, Sinnappah, 'India and the Indian Ocean in the Seventeenth Century', in: Ashin Das Gupta and Michael N. Pearson (eds.), *India and the Indian Ocean, 1500–1800*, pp. 94–130, p. 114, 124.

28. Cf. Arasaratnam, 'India', p. 126.

29. Chaudhuri, *Trade and Civilisation*, p.16.

30. Cf. Kieniewicz, 'Asian Merchants', p. 82.

31. Cf. Das Gupta, 'Malabar in 1740', p. 108f.

32. For a detailed account of Vasco da Gama's travels: Subrahmanyam, Sanjay, *The Career and Legend of Vasco da Gama*, Cambridge, 1997 and Ravenstein: *Journal*.

33. The title of the king of Kōḻikkōṭu is Tāmūtiri, cf. Gundert, *Dictionary*, p. 444, Col. 2. He was called Zamorin by the English.

34. Cf. Chaudhuri, *Trade and Civilisation*, p. 67.

35. Chaudhuri, *Trade and Civilisation*, p. 63. Dale holds the view that attacks by the Portuguese were generally aimed at the Muslim merchants, who resided in the coastal towns—particularly Kōḻikkōṭu. Cf. Dale, Stephen Frederic, 'Trade, Conversion and the Growth of the Islamic Community of Kerala, South India', *Studia Islamica* 71 (1990), pp. 155–75, p. 165.

36. Cf. Innes and Evans, *Malabar*, p. 47. See also Prakash, Om, *European Commercial Enterprise in Pre-Colonial India*, Cambridge, 1998 (The New Cambridge History of India II, 5), p. 44.

37. Cf. Rothermund, Dietmar, *Asian Trade and European Expansion in the Age of Mercantilism*, New Delhi, 1981, p. 19.

38. Cf. Rothermund, *Asian Trade*, pp. 17–20; Kulke, Hermann and Rothermund, Dietmar, *Geschichte Indiens*, Stuttgart, 1982, p. 234.

39. Kieniewicz, 'Asian Merchants', p. 81.

40. For information on the significance of Kocci for Portuguese trade in India, cf. Malekandathil, *Portuguese Cochin* and Innes and Evans, *Malabar*, p. 48f.

41. Cf. Panikkar, K.M., *A History of Kerala 1498–1910*, Annamalainagar, 1960, p. 144.

42. The horse trade was extremely important for Kannūr: The ruler of Vijayanagara also satisfied his need for horses here. Kannūr was also the transhipment centre for elephants from Sri Lanka. Cf. Bouchon, 'Sixteenth Century Malabar', p. 167; Stein, Burton, *Vijayanagara*, Cambridge, 1989 (New Cambridge History of India I, 2), p. 74f. Also see Bouchon's detailed study on the Ali Rājās of Kannūr and their relations to the Portuguese: Bouchon, Geneviève, *'Regent of the Sea': Cannanore's Response to Portuguese Expansion, 1507-1528* (French Studies in South Asian Culture and Society 11), Delhi, 1988.

43. Cf. Das Gupta, 'Malabar in 1740', p. 96. Examples are the description of Kōḻikkōṭu by Cabral in 1500 and the attacks by Vasco da Gama in 1502, as well as further Portuguese attacks in 1504 and 1510. Cf. Sewell, *List of Antiquarian Remains*, p. 246.

44. Cf. Panikkar: 'The Portuguese never had any "Empire" in India. They had a few coastal towns, and their authority never extended beyond a few miles of their naval bases. The only territorial possession of any considerable extent over which they ruled was Goa', Panikkar, K.M., *History of Kerala*, p. 143.

45. The Portuguese period is usually given as 1498 to 1663, thus lasting 165 years. Cf. Innes and Evans, *Malabar*, p. 44.

46. Cf. Chaudhuri, *Trade and Civilisation*, p. 77f.

47. Cf. Rothermund, *Asian Trade*, p. 23f. Mathée gives the work ethic of Catholicism, which was indifferent to value, as an accompanying factor to the decline of the Portuguese. This was superseded by the Calvinistic work ethic of the North Europeans. Mathée, Ulrich, '"*Zu den Christen und zu den Gewürzen*"—Wie die Portugiesen den Indischen Ozean gewannen', in: Stephan Conermann (ed.), *Der Indische Ozean in historischer Perspektive*, Hamburg, 1998 (Asien und Afrika: Beiträge des Zentrums für Asiatische und Afrikanische Studien (ZAAS) der Christian-Albrechts-Universität zu Kiel 1), pp. 181–207, p. 203.

48. Cf. Gaastra, Femme S., 'Competition or Collaboration? Relations between the Dutch East India Company and Indian Merchants around 1680', in: Sushil Chaudhury and Michel Morineau (eds.), *Merchants, Companies and Trade: Europe and Asia in the Early Modern Era*, Cambridge, 1999, pp. 188–201, p. 193f.

49. Cf. Panikkar, K.M., *History of Kerala*, p. 186.

50. Cf. Rothermund, *Asian Trade*, pp. 25, 27; Koshy, M.O., *The Dutch Power in Kerala (1729–1758)*, New Delhi, 1989, p. 207. For details on the conflict between the Portuguese and the Dutch, cf. Vink, Mark, 'Mare Liberum and Dominium Maris: Legal Arguments and Implications of the Luso-Dutch Struggle for the Control over Asian Waters ca. 1600–1663', in: K.S. Mathew (ed.), *Studies in Maritime History*, Pondicherry, 1990, pp. 38–68.

51. Cf. Logan, *Malabar*, vol. 1, p. 338.

52. Cf. Panikkar, K.M., *History of Kerala*, p. 190.

53. Cf. Innes and Evans, *Malabar*, p. 54.

54. Cf. Logan, *Malabar*, vol. 1, p. 390f.

55. Cf. Koshy, *The Dutch*, p. 210: 'During the Dutch occupation of Kerala, Cochin harbour was the nerve-centre of commerce and trade. It served as the chief centre of Malabar and South Indian commerce.'

56. Cf. Innes and Evans, *Malabar*, p. 57.

57. Cf. Logan, *Malabar*, vol. 1, p. 418.

58. Cf. Logan, *Malabar*, vol. 1, p. 506f; Das Gupta, Ashin, *Malabar in Asian Trade 1740–1800*, Cambridge, 1967 (Cambridge South Asian Studies 1), p. 124.

59. Cf. Rothermund, *Asian Trade*, p. 30. The Dutch also held up to 30 per cent of British state loans; cf. Dickson, P.G.M., *The Financial Revolution in England: A Study in the Development of Public Credit 1688–1756*, New York, 1967, pp. 321, 324.

60. Cf. Chaudhuri, *Trade and Civilisation*, p. 87f. Subrahmanyam emphasizes the willingness of all European powers to use violence in order to reach their goals; if at all there was a difference between them it was only to the 'extent to which this conflict and potential for violence remained bounded.' Subrahmanyam, *Political Economy*, p. 254.

61. Cf. Logan, *Malabar*, vol. 1, p. 335.

62. Cf. Logan, *Malabar*, vol. 1, p. 340; Kulke and Rothermund, *Geschichte Indiens*, p. 242.

63. Logan, *Treaties*, i, XVII, p. 15f.

64. Cf. Kieniewicz, 'Asian Merchants', p. 80.

65. Cf. Chaudhuri, *Trade and Civilisation*, p. 86.

66. Cf. Kulke and Rothermund, *Geschichte Indiens*, p. 237.

67. Cf. Schweinitz, Karl de Jr., *The Rise and Fall of British India: Imperialism as Inequality*, London/New York 1983, p. 94 and Marshall, Peter J., 'British Expansion in India in the Eighteenth Century: A Historical Revision', *History* 60 (1975), pp. 28–43.

68. Cf. Arasaratnam, Sinnappah, *Pre-Modern Commerce and Society in Southern Asia. An Inaugural Lecture Delivered at the University of Malaya on December 21, 1971*, Kuala Lumpur, 1972, p. 16.

69. Cf. Marshall, Peter J., 'Western Arms in Maritime Asia in the Early Phases of Expansion', *MAS* 14,1 (1980), pp. 13–28, pp. 24–6. The term *sepoy* is the English variant of the Persian *sipāhī*—used in India as a description for a cavalryman. In line with the European model, the British named trained Indian cavalrymen, who were taken into their service, as *sepoy*. Fisher calls this 'invention' a 'new model'. Cf. Fisher, Michael H., *The First Indian Author in English: Dean Mahomed (1759–1851) in India, Ireland, and England*, Delhi, 1996, p. 122. In the latter eighteenth century, the sepoys constituted the bulk of soldiers in the EIC army; for example, in 1782, a total of 102,233 sepoys and only 5,310 Europeans were in service there. Cf. *British India Analysed: The Provincial and Revenue Establishments of Tippoo Sultaun and of Mahomedan and British Conquerors in Hindostan*, 3 vols., London 1793, reprint New Delhi, 1988, vol. 3, p. 787.

70. Innes and Evans, *Malabar*, p. 55.

71. Cf. Logan, *Malabar*, vol. 1, p. 335; Innes and Evans, *Malabar*, p. 53. The time of the establishment of the trading-post is uncertain; Logan assumes that it happened around 1694/95 or later, at any rate before 24 October 1699. Logan, *Malabar*, vol. 1, pp. 341, 343, 346. Cf. also Rajendran, *Establishment*, p. 48.

72. Cf. Buchanan, *Journey*, vol. 2, p. 530.

73. Cf. Logan, *Malabar*, vol. 1, p. 418.

74. Cf. ibid., pp. 424, 457.

75. Cf. Logan, *Treaties*, i, XXX, p. 27f.

76. Cf. ibid., i, CXIV, p. 103.

77. Kolff divides the English conquest of India into a maritime and a territorial phase. Kolff, Dirk H.A., 'The End of an *Ancien Régime*: Colonial War in India 1798–1818', in: A. de Moor Joop and H.L. Wesseling (ed.), *Imperialism and War: Essays on Colonial Wars in Asia and Africa*, Leiden, 1989 (Comparative Studies in Overseas History 8), pp. 22–49, p. 23.

78. Charles Cornwallis (1738–1805) was Governor General in Council from 1786 and took over command of the army in Madras in December 1790.

79. *Reports of a Joint Commission*, § LXVII; Bowring, Lewin B., *Haidar Alī and Tipū Sultān and the Struggle with the Musalmān Powers of the South*, Oxford, 1899, reprint New Delhi and Madras, 1997, pp. 141–4; Logan, *Malabar*, vol. 1, pp. 456–8. Unlike Cornwallis, the Madras government had considered the incident to have been merely a 'frontier accident'. Cf. Kareem, *Kerala under Haidar*, p. 115f. Bayly cites the British motivation to take on Ṭippu Sulttān militarily not as fear of his despotism or Muslim views, but as fear he might beat them with their own

weapons and gain the upper hand in trade or refuse to join the British-Indian peers. Bayly, C., 'British-Military Fiscal State', p. 344.

80. Cf. Logan, *Malabar*, vol. 1, p. 459.

81. Cf. Nightingale, *Trade and Empire*, pp. 69, 460; Logan, *Treaties*, i, CLVIII, p. 135.

82. Consultation of Covakkāran Mūssa of Talaśśēri dated 20.12.1797, in BC, OIOC F/4/34.

83. Cf. Logan, *Treaties*, i, XCV, p. 85; Aitchison, C.U., *A Collection of Treaties, Engagements and Sanads Relating to India and Neighbouring Countries* (Revised and Continued up to 1929), 14 vols., Calcutta, 5th edn., 1929–1932, vol. 10, p. 125.

84. Cf. Logan, *Malabar*, vol. 1, p. 460: Letter by Lord Cornwallis to the government in Bombay dated 31.5.1790.

85. Cf. Nightingale, *Trade and Empire*, p. 62.

86. Cf. Logan, *Malabar*, vol. 1, p. 465f., idem, *Treaties*, i, XCVI, p. 86f.

87. Logan, *Malabar*, vol. 1, p. 471; cf. idem, *Treaties*, i, CLIX, p. 135f.

88. Cf. Logan, *Malabar*, vol. 1, p. 463. One example is the troop of 1500 Nāyars from Kōṭṭayaṃ who were involved in the British attack on Ṭippu in Katirūr in May 1790.

89. Cf. Logan, *Treaties*, ii, II, pp. 139–46.

90. Cf. Nightingale, *Trade and Empire*, p. 58f. These facts emerge from the written correspondence between Cornwallis and Henry Dundas.

91. Cf. Fisher, Michael H. (ed.), *The Politics of the British Annexation of India, 1757–1857*, Delhi, 1993, p. 122.

92. Cf. Rajendran, *Establishment*, p. 228f.

93. Quote taken from Abercromby's instructions to the Joint Commissioners dated 20.4.1792 in *Reports of a Joint Commission*, § LXXXI.

94. Cf. Nightingale, *Trade and Empire*, p. 69.

95. *Reports of a Joint Commission*, §§ CCLXXXI, CCXXXII.

96. Cf. Rajendran, *Establishment*, p. 159.

97. Cf. Logan, *Malabar*, vol. 1, p. 426; Kulke and Rothermund, *Geschichte Indiens*, p. 257.

98. Cf. Brittlebank, Kate, *Tipu Sultan's Search for Legitimacy: Islam and Kingship in a Hindu Domain*, Delhi, 1997, pp. 24, 27.

99. Cf. Khirmani, Mir Hussein Ali Khan, *The History of Hydur Naik, Otherwise Styled Shums Ul Moolk, Ameer Ud Dowla, Nawaub Hydur Ali Khan Bahadoor, Hydur Jung, Nawaub of the Karnatic Balaghaut*, trans. by W. Miles, London 1842, p. 184. Contrary to this, Dale gives 1763 as the date for the first alliance between Haidar Ali and Ali Rājā. Cf. Dale, *Islamic Society*, p. 79.

100. K.M. Panikkar describes this resistance as 'national resistance'; he thus interprets it as a precursor to the struggles for freedom against the British in the nineteenth and twentieth centuries. I believe that this interpretation goes too far, especially as the 'nation' is an unfamiliar category in eighteenth-century India; the Maisūrian forces targetted their resistance against a foreseeable loss of power. Cf. Panikkar, K.M., *History of Kerala*, p. 339.

101. Kareem, *Kerala under Haidar*, p. 43f.

102. Ibid., p. 38.

103. Cf. Logan, *Malabar*, vol. 1, pp. 410–13. In recent research only Kareem doubts the authenticity of the edict. Cf. Kareem, *Kerala under Haidar*, p. 46f.; idem, 'A Probe into the Veracity of the Malabar Edicts of Haider Ali and Tipu Sultan', *South Indian History Congress*, XVIII Session at Sree Sankaracharya University of Sanskrit, Kalady, Kerala, 1998, pp. 33–9.

104. Cf. Rajendran, *Establishment*, p. 162; Logan, *Treaties*, i, LXXIII, pp. 61–3.

105. Cf. Innes and Evans, *Malabar*, p. 66.

106. Cf. Aitchison, *Treaties*, vol. 9, p. 276f. and Logan, *Malabar*, vol. 1, p. 417.

107. Cf. Kulke and Rothermund, *Geschichte Indiens*, p. 257.

108. Panikkar, K.M., *History of Kerala*, p. 351. French officers and soldiers served in the Maisūrian army both under Haidar Ali and also Ṭippu Sulttān. Cf. *British India Analyzed*, vol. 3, p. 761; *Michaud's History of Mysore under Hyder Ali & Tippoo Sultan*, trans. by V.K. Raman Menon, Paris 1801–1809, reprint New Delhi, 1985, p. 55.

109. Kōṭṭayaṃ supported the English in the defence of Talaśśēri with a troop of 2000 Nāyars. Cf. *Reports of a Joint Commission* § XXX; Rajendran, *Establishment*, p. 168.

110. Cf. Logan, *Malabar*, vol. 1, p. 425.

111. Cf. Innes and Evans, *Malabar*, p. 69.

112. Cf. Panikkar, K.M., *History of Kerala*, p. 352.

113. Cf. Logan, *Malabar*, vol. 1, p. 428. In western India the British feared to lose their influence. Kolff, 'The End', p. 30.

114. Cf. Logan, *Malabar*, vol. 1, pp. 431, 443.

115. Cf. Kareem, *Kerala under Haidar*, p. 78.

116. Cf. Aitchison, *Treaties*, vol. 9, pp. 141–5. Cf. also Leela Devi, *History*, p. 270. Ṭippu Sulttān appointed Arshed Beg Khan as 'commandant and manager of all the civil and revenue concerns of the countries in Malabar, from Nelishur to Cochin inclusive', who was to negotiate with the rājās over the sums to be paid. *Reports of a Joint Commission*, § XXXI. Cf. Chapter 5 for the regulations of Arshed Beg. Cf. also Rajendran, *Establishment*, p. 187.

117. Cf. *Reports of a Joint Commission*, § LIV. The fort was established in Fāṟūkhābād. The people who had been forced to settle there largely originated from Kōḻikkōṭu, but moved back to their home town once Ṭippu had withdrawn. Cf. Logan, *Malabar*, vol. 1, p. 446.

118. Cf. Innes and Evans, *Malabar*, p. 72.

119. *Reports of a Joint Commission*, § LXIV. Cf. also § LII: '[...] he [Ṭippu] proceeded to make known to the Hindoo part of his Malabar subjects, his desires to procure and effect their conversion to his own (the Mahommedan) faith; [...].'

120. Cf. Dale, *Islamic Society*, p. 85.

121. Cf. *Reports of a Joint Commission*, § 67.

122. Cf. Logan, *Malabar*, vol. 1, pp. 449, 451.

123. Cf. Rajayyan, K., 'Kerala Varma and Malabar Rebellion', *Journal of Indian History* 47,1 (1969), pp. 549–57, p. 549; Logan, *Treaties*, p. 86: Logan adds to this

in the remark: 'Karla Warma (...). Better known subsequently as the Palassi (Pychy) Raja. He was left alone in 1788–9 to manage the family dominions as best he could, the rest of the family including the Raja's senior to himself having at that time taken refuge in Travancore.'

124. At the 200-year commemorative ceremonies of the death of Ṭippu, a controversy arose over his policy of 'Islamization'. Cf. *Outlook* 5, 19 dated 24.5.1999. In her study Susan Bayly deals with the reception of Ṭippu's religious policy in Malabar. Cf. Bayly, Susan, *Saints, Goddesses and Kings: Muslims and Christians in South Indian Society 1700–1900*, Cambridge, 1989 (Cambridge South Asian Studies 43), p. 165.

125. Cf. Bowring, *Haidar Alī*, p. 137; Logan, *Malabar*, vol. 1, pp. 453f., 464.

126. Cf. Kareem, *Kerala under Haider*, p. 115; *Michaud's History*, p. 115.

127. Cf. Logan, *Malabar*, vol. 1, p. 454.

128. Khirmani, Mir Hussain Ali Khan, *History of Tipu Sultan: Being a Continuation of the Neshani Hyduri*, s.l. 1864, reprint New Delhi, 1986, p. 73.

129. Cf. *Reports of a Joint Commission*, § LXXVII. According to Panikkar they found it easy, since Ṭippu had fled to Śrīraṅgapaṭṭaṇaṃ and the Maisūrian soldiers thus lacked motivation. Cf. Panikkar, K.M., *History of Kerala*, p. 395.

130. Cf. the peace treaty of 1792 in Aitchison, *Treaties*, vol. 9, pp. 233–40. Cf. Callahan, Raymond, *The East India Company and Army Reform, 1783–1798*, Cambridge (Massachusetts), 1972, p. 224f. The division of the captured Maisūrian state treasures triggered a 'major uproar'.

131. Cf. Brittlebank, *Tipu Sultan*, pp. 24, 27.

132. It is likely that Wellesley provoked Ṭippu Sulttān to this war. Cf. Ingram, Edward, *Empire-Building and Empire-Builders: Twelve Studies*, London, 1995, p. 12. This would tie in with Förster's thesis, that Wellesley was operating a preventive policy of expansionism. His goal was to establish a Pax Britannica, by which the trading interests of the EIC could be pursued in peace. Förster, *Die mächtigen Diener*, pp. 132, 155, 157. Förster describes the fourth Anglo–Maisūrian war as the 'final battle between two aggressive social systems, and their representatives'. Ibid., p. 158.

133. Victory in the fourth Anglo–Maisūrian war was Wellesley's most spectacular success in India. Ingram, Edward, *Commitment to Empire: Prophecies of the Great Game in Asia 1797–1800*, Oxford, 1981, p. 118. For information on Wellesley, cf. Bennell, Anthony, *The Making of Arthur Wellesley*, Hyderabad, 1997.

Four

Clash of Sovereignty

A *clash of sovereignty* is understood here as the conflict that ensues when different powers come into contact with one another, powers that make a claim of sovereignty over the same country, seeking to get hold of the rights connected to the land such as those of tax collection, the structure of trade, and jurisdiction. The following section focuses on Malabar, the Malabar rulers to be more precise, whose rights of sovereignty were disputed both by the Maisūrian rulers and the British. In order to achieve their goal, viz. sovereignty over Malabar, both the Maisūrians and the British attempted to intervene in the administration of the Malabar principalities. These methods were designed to give them an increasing amount of power which was to culminate in sovereignty over Malabar. The extent of change was severe and resulted in the restructuring of the administrative and tax system. For this reason, the changes introduced by Haidar Ali and Ṭippu Sulttān will be considered as well as those by the British government. The differing reactions of the Malabar rulers to these changes will also be a subject of discussion.

Maisūrian Policy Meets Resistance in Malabar

During their occupation of Malabar, the Maisūrian rulers Haidar Ali and Ṭippu Sulttān introduced fundamental changes to Malabar that affected administrative and tax structures. The most important change was the introduction of a central administration which was intended to replace the existing decentralized government in Malabar. The prevailing social system in Malabar was consequently shaken to its very foundations, something which was not accepted easily by the population.

After he had invaded Malabar in 1766, Haidar Ali deprived the *dēśavāḷi*s and *nāṭuvāḷi*s of their rights. In their place he ordered the establishment of a central government for the province of Malabar:[1] Malabar was henceforth divided up into twelve *tukri*s (divisions) which were, in turn, subdivided into *tālūkka*s (subdivisions). The tukris were headed by *tukridār*s and *seristtadār*s.

In 1773, the Maisūrian governor Srinivas Rao assumed direct control of the country. He organized the first tax assessment in Malabar, using the *pāṭṭaṃ* as the basis for calculation of taxes. The level of tax was tied to the actual harvest. Furthermore, from this point on the taxes were to be paid directly to the government to cut out the middlemen, thereby avoiding possible tax losses. The *dēvasvaṃ*s were exempted from taxation, as mentioned earlier.[2]

In 1774, Haidar Ali charged his governor in Malabar with the assessment and collection of tax in the recently acquired province. To this end he made treaties with the individual *rājā*s, under which they agreed to make tributary payments to Maisūr. A *jamā*[3] of 50,000 rupees per annum and a *nazrānā*[4] of two lakh rupees was fixed with the Kaṭattanāṭu Rājā, a jamā of 125,000 rupees and a nazrānā of 268,000 rupees[5] was fixed with the Ciṟakkal Rājā—in place of the Rājā of Kōṭṭayaṃ, since he had refused to negotiate a treaty with Ṭippu: '[...] but the Cotiote Raja would not yield to similar terms'.[6] For this reason the 'expropriated' Rājā of Kōṭṭayaṃ, Ravi Varmma, asked the British in Talaśśēri, in 1778, whether his land could be placed under their protection. The request was passed on to Bombay. In spring 1779, Ravi Varmma took back large parts of Kōṭṭayaṃ and was provided with military supplies from the trading posts in Talaśśēri. However, Ravi Varmma was still defeated by Haidar Ali's troops, which had since pressed forward, and was forced to return to hiding in the jungles.[7]

After the peace settlement of Maṅgalūr in 1784, Ṭippu Sulttān appointed Arshed Beg Khān as governor, who became responsible for the reorganization of land revenue. Arshed Beg Khān made new treaties with the rājās in northern Malabar. The payment of jamā per annum was set with the Kaṭattanāṭu Rājā at 50,000 rupees, with the Kōṭṭayaṃ Rājā at one lakh and with the Ciṟakkal Rājā at 125,000 rupees.[8] The basic assumption regarding all tax payments was that a *paṟa*[9] of seeds would produce an average annual harvest of ten paṟas of cereals, from which five and a half paṟas would be kept by the farmer, three paṟas would go to the Maisūrian government and the *janmakāran* would receive one and a half paṟas. The taxes were collected in cash for coconut palms, pepper bushes, jackfruit trees and betelnut palms.[10]

In southern Malabar the first tax collections by Haidar Ali amounted to approximately 508,280 *hūn*s,[11] 5 *fanam*s[12] and to 499,400 hūns, 4 fanams in 1774/5. In the following years there was so much unrest and so many rebellions in southern Malabar that it was inconceivable for the Maisūrian occupants to collect tax regularly. Only in 959 M.E. (1783/4) was Arshed Beg Khān able to begin regulating tax matters in the south as well. The total jamā for southern Malabar excluding Pālakkāṭu, amounted to 408,265 hūns. The commissioners declared 960 M.E. (1784/5) to be the first year of tax collection for the

Maisūrian rulers in Malabar.[13] All in all, Arshed Beg was probably well regarded as Ṭippu's governor in Malabar if one is to believe the report of the Joint Commission.[14]

In Kōṭṭayaṃ, for example, the first levy of taxes by Ṭippu Sulttān amounted to a payment of one lakh rupees for 1784/5.[15] In 1785 the rājās of the northern division, meaning those of Kōṭṭayaṃ, Ciṟakkal and Kaṭattanāṭu, approached Ṭippu themselves and made new agreements directly with him: The sum agreed for Ciṟakkal was 30,000 rupees of nazrānā and 120,000 rupees of jamā, and for Kaṭattanāṭu it was 62,500 rupees of jamā. Against his will Ṛavi Varmma, the Rājā of Kōṭṭayaṃ, had to cede a part of his principality, that of Vāyanāṭu, to Maisūr.

[...] which after some reluctant delay the said Raja was forced finally to give up by the middle of the next Malabar year, or about February 1787, so that [...] it is stated to have become a new annexation to, and to have been registered as a dependency on, the Cuchery of Seringapatnam, under the name of Chuckloor, from the beginning of 963, or September 1787 [...].[16]

On account of the annexation of Vāyanātu, Ṭippu excused Ravi Varmma of Kōṭṭayaṃ a part of his jamā which had been set previously; from this point onwards, it only amounted to 65,000 rupees (instead of one lakh). Ṭippu countered the rājās' complaint that their land was being too highly taxed with the announcement that he would send his own tax assessors to Malabar in order to check the tax rates, i.e. to confirm that the tax rates were in accordance with those set previously. In spite of Ṭippu's stringency, the rājās were nevertheless able to persuade him to grant them an annual pension.[17]

In 1786, Ṭippu subdivided the post of governor in Malabar into a civil and a military sphere. Arshed Beg received the post of military governor and Mir Ibrahim that of civil governor. Around this time, northern Malabar was subdivided into five tukris: Kurumpranāṭu, Kōḷikkōṭu, Ēṟanāṭu, Veṭṭattanāṭu and Cāvakkāṭu, which were in turn divided into smaller administrative units. The tukridārs were responsible for tax collections on Mir Ibrahim's behalf.[18] After Ṭippu had ordered the forced conversion of Hindus in 1788,[19] he expected a nazrānā totalling twelve lakh rupees from the entire province of Malabar, which was to be paid by the different principalities of Malabar. It is likely that Ṭippu Sulttān received at least a share of the payments made by the rājās.[20]

Varying local customs imposed limits on the Maisūrian target of a single taxation for Malabar. Taxation in southern and northern Malabar was based on different values: in the south the number of pepper bushes served as the basis for taxation, whereas half of the pepper harvest was taken as tax in the north. There were also differences between the north and south in the setting of tax levels for rice. In the south, the level of tax depended on the quantity of rice sowed, whereas in the north it depended on the actual rice harvest.[21]

In 1789 Ṭippu introduced his own tax collectors to Malabar, as he had announced previously in 1785: they were given the same status as the collectors in the southern districts of Malabar. It was only in the beginning of 1791 that the rājās of Malabar regained power; in the meantime it seems that Ṭippu's agents had collected amazingly high taxes.[22]

The problem with using Maisūrian officials for tax collection was that they did not have any knowledge of the land which they were to assess, and they were therefore reliant on information from the locals as to how great the expected yields for their cultivated areas were likely to be. As a result, the door was opened to false assessments. The possibility of Ṭippu's tax collectors lining their own pockets is also something that cannot be ruled out. An important factor not to be overlooked was that the absence of the Malabar janmakārans, most of whom had fled to Tiruvitāṃkūr, made the introduction and execution of Maisūrian taxation of Malabar possible. Due to their absence Ṭippu's actions were initially met with little opposition.

The mints in Kōḻikkōṭu and Fāṟūkhābād were an additional institution brought to Malabar by Haidar Ali and Ṭippu Sulttān in order to make clear their dominance in the province that they had recently acquired. Both places were of strategic importance in the rule of Malabar. Furthermore, control over the mint meant a lucrative source of income.[23] The mint in Kōḻikkōṭu struck gold and silver coins, generally fanams and rupees, as well as copper coins (paisas). However, in 1788, the mint in Kōḻikkōṭu was closed and destroyed, since the Maisūrian administrative centre in Malabar was moved to Fāṟūkhābād. The newly founded mint in Fāṟūkhābād took over the tasks of the one in Kōḻikkōṭu. Gold fanams and copper paisas were struck there. After 1792, following the peace settlement of Śrīraṅgapaṭṭaṇaṃ, the British took both mints and any respective rights away from Ṭippu.[24]

To summarize, Ṭippu taxed the land, collected tolls on trading goods, and also imposed taxes on the production of teak, tobacco, pepper and coconuts, as well as coins.[25] All in all, Ṭippu Sulttān received a considerable amount of taxes from the province of Malabar, which, according to the calculation of the Joint Commissioners, amounted to a total of 944,765 hūns.[26] Yet in spite of gaining a profit through a relatively high tax revenue, Ṭippu Sulttān also had to deal with a number of problems in Malabar.

The economic consequences of the Maisūrian occupation in Malabar were severe: the cultivation of pepper came to a standstill at times, the volume of trade in the coastal towns crumbled and there was a sharp decline in ship-building, a traditional craft of Kēraḷa. K.M. Panikkar believes that the Nāyars suffered the most under the occupation since they were both impoverished and disarmed.[27] The Māppiḷḷas also lost their wealth—indeed the entire population in Malabar was affected by the wars and measures taken by the Maisūrian government, which strove to gain as much as possible from the tributary dependency of Malabar, and aimed to suck dry its economy. Society in Malabar was thus shaken to its very foundations and the administration, the land laws, and the whole way of life were called into question. The districts occupied by Maisūr required many years to recover from this economic strain. The decline in population, the fields which had lain waste, and the ensuing disputes over property and tax amendments exerted a lasting influence on the social structure.

The Reaction of the Malabar Rulers to Maisūrian Innovations

At first glance, the British commissioners had the impression that Haidar Ali's rule was firmly established across southern Malabar, at least since his second invasion of 1774.[28] However, this impression was mistaken: since the end of the 1770s, and in the 1780s, there had been a great deal of unrest and a number of rebellions in the southern districts of the province of Malabar, which the Maisūrian troops were able to suppress only after some considerable effort. Both the rājās and the local élite supported the unrest, instigated by the Tāmūtiri of Kōḻikkōṭu.[29] In 961 M.E. (1785/6), these dissensions culminated in a rebellion to the south of Kōḻikkōṭu, under the leadership of a supporter of the local élite. Arshed Beg and the Maisūrian troops that were stationed in Malabar were unable to suppress this rebellion, which prompted Ṭippu Sulttān to try to gain an ally in the Tāmūtiri family. Ravi Varmma of the Tāmūtiri family declared himself willing to fight against the rebels alongside Arshed Beg—an action which culminated in the flight of the rebel leader. Ṭippu granted Ravi Varmma a pension as a mark of gratitude for this success. The family members of the Tāmūtiri who had fled to Tiruvitāṃkūr then headed back and, at the start of 1788, they travelled with Arshed Beg to Śrīraṅga-paṭṭaṇaṃ in order to discuss the matter of their reinstatement with Ṭippu. However, these negotiations did not produce a positive outcome for the Tāmūtiri family.

Ṭippu's visit to Malabar in April 1788, which resulted in the forced conversions to Islam, plunged southern Malabar into deep unrest for the next two years. Ṭippu took some of the rājās who had been forced to convert to Kōyamputtūr. Many of the Hindus who were to be converted forcibly sought shelter in the house of the Tāmūtiri in Kōḻikkōṭu (three of the Tāmūtiri rājās were present at this time). In October or November 1788, Ṭippu took an important landowner as hostage. In order to free him, Ravi Varmma and a group of Nāyars and Māpiḷḷas mounted opposition against the representative of the Maisūrian government which had taken him into custody, and thereby triggered off a general rebellion. The rebels were able to capture the open land up to Kōḻikkōṭu, thus forcing Ṭippu to send in one of his French generals with a unit of troops. This action did succeed in driving out Ravi Varmma from Kōḻikkōṭu, but he continued to remain active within the land.[30] Furthermore, the spark of rebellion spread like wildfire to northern Malabar. The Ciṟakkal Rājā's attempt to drive Ṭippu Sulttān towards concessions ended in his being threatened with circumcision—i.e. conversion to Islam. Rather than be circumcised he chose to commit suicide.[31]

In general, the Malabar rulers' reaction to the occupation of Haidar Ali and Ṭippu Sulttān was characterized by the attempt to safeguard their own sovereignty as far as possible; this was something that had been called into question by Haidar Ali's and Ṭippu Sulttān's restructure of the economic and social conditions in Malabar society. The reactions of local rulers and the population partly constituted flight, often to Tiruvitāṃkūr, partly a kind of 'passive' resistance, such as making false statements for tax assessments, and partly active resistance, as demonstrated by the various rebellions against the Maisūrian occupation.

The motives for resistance can in part be explained by the rejection of those changes made to social and economic structures. For the Nāyars and rājās especially, these measures were accompanied by a loss of their previous function and privileges, and thus meant a decline in their status within the population and in their influence in political decisions. It was thus out of the question for them to adopt a loyal stance towards, or to submit to, the new system. The entire population suffered from the economic upheavals caused by the tax collections that were introduced by the Maisūrian rulers, but the hardest hit of all were the farmers.

Nevertheless, the Maisūrian rulers—Ṭippu Sulttān in this case—were not able to establish themselves in Malabar for long. The rulers of northern Malabar, and first and foremost the Rājā of Kōṭṭayaṃ, put up the most dogged resistance to Ṭippu's attempts at conquest.

> It has been stated, that Tippoo's government was not so firmly established in the Northern, as in the Southern, parts of the Province—the natural strength of Cotiote in particular enabled the inhabitants of that district to maintain a comparative Independence—this fact is repeatedly asserted, and it is further added (and on the authority of the Raja of Koormenaad), that the Mysorean Government had found it necessary to compromise with the Pyche Raja.[32]

What can we conclude from this development? The rulers and population of northern Malabar had a highly developed sense of freedom and self-government, which was partly due to the geographical situation and limited size of their principalities. The British also had to combat this phenomenon when they strove to achieve territorial rule over Malabar, and they too clashed with the local élite's will to assert itself.

In spite of all the measures taken by Haidar Ali and Ṭippu Sulttān, neither succeeded in establishing fixed central structures in Malabar.[33] Indeed, their rule had removed irretrievably certain elements of the traditional social structure in Malabar, such as the tax system, but the *tar̠avāṭu*s were able to maintain their socio-political function despite years of war and the pattern of flight which accompanied them. Although considerable changes had emerged in Malabar during the Maisūrian hegemony, the local conceptions of rule had remained in place, and these would come into conflict with British ideas of a bureaucratic administrative system. The ensuing problems are dealt with in the subsequent section.

British Policy towards Malabar after 1792

After the British had taken control of Malabar in 1792, by the peace settlement of Śrīraṅgapaṭṭaṇaṃ, they intended to provide the recently won province with institutions capable of government according to British standards. In this they were partially able to fall back on the structures that had been created in Malabar by Haidar Ali and Ṭippu Sulttān. The primary aim was to turn the province into a prosperous source of income.[34] The British paid little attention to traditional structures in Malabar, which they considered to be outdated, and their disregard aroused the displeasure of both the population and the rājās. The most important measures taken by the British in the spheres of administration and taxation will be presented in the following section, and the reactions of the Malabar people to these measures will form the focus of the last subsection in this chapter.

British Administrative Interventions in Malabar

The government in Bombay decided to form a commission in order to assess conditions in Malabar. The commission started its work in Malabar in 1792 and comprised Alexander Dow and William Gamul Farmer from the Bombay Presidency, as well as William Page and Charles Boddam from the Bengal Presidency.[35] They were charged with recording the political situation of the day and its historical background, with producing a summary of the connections already discovered by Messrs Dow and Farmer and with noting the changes made previously by the commissioners from both Presidencies.[36] It is evident from the instructions drawn up by General Abercromby[37] that the aim of the commission was to establish a fully functioning administrative system in Malabar which was to be in a position to collect the taxes levied by the British on a regular basis.

> Wherefore the commissioners from Bombay are required to proceed with such enquiries as may ultimately enable them to establish a system for a regular administration of justice over all ranks; [...] another essential article of immediate discussion pointed out in these instructions, is the Tribute to be paid for the present year (967 Malabar style,) as well as the recovery of such part of last year's revenue as can be acquired [...].[38]

One of the most important aspects regarding the establishment of administration in Malabar was the British government's intention to direct along well-ordered paths the affairs within the province which they viewed as anarchic.

The difficulty for the British in their plans for administration lay in the rājās' assumption that they were to regain their independence after the end of the Maisūrian occupation. The British, however, wanted to gain political control of Malabar themselves. So as not to offend the Malabar rājās outright, General Abercromby instructed the commissioners to adopt a rather cautious approach with the Malabar rājās. This occurred after he had ascertained that the treaties signed with the rājās of northern Malabar in 1790 were not formulated as comprehensively as the British would have liked at that moment. The treaties promised the rājās independence from Ṭippu, but did not pronounce explicitly the dependency of the Malabar rulers on the British.[39] The commissioners had a weighty argument in their favour—from a British viewpoint—which could force the rājās to comply when it came to their demands for independence: from a British perspective the Malabar rulers had not adhered to the most important article of the previous treaties—namely the exclusive supply of pepper to the EIC.[40] Consequently, the commissioners were to stipulate in future treaties with the rājās that the rājās should pay tributes for their protection by the British in natural produce.

> [...] still however it will be necessary to use a mild language with the chiefs, and to claim a Tribute for protection as implied in the treaties; nor can they with propriety insist on a literal construction of them, as they must be conscious they have not adhered to the most essential article—the exclusive trade of the country; [...] that the Tributes or a part of them should be paid in Pepper, Sandalwood, and Cardamums [...].[41]

But the policy of 'mild language' lasted only a few months. From September 1792, a policy of intervention was favoured, one which was to assure the EIC of a monopoly over pepper. A chief characteristic of this policy was to regard the Malabar rulers in the sense of Bengali zamīndārs,[42] i.e. to strip them of their sovereignty and to seal with them appropriate treaties on tax.[43] The aim of the treaties was firstly to refute all claims to sovereignty made by the Malabar rulers and to ensure their long-term dependence on the EIC, secondly, to guarantee their tax collections by restoring the strength of Malabar's economic production through its primary good of pepper, and thirdly, to create an administrative and legal structure.

However, the rājās were not willing to give up their sovereignty to the British that easily. In their first set of negotiations with Farmer and Dow, they assumed that they would be regarded as allies of the British, and therefore insisted upon being returned their principalities. In the end, however, the rājās were forced to give in to British demands: They were only returned governmental sovereignty over their lands on the condition that they permitted the British to collect taxes, and that they themselves regulated internal affairs.[44] Furthermore, the British endeavoured to countermand a large part of the Malabar rājās' basis of legitimation by depriving them of their traditional rights underlining their sovereignty. For example, they forbade the rājās to accept gifts from the people at the festivals of Oṇam and Viṣu[45] and in doing so they struck at one of the fundamental pillars for the basis of legitimation within the redistributive system. The Rājā of Kaṭattanāṭu refused to forfeit his right to *cuṅkaṃ* to the EIC, since this constituted one of the most important sovereign rights in Malabar.[46] Indeed, whilst the Joint Commissioners called themselves sovereign in Malabar on behalf of the EIC,[47] the rājās considered the EIC to be usurpers: '[...] considering the state of this country [Malabar], and more particularly the peculiar situation of the British Government in respect to the exercise of their sovereignty in it (which, to hide nothing, the rajas look upon rather as a usurpation on our part than a legal rule) [...].'[48] But finally none of the rājās were steadfast: the Rājā of Kaṭattanāṭu was the first to accept the conditions of the British, and signed a treaty with them. He was followed by the rājās of Kōṭṭayaṃ and Ciṟakkal.[49]

A particular conflict over the rights of sovereignty led by Paḻaśśi Rājā, focused on the precarious situation of Vāyanāṭu, which had become a bone of contention between the British and Ṭippu Sulttān after 1792. For Paḻaśśi Rājā the most desirable outcome would have been a clear decision in favour of the British, since Vāyanāṭu had for centuries belonged to Kōṭṭayaṃ[50] and its loss would have meant that a large section of the principality no longer came under the sovereignty of Paḻaśśi Rājā. Throughout 1792 correspondence went back and forth between Paḻaśśi Rājā and the British; the commissioners felt that Vāyanāṭu had not become their property and that Paḻaśśi Rājā was thus wrong to make his claim to this section of the land. It is likely that a military dispute had taken place in December 1792 between the Nāyars of Kōṭṭayaṃ and Ṭippu's envoys, yet the commissioners were not able to verify this event. In March 1793, the commissioners informed Paḻaśśi Rājā (and Vira Varmma) that the district of Vāyanāṭu came under the territory of Ṭippu Sulttān and that they expected both rājās to respect Ṭippu's sovereignty in Vāyanāṭu.[51] In their negotiations with Vira Varmma, the British emphasized that it would not be acceptable to serve two masters at the same time. Vira Varmma had to promise the British that he would hand over taxes to them and not to Ṭippu whilst accepting at the same time an obligation not to put up any resistance should Ṭippu march into Vāyanāṭu.[52] The legal situation of Vāyanāṭu was only really clarified in 1799: under the treaty of Śrīraṅga-paṭṭaṇaṃ the EIC took control of the district of Vāyanāṭu, which once again belonged to Kōṭṭayaṃ.[53]

Regarding the civil administration of Malabar, the first significant administrative act to be passed by the commissioners were the guidelines for the new government of what was known as the 'Malabar Province' on 11 March 1793.[54] At the head of the government was the 'Supravisor' (or General Magistrate) to whom two Superintendents were assigned. The northern and southern halves of the Malabar Province, now divided into two, were each under the control of these Superintendents. The Northern Superintendent had his headquarters in Talaśśēri and the Southern Superintendent was based in Cērapulaśśēri. The Superintendents exercised both fiscal and administrative powers.[55] The Supravisor was stationed in Kōḻikkōṭu; he held even greater political, fiscal, and legal power and was in charge of the Superintendents. He alone made decisions about the military forces—except in an emergency—and about the mint. Both he and his Superintendents were obliged to make trips around the country, which were aimed at making it easier for him to exercise administrative control.[56] It was their responsibility to keep the peace, to administer justice, and to collect taxes as well as to keep an eye on the mint.[57]

As a support to the Superintendents and the Supravisor the British took on a certain number of assistants who were employed in public accountancy, as court administrators and in any miscellaneous tasks which may have arisen.[58] The new kind of governmental organization was announced officially to the Malabar rājās and the population on 18 March 1793. William Gamul Farmer was sworn in as Supravisor[59] and Jonathan Duncan took over his post in the Joint Commission.[60] The initial phases of the new government saw the Supravisor and the Joint Commission involved in disputes with one another over respective authority, and these included disputes over the pepper monopoly. This particular problem was settled with the disbandment of the Joint Commission in October 1793.[61]

Analysing the levels of administration introduced by the British, it has to be noticed that they did not take into account the structures that had developed previously in Malabar, apart from in the retention of their names: the old *dēśaṃ*s were brought together into larger administrative units, the *aṃśaṃ*s.[62] In this way the figure of just over two thousand dēśams was reduced to 429 aṃśaṃs by the middle of the nineteenth century.[63] At the head of the aṃśaṃs were *adhikāri*s, administrative officials, who were appointed by the British government. They were each assigned one bookkeeper and two additional assistants. The British frequently recruited their employees from the numbers of old *dēśavaḷi*s and *nāṭuvāḷi*s, who had lost their privileged position due to the new British administration.[64] The primary function of the adhikāris was to collect taxes for the British. They were thus the most important people in British eyes for passing on information to the population and for carrying out orders. In return the aṃśadhikāris were afforded the status of powerful men and were more feared than respected by the local people. The British always strove to satisfy the adhikāris so as to receive their loyalty and subordination. The British also benefited from using them as 'middlemen' in communications with the local population; the adhikāris were well acquainted with the land and its people, which meant that administrative costs could be kept low and that pressure would not be put on the already limited finances of the British.

A British court was founded in Kōḷikkōṭu over which the members of the commission presided. One of the purposes of this institution was to impress the locals with the establishment of a system that guaranteed them rights and property.[65] In cases of dispute the population could choose whether to turn to this court or to the rājās for judgement. The British, however, reserved the right to amend judgements made by the rājā in those cases where the parties concerned were not satisfied with the result.[66] In later years courts were also set up in Cērapulaśśēri and Talaśśēri, and the court of appeal was established in Kōḷikkōṭu. The jurisdiction in these courts followed the Code of Bengal. Furthermore, the British also extended their jurisdiction over the regions of Kannūr, Pantalāyini Koḷḷaṃ, Tiruraṅṅāṭi, Ponnāni, Pālakkāṭu, Tanūr and Cēṟṟavāya, and passed additional regulations to the Bengal Code. Within these seven local judicial administrations, the British also employed local people as policemen and court administators.[67] The British withheld an annual salary for local employees as a kind of 'deposit cum personal commitment' to guarantee their good conduct and integrity when carrying out tasks. In addition, the employees had to swear an oath that they would meet their obligations and not abuse their positions to make financial gain in any way.[68]

With the establishment of British courts and the orientation of jurisdiction towards Anglo-Saxon customs, local law was almost entirely replaced by codified law. Traditional institutions were consequently ignored and replaced by the British system without any thought as to whether this would be suited to the customs of the country.[69] Yet the British government found it impossible to bring about 'law and order' to their satisfaction, since the new system was not efficient enough in British eyes—the population trusted neither the courts nor their staff[70]—and the operation of the system entailed very high costs for the EIC.

A modification was made to the Civil Code in October 1797; this was partially designed to keep in check the growing influence of the rājās, whilst at the same time establishing British supremacy and enabling a reduction in the expenditure of the EIC.[71] At the end of 1797, civil servants and tax assistants who had been sworn in were employed across the entire district.[72] The historian J.K. Ravindran believes that British regulations made in the initial years following the takeover of administration did not actually enjoy any real success, but that they did lay the foundations for a modern legislature based on the Western model.[73]

Still, there were further changes in the administrative structure of British Malabar: in 1800, the British government did away with the posts of the Northern and Southern Superintendent of Malabar, as well as with the division of the province into two parts. Instead they divided the province into ten districts, each run by a revenue collector who also had limited legal authority. In the same year the British government handed over the civil and military administration of Malabar from the Bombay Presidency to the Madras Presidency, although the department of trade still remained with the Bombay Presidency.[74] The British hoped that this measure would abate the rebellious spirit still latent in Malabar, thus allowing them to build up an effective administration in this province.

The second Commission of Malabar Affairs,[75] which had previously taken part in governmental operations, was abolished in the aftermath of Malabar's transfer to the jurisdiction of Fort St. George. The province was placed under the responsibility of a principal collector to whom three subordinate collectors were assigned. The principal collector held civil and military power over Malabar. This form of administrative structure remained in place until the complete reorganization of administration in the Malabar Province.[76] The Cornwallis system for administration was introduced to the Madras Presidency in 1802, but it was only applied in Malabar from 1806 onwards.[77] One of the British government's principal tasks in Malabar was the disarmament of the population. A ban was enacted against the production of weapons and also against the carrying of weapons.[78] Ultimately, the British demanded that all weapons in use be handed over for a small fee—from then on only authorized employees of the government were allowed to own a weapon. The rājās were also supposed to hand over their weapons, but they considered this to be an attack on their sovereignty.[79]

With an administrative structure characterized by British conceptions introduced in Malabar, changes and breaks had occurred in the traditional structure of society. One of the most striking examples of these changes is the restructuring of the Nāyar *ta<u>r</u>avāṭu*s. The British did not recognize their major function and importance within society; they stripped the Nāyars of their political freedom, their right to share in decision-making and also their economic independence. As a result the Nāyars were denied their traditional responsibilities, i.e. the management of the land and its people, and the leadership and implementation of local self-administration. The British also mistrusted the family organization within the Nāyar taṟavāṭus. The women within the taṟavāṭus were hit especially hard: due to legislation introduced by the British they were only allowed to hold the post of *kāraṇavarti* if a court acknowledged their right to have this position. Furthermore, the authorization to hold this post could be taken away from them at any time.[80] At the end of the nineteenth century, the traditional right of women to occupy the position of kāraṇavarti was unheard of for some British judges:

> I cannot agree with the Munsif that the evidence is sufficient to prove a family custom which, though it may be in accord with primitive usage, is opposed to the present usage of every other Nayar family in Malabar. [...], but I have never heard of a case where the headship was claimed as of right by a female [...].[81]

Thus the taṟavāṭus were not actually destroyed in physical terms, but they were broken as a political, social and ritual unit through the fundamental redefinition of their appearance and functions.[82]

The British policy—marked on the one hand by persistent ignorance of existing social structures in Malabar and on the other hand by visions of a state modelled on European bureaucracy—increasingly countermanded the traditional structures in Malabar, which had already been undermined by Maisūrian occupation. This ultimately resulted in the widespread elimination of handed-down traditional structures within the systems of society and state in Malabar, and in their replacement by more British forms of state control. Yet it was not only the changes forced by British policy but also its methods which found little favour with the local population. This is exemplified in the dissatisfaction caused by the British restructuring of administration. The aim of British policy was to achieve greater control over the land and its people whilst also attaining the most effective economic exploitation possible in the form of trade monopolies and tax collections—and all this at the lowest possible cost.[83] Therefore, in the course of negotiations with the British, the

Malabar rulers must have detected that the concessions which were wrested from them were intended to weaken their position and to strengthen that of the British. Some rājās who did not consider it acceptable for the British to slowly take away their rights of sovereignty took a stand against them. The result was a period of rebellions lasting almost ten years, and one of the rebel leaders was Paḷaśśi Rājā.

British Tax Policy

Before the British introduced their own taxation scheme, they first tried to ascertain which sums of money Haidar Ali and Ṭippu Sulttān had collected in their annual tax collections, with the initial intention of adopting Ṭippu's *jamābandī*. After their tours around Malabar and after certain negotiations with the rājās, the Joint Commissioners came to the conclusion that they should not retain all of Ṭippu's sources of revenue.[84] The Joint Commissioners believed that Ṭippu had taxed Malabar too heavily, in particular its northern half, and that he had monopolized internal trade. Maisūrian policy towards Malabar was characterized by tax increases which placed a heavy burden on the farmers—Logan and Warden spoke of up to 50 per cent of the production—and which put the janmakārans in a precarious financial situation.[85] When determining British tax policy, the commissioners rejected both Ṭippu's over-taxation of Malabar and his monopoly of internal trade.[86]

After several negotiations in the spring of 1792, the British sealed treaties with the Malabar rulers, limited to a certain length of time, which entitled the rājās to sovereignty over their regions and yet accorded the EIC the highest level of authority. Two British officials per principality were to be responsible for tax assessment.[87] The Rājā of Tiruvitāṃkūr was also granted the right to collect taxes from the Malabar rājās, something which he had already done on behalf of the EIC in 1790/1.[88] Yet in spite of these agreements the issue of tax assessment was to prove a problematic one.

In October 1792, one-year treaties were signed with the rulers of Malabar.[89] Neverthless, negotiations had not been easy for the British and they had required prolonged discussions, especially with Paḷaśśi Rājā, since he refused to pay the sums of money that were demanded of him by the British. This prompted them to describe him as the 'most untractable and unreasonable'[90] of the rājās. In the end Paḷaśśi Rājā had to agree to the following treaty: firstly, the entire pepper production (at least 500 *kaṇṭi*s) was to be handed over to the British, and secondly, a sum of 20,000 rupees,[91] either in cash or natural produce, was to be paid in two instalments one year in arrears. The sum of 20,000 rupees was regarded as the minimum payment; should the British tax collectors decide that a higher sum be taken then the rājās would receive instructions to collect more tax.[92] In the spring of 1793, the commissioners made amendments to the treaty that they had sealed with Paḻaśśi Rājā in October 1792: in Kōṭṭayaṃ there was to be a tax collection of 55,000 rupees and at least 700–800 kaṇṭis of pepper.[93]

Although the treaty on tax collection had been sealed with Paḻaśśi Rājā, on 18 May 1793, Vira Varmma of Kurumpranāṭu was confirmed as the appointed tax collector of Kōṭṭayaṃ. His subsequent request for an assistant to facilitate tax collection was upheld by the EIC.[94] Thus at that time, two treaties existed with two different rulers over tax collection in Kōṭṭayaṃ; the execution of either treaty was therefore bound to lead to some confrontation. Paḻaśśi Rājā was most annoyed with his relative, Vira Varmma, since he was questioning Paḻaśśi Rājā's sovereignty in his own principality. Paḻaśśi Rājā's resistance to British policy also deepened considerably at this point, because he felt that his previous loyalty to the British was not being honoured.[95]

Although the British made systematic attempts to secure tax collection through contracts, they enjoyed such a low level of success that the Supravisor of Malabar found himself forced to give concessions to the rājās. No taxes were collected in Kōṭṭayaṃ until November 1793. Paḻaśśi Rājā saw to it that all pepper plants were destroyed in case they would be used to calculate taxes and their value taken for estimation.[96] In the end an agreement was reached between Paḻaśśi Rājā and the Supravisor on 20 December 1793, which concerned the taxation of the districts of Katirūr, Paḻaśśi, Kūtiyāṭi and Tamaraśśēri. Additionally, the following points were agreed upon with Paḻaśśi Rājā: estates that belonged to temples were to be exempt from tax for one year, a fifth of taxes were to go towards Paḻaśśi Rājā's upkeep because he had remained loyal to the EIC during the battles against Ṭippu Sulttān, and another fifth of taxes were to be used towards supporting the temples.[97] These more or less liberal conditions which were contained within the treaty managed to bring some stability to the strained situation.[98]

However, the peace did not last because Vira Varmma Rājā of Kurumpranāṭu held governmental sovereignty over Kōṭṭayaṃ on the basis of agreements with the British. The population of Kōṭṭayaṃ did not care to accept the appointment of a British puppet as ruler instead of their own rājā, i.e. Paḻaśśi Rājā; they demanded to be led by the ruler who had stood by them in wartime. Furthermore, Vira Varmma turned the operation of tax collection to his favour in those regions that were under his control: as intended by the British, the population of Kōṭṭayaṃ had to pay him fourfold the amount of taxes expected—this is evident from the complaints issued by Kōṭṭayaṃ's nobility.[99] Many poor settlers left the country for this very reason, which in turn had a negative effect on pepper production. Thus high taxation affected the farmers' way of life fundamentally. The local people of Kōṭṭayaṃ demanded the reinstatement of their king, Kēraḷa Varmma Paḷaśśi Rājā:

So we made a representation about all these affairs to Paḷaśśi Rājā and await his decision. [...] Now we request you, Sahib [Christopher Peile], to be kind enough to entrust Paḷaśśi Rājā to collect the taxes due to the Company from 72 [972 M.E./ 1796–97 A.D.] onwards and to remit the same to the Company. This would solve our problem and save us.[100]

Nevertheless in April 1797, when the British were busy signing new treaties, tax collection in Kōṭṭayaṃ was once again entrusted to the Kurumpranāṭu Rājā. This was allowed to happen despite clear knowledge of the resulting and ongoing conflicts, documented in the aforementioned petition by the nobility of Kōṭṭayaṃ. Paḷaśśi Rājā was summoned to Talaśśēri on account of outstanding payments. But he did not appear and as a result Colonel Dow assumed full authority for tax collection in June 1797.[101]

James Stevens, the Northern Superintendent, reported to Colonel Dow in August 1798 that he had not received any payment whatsoever from Paḷaśśi Rājā. Furthermore, Paḷaśśi Rājā was reported to have prevented attempts by British officials in Kōṭṭayaṃ to collect taxes there. He opposed the taxation of houses in particular.[102] In the spring of 1799, Paḷaśśi Rājā was largely able to prevent the payment of pepper tax.[103] The government in Bombay expressed its dissatisfaction over the level of taxes being brought in by the province of Malabar, and the government in Malabar was ordered in turn to take appropriate measures and to increase levels of tax:[104] the Superintendents called together local officials who came from Malabar to submit reports on tax collection, and to face questions on the state of affairs within the country.[105] On the basis of the current tax situation, which was no longer viable for the British, the inhabitants of Kōṭṭayaṃ were instructed to hand over their taxes to none other than the EIC collector s.[106]

In 1802, a new tax assessment was made, and W. Macleod headed a redefinition of the exchange rate in Malabar.[107] This meant an increase in taxation for each individual by 20 per cent in gold fanams and by 10 per cent in silver fanams, on top of the increase in the government's share of rice production from 35–40 per cent. This increase was based on a seriously incorrect assessment of farming production. The yield for one coconut palm, for example, was put at 48 nuts instead of a realistic estimate of 24 nuts.[108] As a result the finanical situation of the Malabar population became even more precarious—many of them had to sell all of their movable property just to cover tax payments.[109] Macleod had stated in the previous year that the province had reached a slump in economic and demographic terms; he even admitted that the British government could also have made some errors in this regard. He appeared to have forgotten that fact, however, when he implemented the tax increases in Malabar in 1802. Instead he cited the subjection of the population to their rājās as one of the causes of the precarious situation:

> The constant scenes of Rebellion and murder which agitated the Province since the invasion of Hyder thirty seven years ago, have caused a great depopulation & decrease in its resources—Cottiote, Wynaad and Chericaul, are the Districts that suffered most, and their misfortunes may be partly attributed to the errors of Governm[t]., and to the infatuated submission to the will of their Chiefs, for which people governed by a feudal system, have ever been conspicuous.[110]

The commissioners, W.G. Farmer perhaps most of all, took advice from Murdoch Brown (1750–1828), one of the wealthiest and most experienced British merchants on the coast of Malabar. Initially he transacted his business in French Mayyaḻi, but he came closer to the representatives of the EIC in Talaśśēri after 1792.[111] The commissioners partly took his advice because they considered him to be 'the most considerable of British subjects' on the coast.[112] Murdoch Brown played an important if not clearly defining role in British policy towards Malabar. It is likely that he influenced both the commissioners and later on the respective Superintendents in accordance with his financial interests.[113] At the end of 1797, in Añcarakaṇṭi, near Talaśśēri, Brown founded the first English plantation in Malabar and assumed the position of manager. The products grown there were sold exclusively to EIC traders. Brown cultivated coconut palms, betel-nut palms, cinnamon, nutmeg and sandalwood.[114] From 1817, Brown leased the plantation over ninety-nine years in a contract, and subsequently cultivated pepper, cotton, and coffee too.[115]

The aforementioned events show that, despite announcements to the contrary, the British pursued similarly uncompromising policies to those of Ṭippu Sulttān when it came to tax and land law. The result was that the economy in Malabar suffered severely, something which the majority of the population did not take lying down. The rājās exhibited differing reactions to the British policy of monopoly through treaties: whilst Kēraḷa Varmma Paḻaśśi Rājā repeatedly insisted on respect for his authority as rājā, existing sources allow us to infer that Vira Varmma probably preferred the personal advantages of a separate autonomy in his kingdom.

The Central Role of Pepper in the Dispute over Malabar

Pepper played a key role both at the time of the Maisūrian invasions and also during the British appropriation of rule. Each foreign power strove to take control of the pepper trade, and yet not even direct political control of Malabar could guarantee the monopolization of pepper. Profits in trade were attempted also by political interventions; trade and politics were not separable.[116]

Upon his departure from Malabar Ṭippu Sulttān had ordered, where possible, the destruction of pepper plants so as to deprive the EIC of the foundations of the pepper trade. The commissioners decided to propose a reduced level of tax upon new plants in order to revive pepper cultivation. The EIC had paid Malabar traders 165 rupees per kaṇṭi of pepper since September 1792, i.e. 10 rupees less than in Mayyaḻi. A proclamation was announced on 20 December 1792 which served to establish and guarantee freedom of trade, though this excluded pepper. The EIC obliged the rājās of northern Malabar to collect half of the harvest from pepper cultivation and sell it to the EIC supervisors in Talaśśēri for 100 rupees per kaṇṭi, i.e. for approximately 70 rupees less than on the free market. This agreement did not enjoy any great success in practice,[117] however, despite the fact that those caught by the EIC selling pepper to other parties had to reckon with a fine of 250 rupees per kaṇṭi.[118] In spite of the threat of fines the majority of pepper produced in Malabar did not go to the EIC, but was sold on the free market. The commissioners concluded that the rājās were not to be trusted. They therefore employed local merchants, accompanied by British civil servants, to seize pepper in Ciṟakkal and Kōṭṭayaṃ. They were able to collect 1,330 kaṇṭis of pepper in this manner, some 200 kaṇṭis less than expected. The results in southern Malabar were considerably worse: instead of an expected 1,500 kaṇṭis of pepper they only managed to collect 424 kaṇṭis. Thus the idea of a pepper monopoly did not match up to the hopes of the EIC officials, and consequently, only four months after the initial proclamation on free trading for all goods except pepper, the monopoly was lifted on pepper as well.[119]

One of the EIC's principal suppliers of pepper was the merchant Covakkāran Mūssa from Talaśśēri.[120] Pepper—called 'Malabar money'[121] by the commissioners—was one of the chief products of Malabar, yet pepper production had declined steadily since the Maisūrian invasions. Mūssa reported that it had been possible to harvest 20,000 kaṇṭis of pepper in the region surrounding Cāvvāya in the years prior to Haidar Ali's invasion of 1766—this traded at a price of 70–80 rupees per kaṇṭi—whereas only 11,000–12,000 kaṇṭis, at 130 rupees per kaṇṭi, were available in 1784. According to his estimate, the best case scenario for 1792 would expect 7,000–8,000 kaṇṭis of pepper for the area under EIC control, i.e. the Malabar Province, and such a prosperous harvest would only come about every three to four years. With purchases from Tiruvitāṃkūr the EIC would thus achieve an optimum result of 18,000 kaṇṭis at 200 rupees per kaṇṭi.[122] In spite of this negative development in pepper production, pepper still constituted the chief export product of Malabar in 1804 at 45 per cent of exports.[123] The failure of British policy on pepper can be attributed to three factors: the strong influence of the rājās on the pepper producers and their opposition to the British monopolization of pepper, the activities of Brown, and also the private trading affairs of EIC officials. As a result, the EIC did not achieve the economic advantages that they had hoped would come from the conquest of Malabar.[124]

The Maisūrian invasions, particularly those of Ṭippu Sulttān, resulted in a slump not only in pepper production but also in the pepper trade: Exports from Malabar to other countries declined, as did imports. The prices of imported goods increased proportionately[125] and the Malabar Commission did away with the relatively high domestic duties on cereals, fish and vegetables that had existed to date.[126] The duties levied on goods flowing between the three presidencies of Bengal, Bombay and Madras were also dropped. Contrarily, however, the English levied a customs charge of 4 per cent of the value of goods imported from other parts of India, China and the Persian Gulf, of 3.5 per cent on imports from Great Britain, and of 8 per cent on imports from the rest of Europe. Exempted from duties were metals, cutlery, glasses, glass goods and certain cloths imported from Great Britain. Also free from duty were pepper, cardamom, sandalwood and nutmeg, which were imported over land, whilst all other imported goods were subject to a customs duty of 2.5 per cent. An import charge was to be imposed on imports from Maisūr, but this had not yet been fixed. Taxation on exports was set at 10.5 per cent for pepper, 6 per cent for sandalwood, 5 per cent for cardamom, 5 per cent for nutmeg, 4 per cent for cinnamon, and 2.5 per cent for all other export goods from Malabar *ad valorem.* The commission declared a trading ban on the export of bondsmen, weapons and ammunition. The supervisors in Talaśśēri are reported to have put this new system into practice from September 1793.[127] Even the most elaborate attempts of Europeans to control or monopolize the pepper trade in Malabar did not succeed—and this not only in pre-colonial times but right into the early nineteenth century.

The Issue of Land Law

Besides the difficulties involved in collecting taxes after 1792, conflicts also emerged between locals and the British, and even amongst the population itself, as a result of the British reorganization of land law. British financial and economic policy in Malabar was characterized by two features: On the one hand, the largest share of production was set aside for the state, and on the other, the janmakāran was regarded as the absolute owner of the land.

> [...] and the *jenmkars* [sic], free from all interference of this kind, were the independent owners of the land. They held, by right of birth, not of the prince, but

in common with him, and therefore may be considered as having possessed a property in the soil more absolute than even that of the landlord in Europe.[128]

The British conception of law equated the janmakāran to the Roman *dominus*; accordingly, they treated the *janmaṃ* as the *dominium*.[129] In doing so, however, they overlooked the fundamental difference between the dominus and the janmakāran: The dominus owned the land himself whereas the janmakāran owned not the land but the janmaṃ with the laws and titles that went with it—the *sthānamānaṅṅaḷ*. The actual ownership of land was not the decisive criterion when it came to distributing land in Malabar; instead the spiritual, political and ritual functions of the janmakāran that were connected with the land and that were represented in the redistributive system played the decisive role. Only a few British administrators recognized the local system, i.e. the principle of sharing the produce and no one being the landlord in the western sense,[130] but usually those who grasped the difference were not the ones to take the final decisions about the British tax policy in India.

An additional problem within the context of laws regarding land and ownership was that a large number of janmakārans were no longer masters over their land *de facto* due to long periods of exile, and *kāṇakkāran*s were in control of farming affairs instead. British policy, which fundamentally acknowledged the returned janmakārans—a large percentage of whom were Hindus—as landowners, made things difficult for the kāṇakkārans, who were Māppiḷḷas in many regions. Despite the fact that kāṇakkārans had farmed the fields and prevented farming production from coming to a complete standstill, even in the turbulent years of the Maisūrian invasions, they came away empty-handed from the British government. They were actually supposed to continue working the land, but they did not receive any rights at all—contrary to the period prior to the invasions when they were able to assert proportional rights to the land compared to those of the janmakārans. As a result, conflicts arose between janmakārans and kāṇakkārans. The reason for these conflicts was originally financial, but a religious connotation was also at play, particularly during the nineteenth century.[131] The British used the following period to redefine all of the laws associated with land such as the *kāṇaṃ* and the *pāṭṭaṃ*.[132]

This major error on the part of the British—to ignore the basic principles of land law in Malabar—had dire consequences for the local people, since social spheres which had previously been closely linked were dissociated from one another and thus rendered meaningless. Furthermore, the British concept of justice was based on codified law, which provided for treaties to create land law. Contrary to this, the *maryyāda*[133] was based on the Malabar concept of justice. However, the British did not recognize the maryyāda as a law of equal standing; they judged the Malabar state system to be anarchic and thus in need of reform. An essential aspect of their conception of the state was its legitimation through technical administrative legal proceedings. In this context 'legal proceedings' should be understood 'as the logical cohesion of real actions [...], legitimation as a transfer of binding decisions into a separate decision-making structure.'[134] Niklas Luhmann assumes that the proceedings are not a criterion of 'truth' itself, but that they promote decision-making and its correctness, that they enable and channel communication, and that they also help to avoid foreseeable disruptions to the ascertainment of the 'truth'. The aim of proceedings is to find true justice. However, truth in such a narrowly defined sense does not always guarantee the resolution of problems, since legal proceedings do not call in all the elements of a case when seeking to ascertain the 'truth'.[135]

Indeed this was clearly evident in Malabar itself: with the aid of legal proceedings as a basis of legitimation, the British did work on an administrative and tax structure which corresponded to their conceptions, but they ultimately were only able to implement it by force and against the wishes of a large part of the local population. The pre-colonial state system in Malabar was brought to collapse due to British unwillingness to use and add to the existing system, their intention of adopting their own model—which they were used to and which corresponded to their own conception of state—and implementing it in Malabar as far as possible and without modification. Admittedly, some elements of the pre-colonial structures of society did remain in place, such as the tar̲avāṭus, but they were given completely new functions which scarcely had anything to do with their original purpose.[136]

The result of British interventions in administration and their policy on land law and tax was to force the local population to live in economically unstable conditions. This in turn aroused a considerable desire amongst the local people to rebel.[137] The ruler was denied the very basis of his income, which had primarily been made up of trade taxes and royal prerogatives. The result was to foster the collaboration of the entire population with their ruler in opposition to the British: '[...] their mistaken revenue policy retarded for years the pacification of the province and resulted in the fierce blaze of the Pazhassi [sic] Rebellion.'[138]

Aside from their claim to sole sovereignty, the economic squeeze imposed by the British (particularly the heavy taxation of the entire population, whether in trade or farming) can thus be regarded as an explanation for the rebellions of Kēraḷa Varmma Palaśśi Rājā and his followers. Rebellions, social unrest and the like had been relatively absent from Malabar until the eighteenth century. The first rebellions in the region took place during the Maisūrian rule, but it was only under British colonial rule that Malabar developed into an enduring trouble-spot within the British Empire in India, and this can be traced back to the British intention to restructure its society.[139] The colonial establishment of law and legislation[140] forced a clear separation of the traditionally interwoven spheres of politics, economy, society, and religion. In place of the indigenous structure the British aimed to create an entirely new kind of order for Malabar based on the Western model, and they consequently fostered a situation of tension.

Conflicts Between the Local Élite and the Colonial Administration

The administrative actions taken by the British as described in the previous section, triggered off varying reactions from the Malabar rulers. One reaction was to refute British claims to power and to fight them, whilst another option was to cooperate with them, thereby supporting the establishment of British rule. These two divergent reactions are exemplified in the respective patterns of conduct of Kēraḷa Varmma Paḻaśśi Rājā and Vira Varmma of Kurumpranāṭu. After several attempts by diplomatic means, Paḻaśśi Rājā decided to mount resistance against the British. Vira Varmma, however, opted to cooperate with them. This subsection will examine the roles exhibited by these two personages, which exemplify the patterns of conduct of all other rājās in Malabar. The main focus will be placed on the behaviour of Paḻaśśi Rājā on account of the source materials available.

British source texts give several instances where both rulers are described by officers or officials of the EIC. The recurrence of *topoi* is striking in these descriptions, the significance of which can be summarized in the subsequent examples:

> Kerola Vurma [Kēraḷa Varmma] is stated to have been a Man of very shallow intellects and as uniformly and unequivocally acknowledged by himself, inexperienced and totally unfit to govern. His conduct and his professions were however often at variance.—This acknowledged incapacity to manage the affairs of Cotiote [Kōṭṭayaṃ] could appear to have been, in reality, an indisposedness to assist the Company's Servants in the introduction of the authority of their Masters into the Province.[141]

In this judgement it becomes evident that the behaviour of Kēraḷa Varmma Paḻaśśi Rājā did not always seem unambiguous and that the British did not think him capable of ruling his country. It is interesting to note here that the British correlated what they viewed as Paḻaśśi Rājā's inept behaviour as a possibly deliberate act designed to hinder their own claim to sovereignty.

From the point of view of Paḷaśśi Rājā a ruler could only fulfil his duties in the sense of the *rājādharma* if he displayed a will for freedom and if he stood by his own sovereignty.

Contrary to Paḷaśśi Rājā, Vira Varmma was seen by the British as a rājā with whom it was comparatively easy to make agreements, one who conformed to British ideas about their rule in Malabar. Admittedly the British were not completely convinced of Vira Varmma's honesty, but they nevertheless considered his receptiveness to their treaties to be an effective way of gaining an insight into and, where possible, of exerting an influence over the policies of the Malabar rulers.

> Vira Varmma appears to have been an intriguing sort of individual always ready to grasp at personal advantage. [...] And it was certainly a self-seeking arrangement which he now made with the Bombay Commissioners. They and the Bengal Commissioners who joined them subsequently found him to be a very convenient stalking horse (so to speak) for bringing the Zamorin and the other Rajas to terms for he was apparently willing to accept the management of any districts belonging to the people on any terms so long as these promised to be of advantage to himself personally.[142]

Even though this judgement of Vira Varmma was only put down in writing by William Logan some eighty years later, it is clear to see just how comfortable it must have been for the Joint Commissioners to have had such a willing contact amongst the Malabar rulers. As indicated above, Vira Varmma functioned in some respects as a stalking-horse for the British by readily coming to agreements with them, assuring them repeatedly of his dependability, and calling them to aid in internal affairs when problems arose.[143] Obviously Vira Varmma considered economic advantages to be more important than the preservation of his sovereignty at the time of these agreements.

The particular connection between these two rājās was in their blood relation and the entwined legal issues which affected both of their principalities. One of the most striking discrepancies between Kēraḷa Varmma Paḷaśśi Rājā and Vira Varmma of Kurumpranāṭu, in the eyes of the inhabitants of Malabar, was that Vira Varmma went into exile in Tiruvitāṃkūr at the time of the Maisūrian invasions, whilst Paḷaśśi Rājā remained in Malabar and took care of the affairs of his principality and its people. This gave a considerable boost to Paḷaśśi Rājā's reputation both in and around Kōṭṭayaṃ.[144] Furthermore, he considered the fulfilment of religious duties to be one of his most important tasks, and the local population felt likewise.[145] Paḷaśśi Rājā took on the legacy of the senior rājā: the old king still lived in Kōṭṭayaṃ and continued to be the final authority on certain governmental matters. He wanted to see religious festivals adhered to and practised once again; they had been neglected due to the disruption caused by ongoing conflicts ever since the arrival of the British. He thus supported Paḷaśśi Rājā's conviction over matters of religious duty.[146]

Historical Background of the Rebellions in Kōṭṭayaṃ

In 1794, the British made five-year agreements with the rulers, instead of the previous one-year agreements. Here the intention of the British was to assure themselves of trade privileges on the one hand, whilst reaping tax revenue on the other.[147] Yet when he made these agreements the British representative repeated the mistake of seeing Kōṭṭayaṃ as a part of Kurumpranāṭu and, in turn, of putting it under Vira Varmma's supervision.[148] On top of this Vira Varmma announced his willingness to go along with the British request that he might also collect taxes in Vāyanāṭu—an enticing offer for the British but a bone of contention for Paḷaśśi Rājā, since Vāyanāṭu had belonged to Kōṭṭayaṃ since ancient times. Despite official treaties, however, Vira Varmma was not recognized by the population in Kōṭṭayaṃ because he exploited them over taxes.[149] He asked the British to help establish his authority so they stationed troops in Kōṭṭayaṃ and Maṇattaṇa. This action of seeking help from the British instead of facing up to the actual ruler of Kōṭṭayaṃ, not only aroused the displeasure of Paḷaśśi Rājā but also that of the population of Kōṭṭayaṃ, and created a precarious situation for Vira Varma.[150]

The new agreements which Jonathan Duncan[151] made at the end of 1795 with the rājās in Malabar were another reason for Paḷaśśi Rājā's disgruntlement with the British. Their aim was to accustom the rājās to regular payments by introducing interest payments for any taxes handed over late. If the delay in payment totalled one month then the British were entitled to collect taxes directly from the farmers in that particular area, an act which amounted to an invasion into the rulers' territory—another display of the British failure to recognize the rājās' sovereignty. It was one British official *on the spot*, Alexander Walker, who first admitted that the rebellions might not have taken place if the British had conducted themselves in a more moderate manner.[152] At the end of the nineteenth century Logan followed his line of argument remarking that the British system was 'very unsuited to the circumstances of the country',[153] and that it was partly responsible for bringing about the rebellions of subsequent years. So it was that, during the period 1792 to 1796, an explosive mixture of misunderstandings emerged between the rājās and the British, which then erupted into disturbances and rebellions against British colonial power.

The Initial Phase of Rebellion (1796/7)

On 19 April 1796, under second lieutenant James Gordon, 300 men from the

British 3rd Home Infantry marched from Talaśśēri to Paḷaśśi where they surrounded and stormed the royal palace at daybreak. The British troops looted Paḷaśśi Rājā's palace and appropriated its treasures. Yet the British were unable to take Paḷaśśi Rājā prisoner, because he had fled into the woods around Maṇattaṇa before the attack. The temple located there was one of Paḷaśśi Rājā's preferred places of retreat in times of unrest. It seems likely that he had been relayed information about the imminent raid and had therefore been able to flee in time. According to British sources the palace was stormed because Kēraḷa Varmma Paḷaśśi Rājā had refused to give the EIC the taxes collected by Vira Varmma of Kurumpranāṭu. By this refusal Paḷaśśi Rājā fought against the exploitation of his subjects, supporting their material and spiritual well-being as befits the role of the rājā according to the rājādharma:

> I brought people in and gave loans to them having taken loan from Talaśśēri. I paid money for cattle to be brought to the settlements for agriculture. This is how I looked after the country and the people. So when people were tormented [...] in an unprecedented manner I was very much pained. That's why I objected to the collection of wealth from the country. Besides this, I have done no harm to the country nor shall I do anything in the future.[154]

In addition to accusations of having held back taxes and committed injustices against his people, the British considered Paḷaśśi Rājā responsible for the murder of three Māppiḷḷas.[155] One can assume that the actual reason for storming the palace was the wealth presumed therein, valued at approximately 17,000 rupees,[156] and that the alleged murder of the Māppiḷḷas by Paḷaśśi Rājā served only as a welcome excuse for British actions.[157] In a letter to the British Paḷaśśi Rājā stressed that he had not infringed their rules on previous occasions. Following the looting of the palace the British made it known by proclamation that they had come to protect the local people from suppression by the rājā. In this way they hoped to gain authority in the eyes of the population and to turn them away from Paḷaśśi Rājā, but they did not succeed in doing so. Paḷaśśi Rājā had not been safe in the lowlands of Kōṭṭayaṃ since the storming of the palace, so in May of the same year he moved along with his family and supporters into the forests of Vāyanāṭu.[158] Since the poor supply situation rendered life in the highlands very difficult, Kēraḷa Varmma Paḷaśśi Rājā expressed in a letter to Colonel Dow his readiness to return to Kōṭṭayaṃ on condition that the property which had either been confiscated or plundered was returned to him. In July 1796, following a meeting with Kēraḷa Varmma Paḷaśśi Rājā, Dow agreed to this request: Kēraḷa Varmma was to be returned his property, or given appropriate compensation, so long as he in return accounted for the death of the Māppiḷḷas in Bombay, recognized the supremacy of Vira Varmma, and displayed 'a more reasonable conduct' in future.[159] In anticipation of this agreement being kept, Palaśśi Rājā returned to Palaśśi under British escort where he was able to receive all of his property except the state reserves.

The reinstatement of Palaśśi Rājā was confirmed by the government in Bombay in the summer of the same year.[160] It did not, however, send the orders directly to Kēraḷa Varmma, but via Vira Varmma of Kurumpranāṭu. His agent Palavīṭṭil Cantu did not pass on the orders to the rightful recipient, and misappropriated the promised British cash compensation for the plundering of the palace treasures.[161] At the same time Vira Varmma dismissed Kaiteri Ampu, an employee of Palaśśi Rājā, despite the fact that he had been expressly employed by Palaśśi Rājā to collect taxes in Kōṭṭayaṃ. Kaiteri Ampu then moved away with some of his supporters to settle in Kannavaṃ, from where he and his men roamed through the land causing unrest. Kaiteri Ampu would later join Palaśśi Rājā during the rebellions.[162]

Since the matter of returning the palace treasures had not yet been settled to his satisfaction, Palaśśi Rājā made a written complaint in October 1796 to Christopher Peile, the Northern Superintendent of Malabar. He also related that it was impossible for his people to pay the high level of taxes which the British demanded of them: 'But on arriving in Nittūr, only a part of the wealth taken away from Palaśśi was brought back. That, too, is with a third party. Besides this, people who believe and stick to me, are compelled to pay money over and above the normal taxes in the country. Some have already left the country because of this unbearable taxation.'[163]

Palaśśi Rājā criticized the way in which Palavīṭṭil Cantu (the agent of Vira Varmma) went about collecting taxes: He had settlements destroyed and money and pepper collected without prior assessment,[164] which resulted in poverty and misery for the population. This prompted the Nāyars and noble people of Kōṭṭayaṃ to submit a petition to the British.[165] In another letter Palaśśi Rājā once again insisted vigorously that the purloined property be returned and that, despite all the serious shortcomings thus far, he was prepared in return to declare his loyalty to the British as long as his conditions would carry weight in the basis for an agreement.[166]

After several futile written attempts by Peile to change Kēraḷa Varmma's mind about his conditions for cooperation with the British,[167] he pushed to hold discussions with Kēraḷa Varmma Palaśśi Rājā, possibly to reach an amicable settlement. By that time, however, Palaśśi Rājā had moved back into the forests because he felt that the British had betrayed him.[168] In all probability it seems that the incomplete return of the palace treasures was the straw that broke the camel's back: Palaśśi Rājā was no longer prepared to come to any amicable agreement with the British and Vira Varmma because he was now bound to doubt the integrity of his opponents, bearing in mind the looting of the palace, the subsequent conflicts with the British and the presumptions of Vira Varmma. Futhermore, he feared that the commissioners wanted to do him an injustice. Such suspicions arose because Paḷaśśi Rājā was still unaware of the official orders from Bombay concerning his reinstatement and rehabilitation. They were finally sent to him via a trustworthy messenger only on 26 October 1796.[169] The many letters and petitions, eloquent witnesses to Paḷaśśi Rājā's intention to reach an agreement by diplomatic means, had not led to any recognizable compromise for both parties. Although the Northern Superintendent always insisted upon reaching an agreement,[170] Paḷaśśi Rājā suspended future tax payments and would only consider further payments once he had actually received the compensation to which he was entitled:

In the earlier letter from Bengal and Bombay of which a copy was sent to me earlier [this had been withheld from him], it was written that the country and the wealth taken from Paḷaśśi should be returned to me. [...] Regarding the wealth taken away from Paḷaśśi now I have made up my mind that I shall wait till the Company pleases to pay it.[171]

After the Superintendent had once again sought the advice of Vira Varmma on the 'matter of Paḷaśśi Rājā',[172] and he had recommended that the Superintendent suppress the rebel and his supporters,[173] a proclamation was drawn up at the end of December 1796 by the Superintendent under which it was forbidden to meet with or gather around Paḷaśśi Rājā.[174]

A meeting ultimately took place between the Superintendent and Kēraḷa Varmma Paḷaśśi Rājā on 27 December 1796 in Nittūr, where Paḷaśśi Rājā had the opportunity to express his concern over what had happened in the country. His chief complaint was that the British did not regard him as the rightful ruler of Kōṭṭayaṃ and had instead placed him under Vira Varmma's overall supervision. Paḷaśśi Rājā arrived at the meeting with 1,200–1,500 armed men in order to demonstrate his strength. He demanded direct government of Kōṭṭayaṃ, as was his rightful entitlement,[175] but this demand was refused by the Commissioners. Furthermore, one week of attempts by the Superintendent to bring the opposed views to some acceptable compromise were all in vain, because the agreements between the British and Vira Varmma were unacceptable to Paḷaśśi Rājā. Instead of meeting Paḷaśśi Rājā's demand, British troops remained stationed in Kōṭṭayaṃ to keep the peace—from a British perspective—and to guarantee tax collection using agents of the Kurumpranāṭu Rājā.[176] In spite of Paḷaśśi Rājā's readiness to discuss matters with the British they were once again unwilling to cooperate with him, which resulted in resignation and anger on the part of Paḷaśśi Rājā[177] and in a deepening enmity between the two parties.[178]

The events after the turn of the year exposed the opposing positions of the two parties clearly. On 8 January 1797 Kaiteri Ampu and his supporters attacked the palace of Paḷaśśi, which was still occupied by British guards. All but one of the British soldiers were killed. Kaiteri Ampu and his supporters carried out more attacks on several British troop movements travelling to Pēriya and Mānantavāṭi. The rebels were widely supported by the population in their actions; they received money from the Māppiḷḷas, for example,[179] and were able to acquire weapons or ammunition from them in exchange for pepper.[180] The tribes of the Kuṟiccyars and Kuṟumbars who lived in Vāyanāṭu fought on the side of Paḷaśśi Rājā.[181] He also strove to gain support from outside: several meetings with Ṭippu Sulttān resulted in concrete cooperation. Ṭippu came to Paḷaśśi Rājā's aid with ammunition; he stationed 6,000 Maisūrians in Karkaṇkōṭṭa and also delivered 2,000 horses. Paḷaśśi Rājā was also to receive fresh supplies of ammunition in cases of emergency.[182] Furthermore, it is likely that Paḷaśśi Rājā had associations with Carnatic rebels and the *pāḷaiyakkārar*s in the Tamiḻ land.[183]

Shortly after Kaiteri Ampu's attacks against the British and Paḷaśśi Rājā's agreement with Ṭippu Sulttān, open hostility broke out between the rebels and the British, who had received fresh troops from Bombay following the unrest in February 1797. The battle between a British regiment and Paḷaśśi Rājā and his supporters, from 9 to 11 March, resulted in heavy losses for the British and formed a prelude to the military clashes. Several skirmishes ensued between the opponents after which the rebels controlled the whole of Vāyanāṭu.[184] This was a triumph for Paḷaśśi Rājā and his people since Vāyanāṭu, which had always been linked closely with Kōṭṭayaṃ, had long been a bone of contention between the British, Ṭippu Sulttān and the royal family of Kōṭṭayaṃ. The success of Kēraḷa Varmma Paḷaśśi Rājā and his people can be explained partly by their alliance with Ṭippu Sulttān who had sent troops from Maisūr to support Paḷaśśi Rājā. A further reason was the British unfamiliarity with the mountainous and densely wooded terrain of the Ghats. The fear of scheming on the part of Ṭippu Sulttān and the French also contributed to British insecurity, which resulted in attempts by the commissioners to reach a peace agreement in Malabar as swiftly as possible.[185] The peace settlement came in July 1797, when Kēraḷa Varmma Paḷaśśi Rājā and the British were able to sign a treaty thanks to the mediation of Ravi Varmma, Rājā of Ciṟakkal.[186] The treaty provided for the transfer of tax collection in Kōṭṭayaṃ to the Rājā of Tiruvitāṃkūr, to which Paḷaśśi Rājā agreeed. In return the British guaranteed Paḷaśśi Rājā an annual pension of

8000 rupees, compensation for having plundered the palace and gave him an apology[187] because the commissioners had since learned that Vira Varmma Rājā had misappropriated letters from the Governor General to Paḷaśśi Rājā as well as the cash payment intended as compensation.

There were no large-scale military conflicts between the British and Paḷaśśi Rājā in the years 1798/9, although smaller acts of provocation bounded back and forth between the two parties; Paḷaśśi Rājā refused to pay taxes on houses,[188] for example, but confirmed that he would keep to the terms of the agreed treaty.[189] In the spring of 1799, the commissioners assessed that the situation in Kōṭṭayaṃ was still unstable and stressed in the same breath that the honour and rightful interests of the EIC would have to be defended.[190] The commissioners pushed the senior rājā of Kōṭṭayaṃ to withdraw from managerial affairs in Kōṭṭayaṃ, but he refused on the grounds that a withdrawal would not be customary in the country: 'he could never consent to a renunciation of what might be deemed his family rights & inheritance of the country.'[191] Consequently he kept his position as the senior rājā of Kōṭṭayaṃ, supporting Paḷaśśi Rājā in ruling the country.

The Second Phase of the Rebellion (1800/1)

During the fourth Anglo–Maisūrian war in 1799, Ṭippu had received troops and supplies from Kēraḷa Varmma Paḷaśśi Rājā and Ravi Varmma of Ciṟakkal. Paḷaśśi Rājā saw the association with Ṭippu Sulttān as a means of safeguarding local inhabitants against further military conflicts in the country, and with providing the peace that was so desperately needed after the decades of unrest.[192] The war ended in British victory and in the death of Ṭippu Sulttān. According to the peace treaty of Śrīraṅgapaṭṭaṇaṃ, Vāyanāṭu and Kōyamputtūr came under British occupation, and the Lakkadives were handed over on a rent basis to the earlier mentioned merchant Covakkāran Mūssa of Talaśśēri who secretly supported Paḷaśśi Rājā.[193] According to the British official Alexander Walker, other merchants also supplied the rebels with arms and ammunition as well as with saltpetre and brimstone.[194]

Over the following months the question of Vāyanāṭu's administration remained unresolved—should it be put under the administration within the province of Kanara or Kōyamputtūr, or should any rājā's authority be trusted at all? Paḷaśśi Rājā set about energetically maintaining his claim to power in Vāyanāṭu and gathered Nāyars, Māppiḷḷas, and those soldiers from Ṭippu's troops who had remained behind in case of British attack.[195] The majority of the population in Vāyanāṭu also joined the rebels in support of Paḷaśśi Rājā, even though they risked the deportation of their families and the confiscation of their property if captured. The new developments in Malabar were a source of intense annoyance to the government in Bombay; thus Edward Clive[196] gave orders to station troops to the north and south of Vāyanāṭu, to drive out Paḷaśśi Rājā from Vāyanāṭu immediately, and to make him submit to EIC orders.[197] In order to strengthen their military position, which was seen as rather weak at that point of time, the British constructed roads to Kannavaṃ and Maṇattaṇa and stationed several battalions in Vāyanāṭu.[198] Paḷaśśi Rājā had positioned his people at junctions of the road network with instructions to block the path of the British.[199] Once they had consulted the oracle in the Bhagavati temple in Mānantavāṭi, and in spite of the coming monsoon, the rebels were able to capture the lowlands of Kōṭṭayaṃ in July 1800.[200] They attacked the plantation in Añcarakaṇṭi, which belonged to the British merchant Murdoch Brown, partially destroyed it and besieged the smaller outposts of the British army, most notably in Kūṭāli and Maṇattaṇa.[201] Arthur Wellesley's[202] response was to mass new troops in Talaśśēri. He ordered the construction of military roads in Malabar, set up two additional military posts and set down large quantities of supplies in Kūttupaṟambu under the protection of two *sepoy* regiments. His aim was to subjugate the rājā, and thereby the entire population of Malabar after attempts to buy the neutrality of the population had failed:[203]

The conquest of Mysore will, I trust, enable us to settle Malabar and Canara on a systematic and durable plan of government. [...] One principle, however, I am persuaded will appear as evident and incontrovertible to your mind, as it does to mine: that, whatever may be our ultimate determination with respect to the power of the several rajahs, it must appear to flow from the generosity, justice, and power, of the British government; and not be derived from a timid submission to the refractory spirit of any rebellious tributary.[204]

Wellesley finally attacked Kōṭṭayaṃ and Vāyanāṭu in November 1800; he chose to invade from Maisūr and from the coast so as to encircle the rebels. The British were helped by the fact that Pallur Eman Nāyar, a follower of Paḷaśśi Rājā, had defected to the British.[205] With his support the British were able to capture Pēriya in January 1801. This victory marked the turning point in favour of the British. The reasons for the rebels' weakness lay partly in the defeat of the Carnatic rebels, which caused supply problems for the Malabar rebels, and partly in the advance of a British unit from Tiṇṭukkal, which cut off the supply line of *pāḷaiyakkārar*s from Kōyamputtūr and brought the Māppiḷḷa resistance in southern Malabar to a standstill.[206] During the next few months Paḷaśśi Rājā became a 'wanderer in the jungles',[207] but he did not give up:

In adverting to the present state of the District [...] it is to be observed in regard to Cotiote, that the turbulent and refractory dispositon of Kerula Werma (commonly called) the Pychy Rajah, and that independent spirit which has marked the character of this Malabar chieftain, supported by the firm attachment of the inhabitants of the country to his person, instigated him, in various ways to counteract, and oppose the full introduction of the Honourable Company's Government in the district [...].[208]

In March 1801, the British carried out a large-scale pursuit of the rebels, but Palaṣ̈ṣi Rājā was able to escape with his people.[209] Already by May of the same year all the posts which Palaṣ̈ṣi Rājā had taken from the British were back in English hands.[210] For the first time the British announced a reward for the betrayal or extradition of Palaṣ̈ṣi Rājā.[211] In addition to this, the British carried out an arrest in July 1801; the man in question proved to be one of Palaṣ̈ṣi Rājā's supporters and was hanged. This was meant as a public example to show how rebels would be dealt with in the future. Meanwhile, British soldiers used rice and sandalwood, which they found in the vacated houses of the fleeing rebels, for their own ends.[212] But at the same time the British were keen to impress the locals with 'the Justice and Impartiality of the Character of a British Administration; the Protection of Persons and Property in the Test of this System'.[213] The wave of measures taken by the British was continued in a proclamation of August 1801, which guaranteed the return of all property to those rebels who submitted and swore allegiance to the British. Any disobedience would be punished, however.[214] Palaṣ̈ṣi Rājā and four of his supporters, who would still face the death penalty if caught, were excluded from this policy of returning property. This 'offer' was valid for six weeks, but the success which the British had hoped for did not materialize.[215] Nevertheless they persisted in their belief that the province must be subjugated, since they could only set up a British-style administration once this had been achieved.[216] During the second phase of unrest the rebels hit a low point: The power which the rebels had exerted in 1796 and 1797 was no longer attainable. They had also dwindled in number: Palaṣ̈ṣi Rājā apparently travelled with only six supporters and 20–25 'musquet people'.[217]

British action against the rebels in Malabar gave conflicting signals: On the one hand they wanted to impress the locals with their justice, but on the other they themselves did not always honour promises and they regarded Malabar as their guinea-pig for administrative measures.[218] And neither the population, which had been looted for centuries by wars and foreign rulers, nor their rājās were prepared to bow to the British claim to power without a challenge.

The Third Phase of the Rebellion (1802–05)

Macleod, the new Principal Collector, ordered the disarmament of the country in January 1802.[219] Any contravention would meet with heavy punishment. Wellesley commanded that additional troops be stationed in Malabar.[220] The

British also offered a reward for whoever could bring them Paḻaśśi Rājā—in the meantime, the reward money had risen to 10,000 rupees. The British commandants in Malabar were forced to conclude, however, that in spite of this publicized reward and the threat of punishment, the populations of Kōṭṭayaṃ and Vāyanāṭu were standing by their rājā and were giving him shelter and supplying him with provisions.[221]

Since the end of 1801, the British had been using two Malabar prisoners as spies whose task it was to find out where Paḻaśśi Rājā was staying and, if possible, to learn about any rebel movements. However, the spies' reports sounded so improbable to British ears that they were sent back to prison in Kannūr in March 1802. The precarious situation in which the British found themselves was intensified still further by the rebellions breaking out in southern Malabar led by Unni Mūta Mūppan. Yet this unrest never quite reached the extent of the rebellions in northern Malabar, with the result that British actions towards the pacification of Malabar remained concentrated on the northern region of Malabar.[222]

The subsequent administrative measure to be taken by the British—Macleod's August amendment of the exchange rate, which signalled higher taxes—led to fresh difficulties (as mentioned earlier). Since tax collection was carried out in a harsh way, unrest soon followed; large parts of the population were opposed to British government.[223] The rebels, battered and reduced in number, led and organized the resistance from their meeting place in the temple of Kūttupaṟambu.[224] In October 1802, the population of Kōṭṭayaṃ and Vāyanāṭu rose up against the British *en masse*; indeed they dropped social barriers between communities and social classes.[225] A troop of Nāyars of perhaps three to four hundred men were able to notch up successes against the British in different places within Vāyanāṭu, which caused the English to call in a new supply of troops.[226] A bitter disappointment for the British was the return of Pallur Eman Nāyar to Paḻaśśi Rājā in December 1802, which seemed to indicate that Pallur Eman had been a spy for Paḻaśśi Rājā.[227] Once he had deserted the British, the intensity of the rebellion grew: 'The insurrection in Malabar has been increasing to a degree of an alarming nature.'[228] The British government in Talaśśēri reacted to the rebellion by proclaiming martial law in Vāyanāṭu on 19 January 1803.[229] The series of military successes by the rebels under Paḻaśśi Rājā lasted well into 1803—even in southern Malabar under Unni Mūta;[230] in July, Rickards, the new Principal Collector, reported that Kōṭṭayaṃ was firmly in the hands of the rebels.[231]

Since the beginning of 1804, subcollector Thomas H. Baber had been trying to ascertain the movements of Paḻaśśi Rājā and his supporters.[232]

Baber's intention was to prevent the delivery of supplies to the rebels. The restriction of pepper exports served for this purpose: licences for the export of goods were only given out to a very limited number of people and the transport routes were checked.[233] Furthermore, Baber called upon the inhabitants of the country to denounce the rebels and any suspicious persons. Indeed his methods bore fruit relatively soon: by April 1804, there was no longer any sign of concrete resistance, because the rebels were keeping themselves hidden in their camps, not carrying out any attacks. In May the British made a proclamation to the effect that any of Paḷaśśi Rājā's supporters who wanted to return would be punished if they withheld information about the rebels' movements or supplied the rebels with weapons or provisions. On 16 May the British issued a new 'wanted persons list' which promised a reward for the capture of twelve rebels. The first name on the list was that of Paḷaśśi Rājā.[234]

Once Baber and his troops occupied Kōṭṭayaṃ, the British forbade trade with foreigners in all cases where the goods amounted to more than the value of a silver *fanam*; the transport of goods was only permitted on public roads.[235] This trade restriction caused such huge supply difficulties for the rebels that they were left with no other option but to flee from the lowlands into the Ghats and forests of Vāyanāṭu.[236] Besides supply problems, their numbers, fewer than in previous years, indicated a group that had not grown in line with the superior strength of the English—i.e. one that was in no position to defeat them. There were not enough of them even for partisan war:[237] they rarely received extra supplies and they were so scattered that it became impossible to exchange any information.[238] This allowed Baber to mount a successful expedition against the rebels in August 1804.[239]

Paḷaśśi Rājā, however, escaped from British troops near the Ghats. The British received reliable information that Kēraḷa Varmma Paḷaśśi Rājā was on a pass between South Vāyanāṭu and southern Malabar and they took up the chase. On 7 September 1804, the British actually found his camp, but the dense jungle slowed them enough for the rebels to make an escape. Only two of Kēraḷa Varmma Paḷaśśi Rājā's supporters and a few objects of value fell into British hands. Paḷaśśi Rājā managed to remain hidden in the forests of Vāyanāṭu for another year without being caught by the British. The temples described in Chapter Two played a very important role as places of refuge for the few remaining rebels. It was also to Paḷaśśi Rājā's advantage that the local people in Vāyanāṭu, who knew about his places of refuge, did not give him away despite the numerous proclamations which forbade any kind of support for Paḷaśśi Rājā.[240]

Ultimately, after a fifteen-hour struggle in the forests around Pulpaḷḷi, British troops under the leadership of Baber were able to capture Paḷaśśi

Rājā on 30 November 1805.[241] His death remains something of a mystery: in the vernacular it is believed that on seeing the British captors, and realizing any escape to be impossible, Paḻaśśi Rājā committed suicide by taking his diamond ring from his finger and swallowing it.[242] A second legend goes that he took his own life with the golden dagger that he always used to carry with him.[243] Contrary to this, the British boast about eliminating him themselves, and thereby crushing the resistance against their rule in Malabar.[244] Whilst nine nephews of Paḻaśśi Rājā did manage to escape[245] the majority of his supporters were either captured or committed suicide in the following months. Their property was confiscated.[246] On 30 November 1805, Baber addressed the government in Madras with the following report on the victory against the rebels:

> It is with infinite satisfacton that I report to you, for the information of the Right Honorable the Governor in Council, that this forenoon, [...], I had the good fortune to come up with the Cotiote Kerula Werma Rajah alias the Pyche (Palassi) Rajah [...] to chastize this Rebel Chieftain, by destroying him and five of his followers.[247]

Obviously, it was the policies of Baber that led to the ultimate suppression of the rebels.[248]

On 8 December 1805, the Principal Collector of Malabar issued an official proclamation by which the death of Paḻaśśi Rājā was made known to the population. He emphasized that any kind of rebellion against the British would be useless, and pointed to Paḻaśśi Rājā as an example. The proclamation stated that it was therefore in the local population's own best interests to place itself under the authority and protection of the British.[249] To keep up appearances the British granted Paḻaśśi Rājā a burial with full honours, and he was laid to rest in Mānantavāṭi.[250] His gravestone can still be seen today.[251]

Although the question considered in this chapter—what was it that motivated the two rulers of Malabar, Kēraḷa Varmma Paḻaśśi Rājā and Vira Varmma of Kurumpranāṭu, to behave in such different ways—is not one that can be resolved with a single answer, it is possible to draw some conclusions from the sources.

Paḻaśśi Rājā was firmly convinced that the sovereign rights over Kōṭṭayaṃ and Vāyanāṭu were rightfully his, and he shared the same conviction in the duty of looking after his people's needs in a way as would befit the rājādharma. For him any renunciation of his sovereign rights, thus being a renunciation of his responsibility for governmental affairs in Kōṭṭayaṃ, would have signified a neglect of duty on his part as ruler. He was not prepared to give up these rights voluntarily. Yet over a period of several years he did try to use diplomatic means when negotiating with the British over areas of responsibility and power in Kōṭṭayaṃ and Vāyanāṭu. Once these attempts had finally failed, however, he was forced to acknowledge that it would be impossible to make any alliances with the British as equal partners. His attitude towards the British, which had initially been one of loyalty, was shattered as a result of their failure to hold to a number of different agreements. Thus Palaśśi Rājā mounted resistance, which took the form of guerilla warfare, from 1796 through to 1805. The rebellions he led were a danger which had to be taken very seriously by the British, and one from which they would not be freed for many years. Had Palaśśi Rājā not given in to the English desire for peace in 1797, it would have been almost impossible for them to have consolidated their power in Malabar at the beginning of the nineteenth century. The rebellions of Palaśśi Rājā and his supporters cast serious doubt over the British position in Malabar.[252] Only after a colossal military armament in Malabar and the stubbornness of Subcollector Thomas H. Baber, who pursued the rebels into the farthest corners of Vāyanāṭu, was it possible for the British to gain control over the politically unstable situation. Ultimately it took the elimination of Palaśśi Rājā to seal British dominance, as it was his death that broke the spirit of resistance amongst the local population.

Vira Varmma of Kurumpranāṭu pursued the opposite strategy to Palaśśi Rājā. He was usually one of the first to sign treaties proposed by the British, which he believed would increase his power. It is no longer possible today to reconstruct with any great certainty whether Vira Varmma's gain in material goods led him to overlook the fact that the price to be paid was a loss of sovereignty, or whether he knowingly accepted this loss. The assessment of Vira Varmma in British source texts is one of a ruler who was concerned only with material gains and who neglected his traditional commitments. At the least he seems to have spotted the chance to make personal gains, whether financial or political, from the conflict with the British. To this end he also schemed against Palaśśi Rājā. It seems likely that he attempted to turn Palaśśi Rājā against the British; Palaśśi Rājā had actually been on good terms with the British up until 1792.[253] One could suspect that Vira Varmma's enigmatic behaviour was often the cause of misunderstandings between Palaśśi Rājā and the British.[254] When Palaśśi Rājā turned towards resistance, Vira Varmma was able to portray himself to the British as the comparatively 'good' rājā, always at their service. Another tactic used by Vira Varmma was his speedy compliance with British orders: he gave the British daily reports about the course of events in Kōṭṭayaṃ and recommended that they crush the rebels.[255] Such policy made it easier for the British to take control of Malabar.

These examples of the rulers' reactions to British claims over rulership and land in Malabar show that the patterns of conduct towards the British could vary considerably. As far as the British were concerned, they found it hard to overcome Paḷaśśi Rājā's conduct, which was a hindrance to their aspirations to power, whilst Vira Varmma's policy of cooperation actively smoothed their way into the circle of Malabar rulers.

Notes

1. Haidar Ali and Ṭippu Sulttān strove for a centralization of government not only in Malabar but in the entire empire. Around Maisūr and Śrīraṅgapaṭṭaṇaṃ the elimination of *pālaiyakkārar*s seemed to have been carried out with relative success. Bayly, Christopher and Bayly, Susan, 'Eighteenth-Century State Forms and the Economy', in: Clive Dewey (ed.), *Arrested Development in India: The Historical Dimension*, Delhi 1988, pp. 66–90, p. 79.

2. Cf. Chapter One.

3. From the Hindi *jamā*, 'collection, capital'; *jamābandī*, 'revenue accounts, government revenue from land'. The English used the forms *jummabundy* and *jumma*. Cf. Maclean, *Manual*, vol. 3, p. 396, col. 1: 'annual settlement of fluctuating items in ryotwarry land revenue, coupled with a personal investigation into all manner of subjects connected with the land revenue system.' (The shortened form of *jamābandī* is *jamā*.).

4. From the Hindi *nazrānā*: 1. a customary payment, 2. a bribe, 3. an offering, gift (to a superior). Cf. Maclean, *Manual*, vol. 3, p. 603, col. 2; Yule and Burnell, *Hobson-Jobson*, p. 634, col. 2.

5. The number is not confirmed beyond doubt, it could also have been 375,000 or 4 lakh rupees. Cf. *Reports of a Joint Commission*, § XXII.

6. *Reports of a Joint Commission*, § XXII. Kareem gives the incorrect date of 1766–8 for the sealing of this treaty. Kareem, *Kerala under Haidar*, p. 146.

7. Cf. *Reports of a Joint Commission*, § XXVIII.

8. Cf. *Reports of a Joint Commission*, § XXXIII–XXXV.

9. Cf. Maclean, *Manual*, vol. 3, p. 655, col. 2: unit of measure on the west coast: 10 *iṭaṅṅaḷi*s equal 1 *paṟa*, 2.5 paṟa equal 1 *mūṭa*. Thus 1 paṟa amounts to 18.696 litres.

10. Cf. *Reports of a Joint Commission*, § DLI.

11. A *hūn* was a gold coin. Cf. Yule and Burnell, *Hobson-Jobson*, p. 425, col. 2. Since the *jamā* was paid in hūns and not in rupees, the exchange rate was an important factor. Yet this was in a constant state of flux. A cited example of this is taken from: *Reports of a Joint Commission*, § LVI: '[...] the value of a Rupee being five Billee or silver fanams; gold fanams not having been introduced there as they had always been in the southern part of Malabar: but as the ascertainment of the Jumma in the last mentioned division in the country, had been made long before in Hoons, it was therefore ordered that, to render all the accounts uniform, this Rupee Jummabundy of Chericul should also be turned into the settled denomination of Sultany Hoons, then established in the revenues, which accordingly took place at the rate of 3 1/8 Rupees to the Hoon, [...].'

12. A *fanam* is a gold or silver coin. In Malabar it was known as a *paṇaṃ*. Cf. Yule and Burnell, *Hobson-Jobson*, p. 348, col. 1. In the following text, the most common form of the term fanam, which comes from the Arabic, will be used. The commissioners drove up the exchange rates during the course of the eighteenth century. Cf. *Reports of a Joint Commission*, §§ XCV–CI. Logan and Buchanan cite different values for the fanam. Cf. Logan, *Malabar*, vol. 2, p. clxxix; Buchanan, *Journey*, vol. 2, p. 539 and vol. 3, p. 25.

13. Cf. *Reports of a Joint Commission*, § XXVII–XL, XXXV.

14. *Reports of a Joint Commission*, § XXXII.

15. Cf. *Reports of a Joint Commission*, § XXXV.

16. *Reports of a Joint Commission*, § XLIII.

17. Cf. *Reports of a Joint Commission*, § XLIII.

18. Cf. *Reports of a Joint Commission*, § L.

19. See below.

20. Cf. *Reports of a Joint Commission*, § LIII. Arshed Beg had been relieved of his office by Ṭippu Sulttān. Hosayne Ali Khān was the new commandant of the Maisūrian troops in Malabar, Shere Khān was responsible for the administration of taxes.

21. Cf. *Reports of a Joint Commission*, § LIX.

22. *Cf. Reports of a Joint Commission*, § LXVIII.

23. Cf. Deyell, John S. and Frykenberg, Robert E., 'Sovereignty and the "SIKKA" under Company Raj: Minting Prerogative and Imperial Legitimacy in India', *IESHR* 19,1 (1982), pp. 1–25, p. 7.

24. Henderson, J.R., *The Coins of Haidar Alī and Tīpū Sultān*, Madras, 1921, reprint New Delhi and Madras, 1989, p. 8f., 96, 100.

25. *Reports of a Joint Commission*, § CCCCXLIV.

26. *Reports of a Joint Commission*, § CCCCLXXI. This sum was applicable to 1793/4.

27. Panikkar, K.M., *History of Kerala*, p. 415.

28. Cf. *Reports of a Joint Commission*, § XXI.

29. *Reports of a Joint Commission*, § XXXVIII.

30. *Reports of a Joint Commission*, § LXIV.

31. *Reports of a Joint Commission*, § LXVII.

32. Summary of the Events in Kōṭṭayaṃ (miscellaneous) 1796–1798, in HMS, OIOC H/607.

33. Brittlebank speaks of the 'centralising drive' in the governmental administrations of Haidar Ali and Ṭippu Sulttān. Cf. Brittlebank, *Tipu Sultan*, p. 90.

34. Nightingale says that the trade interests of the officials in Bombay were chiefly prominent. Malabar was seen as a 'market of opportunities'. Cf. Nightingale, *Trade and Empire*, pp. 80f., 113.

35. Alexander Dow had been military commander in Talaśśēri since 1789. W.G. Farmer had served almost thirty years in the Bombay Presidency, during which time he had been resident of Fort Victoria. Dow and Farmer had been in Malabar since April 1792. Charles Boddam and William Page had been in Malabar since September and December 1792.

36. Cf. *Reports of a Joint Commission*, § II. In spite of the relatively wide-ranging report by the commissioners, which was concluded in October 1793, there were still some points, such as the procurement of geographical data, which never found their way into the report—they remained a desideratum until into the late nineteenth century. After the Joint Commission had completed their work and the presentation of its report, it was dissolved in October 1793. In February 1794 a supplementary volume was published by Messrs Boddam and Duncan.

37. Robert Abercromby (1740–1827) was the supreme commander of the British in Bombay and in this capacity he led troops from Bombay against Ṭippu Sulttān.

38. *Reports of a Joint Commission*, § LXXXI.

39. Quote from Abercromby's instruction to the Joint Commissioners dated 20.4.1792 in *Reports of a Joint Commission*, § LXXXI.

40. Cf. *Reports of a Joint Commission*, §§ CXXXIX, CXLV: In Mayyaḻi the pepper merchants received 175 rupees per kaṇṭi of pepper, but only 130 rupees from the EIC (in 967 M.E.).

41. Quote from Abercromby's instruction to the Joint Commissioners dated 20.4.1792 in *Reports of a Joint Commission*, § LXXXI.

42. Cf. Yule and Burnell, *Hobson-Jobson*, p. 980, col. 1: From the Persian. A land owner who pays his taxes directly to the government (with no middlemen). On 28.10.1793 the British passed a proclamation, which named the janmakārans as landowners and kāṇakkārans as fief owners, whilst the local rulers were made tax collectors. Cf. Logan, *Malabar*, vol. 1, p. 612.

43. Cf. Nightingale, *Trade and Empire*, p. 87.

44. Cf. *Reports of a Joint Commission*, § LXXXIII.

45. Cf. *Reports of a Joint Commission*, §§ CCLVII, CCLXII; Logan, *Treaties*, ii, XXV, p. 173.

46. Cf. *Reports of a Joint Commission*, § CCCXIV.

47. Cf. *Reports of a Joint Commission*, § CCCVIII.

48. *Reports of a Joint Commission*, § CCCIX.

49. Cf. Logan, *Treaties*, ii, V and ii, VI (the treaty for Ciṟakkal is not published). Iruvaḻināṭu and Raṇṭutaṟa were placed under the supervisors in Talaśśēri. *Reports of a Joint Commission*, §§ LXXXIV, LXXXV. Agreements were also made with the Kannūr Bibi and with the rājās of southern Malabar. Cf. *Reports of a Joint Commission*, § LXXXVI and Logan, *Treaties*, ii, XIII, XV, XVI.

50. Cf. *Reports of a Joint Commission*, § CCLXXX: '[...] at the same time that, as an old inheritance, his family cannot think of giving it [Vāyanāṭu] up, [...].'

51. Cf. *Reports of a Joint Commission*, §§ CCXXXI–CCXXXV; Letter from Fort William to John Spencer dated 6.8.1798, in MCR 1729 (TNSA).

52. Cf. *Reports of a Joint Commission*, § CCLXXXI.

53. Logan, *Treaties*, ii, CXCI–CXCIII, pp. 318–22. For more information on the conflict in Vāyanāṭu cf. OIOC F/4/9.

54. *Reports of a Joint Commission*, § CCXII; cf. also Aitchison, *Treaties*, vol. 10, p. 150.

55. The following districts belonged to the area of the Northern Superintendency: Ciṟakkal, Kannūr, Kōṭṭayam, Iruvaḻināṭu, Kaṭattanāṭu, Kurumpranāṭu, Kurg; and

the following to the Southern Superintendency: Rāmnāṭu, Paṟappanāṭu, Veṭṭattanāṭu, Ēṟarnāṭu, Cāvakkāṭu, Śanaṅganāṭu, Pālakkāṭu. The Supravisor's headquarters, Kōḻikkōṭu, formed, with its surrounding suburbs, its own sub-unit. Cf. *Reports of a Joint Commission*, § CCXII.

56. Cf. *Reports of a Joint Commission*, § CCCLXIV. Additional instructions for Supravisor and Superintendents can be found in §§ CCCLXIV–CCCLXXI.

57. Cf. *Reports of a Joint Commission*, § CCXI.

58. Ibid.; Logan, Malabar, vol. 1, p. 489; Ravindran, T.K., *Malabar under Bombay Presidency*, Calicut, 1979, p. 7. This refers to *tahsīldārs*, *kānūṅgos* and *pārapattis*. Cf. *Reports of a Joint Commission*, § CCCXVI. So as not to give preference to any one religious group, the Canongo offices were each occupied somewhat later by a Hindu and a Māppiḷḷa. Cf. *Reports of a Joint Commission*, § CCCCLVI.

59. Cf. *Reports of a Joint Commission*, § CCXIV. Stevens assumed the office of Southern Superintendent, Augustus William Handley was employed as senior assistant in Kōḻikkōṭu—whose function was to support the Supravisor. There is no record as to who was given the position of the Northern Superintendent. Edward Galley was Northern Superintendent from 19.9.1793.

60. At the time this consisted of Duncan, Dow, Boddam and Page.

61. Cf. Logan, *Malabar*, vol. 1, p. 490.

62. Gundert, *Dictionary*, p. 513, col. 1: *aṃśaṃ* is defined as the largest administrative unit of the *dēśaṃ*s. This reflects the situation in the mid-nineteenth century. Cf. also Logan, *Malabar*, vol. 1, p. 87. For information on the *dēśam*s cf. Chapter Two. Between the levels of district and *aṃśaṃ* the land was split up into *hōbali*s (Cf. Gundert, *Dictionary*, p. 1081, col. 2: sub-division of a district, also *hōvali*). For this the old *taṟa*s had been enlarged, something which caused displeasure amongst the local people and which, as a result, was undone shortly after it was introduced. Cf. Logan, *Malabar*, vol. 1, p. 89.

63. The former borders between the administrative units were thus no longer there. The development was a long process, which meant that in the early stages several old *dēśavāli*s were responsible for one *aṃśaṃ*. The objective however was the abolition of the *dēśaṃ* as an administrative unit. Cf. Logan, *Malabar*, vol. 1, p. 89. Miller, 'Caste and Territory', p. 418.

64. Cf. Santha, *Local Self-Government*, p. 6. Yet besides *nāṭuvāḻi*s and *dēśavāḻi*s, other qualified people were also employed. Cf. Mayer, Adrian C., *Land and Society in Malabar*, Oxford, 1952, p. 33.

65. The establishment of the court was resolved on 31.12.1792. Cf. *Reports of a Joint Commission*, § CLVI.

66. Cf. *Reports of a Joint Commission*, § CXCII.

67. Cf. *Reports of a Joint Commission*, §§ CCCLXXIV, CCCLXXXII, CCCLXXXIV, CCCLXXXV; Logan, *Malabar*, vol. 1, p. 495f.; Ravindran, *Malabar under Bombay*, p. 8.

68. Cf. *Reports of a Joint Commission*, § CCCLXIII. This oath was known as *muchalkā*. Cf. Yule and Burnell, *Hobson-Jobson*, p. 578, col. 2.

69. Cf. Ravindran, *Malabar under Bombay*, p. 24f.

70. Cf. Ravindran, T.K., *Institutions and Movements in Kerala History*, Trivandrum, 1978, p. 85.

71. Cf. Ravindran, *Malabar under Bombay*, pp. 38–41.

72. Cf. Logan, *Malabar*, vol. 1, p. 522.

73. Cf. Ravindran, *Malabar under Bombay*, p. 62.

74. This measure was a reaction to a decision by the Governor General in Council. Cf. Extract from a political letter from Fort St. George to the Bombay Presidency dated 9.10.1800, in OIOC F/4/117; correspondence between Henry Dundas and Arthur Wellesley, in: Ingram, *Two Views*, p. 292; Logan, *Malabar*, vol. 1, p. 528f.

75. The second commission had been founded in 1796. Instructions by Jonathan Duncan dated 8.5.1796, in SPP, OIOC P/E/9.

76. Cf. Extract from a political letter from Fort St. George to the Bombay Presidency dated 15.10.1800, in BC, OIOC F/4/117; Logan, *Malabar*, vol. 1, p. 534.

77. Cf. Ravindran, T.K., *Cornwallis System in Malabar*, Calicut, 1969, p. iif.; idem, *Institutions*, p. 87.

78. Cf. Letter from the government in Fort St. George dated 11.4.1801, in BC, OIOC F/4/119. The most commonly used weapons produced domestically were swords, pikes and Nāyar knives. In contrast firearms were generally made in England. Cf. Letter by the commissioners J. Spencer and J. Smee to Fort St. George dated 30.4.1801, in BC, OIOC F/4/120.

79. Cf. Proclamation of 30.1.1802/M.E. 19. Makaraṃ 977, in BC, OIOC F/4/156. For example, the British had collected in 1801, amongst other things, 11 iron cannon, 7872 swords and 9784 stone catapults in Malabar, in BC, OIOC F/4/121.

80. Cf. Arunima, 'Multiple Meanings', p. 298.

81. Statement by judge Herbert Wigram (in the civil court) on the case A.S. 434 1878 (South Malabar), cited in Moore, L., *Law and Custom*, p. 121.

82. Cf. Moore, M., 'A New Look', p. 538. The question of language caused further problems, cf. letter by W.G. Farmer to the Joint Commissioners dated 22.6.1793, in BRP, OIOC P/366/15, as did the system of time: The Malabar calendar was structured in a completely different way from the Western calendar, cf. letter by W.G. Farmer to James Stevens dated 9.9.1793, in BRP, OIOC P/366/15. For more information cf. also Bayly, C., *Empire and Information*, p. 6f.

83. Cf. Marshall, 'British Expansion', p. 43.

84. Cf. *Reports of a Joint Commission*, §§ CXXXII, CCCCLIII.

85. Cf. Logan, *Malabar*, vol. 1, p. 638; Extracts from the Minute of the Board of Revenue, in: Panikkar, K.N., *Peasant Protests*, p. 24; Ganesh, 'Ownership', p. 320.

86. Cf. *Reports of a Joint Commission*, §§ CCCCLXIX–CCCCLXXI.

87. Cf. Logan, *Treaties*, ii, IV–VII, pp. 147–51.

88. Cf. Logan, *Malabar*, vol. 1, p. 477f.

89. Cf. *Reports of a Joint Commission*, §§ CXXXII–CXXXVII; Logan, *Treaties*, ii, XVIII–XX, p. 166–70.

90. *Reports of a Joint Commission*, § CXXXVI.

91. Spencer, Smee and Walker, however, speak of 25,000 rupees. Cf. Spencer, J. and Smee, J. and Walker, A., *A Report on the Administration of Malabar: Dated 28th July 1801*, Calicut, 1910, p. 19.

92. Cf. Logan, *Treaties*, ii, XX, S. 169f.

93. Cf. *Reports of a Joint Commission*, § CCLXII.

94. Cf. Logan, *Treaties*, ii, XLII, p. 188f.

95. Cf. Rajayyan, 'Kerala Varma', p. 549.

96. Cf. Nightingale, *Trade and Empire*, p. 106.

97. Cf. Logan, *Treaties*, ii, LXXIV–LXXV, p. 215f.

98. Cf. Logan, *Malabar*, vol. 1, p. 499.

99. Complaints by the noblemen of Kōṭṭayaṃ dated 10.11.1796, PR 57 B; cf. also *arjī* (Petition) of the noblemen of Kōṭṭayaṃ dated 19.11.1796, in BRP, OIOC P/366/19: 'In the year 970 Malabar Style or 1794 of the Christian Era, Chundoo [Paḷavīṭṭil Cantu] collected more from us than what had been usual and in the same year [...] Chundoo took from us four times the quantity of pepper which we had agreed to give the Company [...].'

100. PR 57 B.

101. Cf. Logan, *Treaties*, ii, CXXXVIII, p. 274.

102. Cf. Letter by James Stevens to Alexander Dow dated 21.8.1798, in MCR 1715 (TNSA).

103. Cf. Letter by James Stevens to John Spencer dated 1.3.1799, in MCR 1716 (TNSA).

104. Cf. Letter by Governor in Council to the Malabar Commission dated 29.8.1799, in OIOC F/4/62.

105. Cf. Report by John Smee dated 16.10.1799, as an enclosure to the letter by John Spencer to Jonathan Duncan dated 24.10.1799 and consultation of the *pārapatti*s in mid-October 1799, in BC, OIOC F/4/62.

106. Cf. Logan, *Treaties*, ii, CCXIX, p. 338. In spite of these difficulties, Duncan reported a growth in tax revenue in Malabar: In 1793 it amounted to 334,000 rupees, in 1800 to 484,058 rupees. Letter by Jonathan Duncan to the Court of Directors dated 28.4.1800, in BC, OIOC F/4/90.

107. In the Bombay Presidency the exchange rate came to 7 gold fanams for a star pagoda, 15 silver aṇās for a rupee, whilst in the province of Malabar a star pagoda cost $5^{7}/_{8}$ gold fanams and a rupee cost only 5 silver fanams or 14 aṇās. Thus the exchange rate was to be adjusted. A rupee should cost around $4^{7}/_{32}$ gold fanams or $5^{1}/_{2}$ silver fanams, a star pagoda $14^{49}/_{64}$ gold fanams or $19^{1}/_{4}$ silver fanams. Logan, *Treaties*, ii, CCXXXVI, p. 350; Logan, *Malabar*, vol. 1, p. 534.

108. Cf. Logan, *Malabar*, vol. 1, p. 535.

109. Cf. Kumar, *Land and Caste*, p. 88; Abdurahiman, A.P., 'Macleod's Paimash and the Malabar Rebellion of 1803', *Journal of Kerala Studies* 4,1 (1977), pp. 65–71, p. 66.

110. Letter by William Macleod to Fort St. George dated 15.7.1802, in BC, OIOC F/4/156.

111. Cf. Logan, *Malabar*, vol.1, p. 495.

112. Cf. *Reports of a Joint Commission*, § CCCCXX.

113. Cf. Nightingale, *Trade and Empire*, pp. 77–127 passim.

114. Cf. Logan, *Treaties*, ii, CLIX, pp. 286–9. Cf. also the correspondence between the commissioners in Malabar and the government in Bombay dated 1.1.1798, in BC, OIOC F/4/38.

115. Cf. Logan, *Treaties*, ii, CCLXIX, pp. 381–3. Buchanan also visited the plantation in Añcarakaṇṭi, cf. his description in Buchanan, *Journey*, vol. 2, p. 544f.

116. Cf. Subrahmanyam, *Political Economy*, p. 298–300, 327, 337–42.

117. Cf. *Reports of a Joint Commission*, §§ CXLII–CXLV, CXLVII.

118. Cf. Letter by the commissioners to W.G. Farmer dated 14.8.1793, in BRP, OIOC P/366/15.

119. Cf. *Reports of a Joint Commission*, § CCX. The lifting came into force on 13.4.1793.

120. More details on Mūssa's strategies are to be found in Banerjee, Ruchira, 'A Wedding Feast or Political Arena? Commercial Rivalry between the Ali Rajas and the English Factory in Northern Malabar in the 18th Century', in: Rudranghshu Mukherjee and Lakshmi Subramanian (eds.), *Politics and Trade in the Indian Ocean World: Essays in Honour of Ashin Das Gupta*, Delhi, 1998, pp. 83–112.

121. *Reports of a Joint Commission*, § CCCCX.

122. Cf. *Reports of a Joint Commission*, § CCCCX.

123. Cf. Clementson, *Report*, pp. 19–23.

124. Cf. Nightingale, *Trade and Empire*, p. 111. See also Kieniewicz, 'Pepper Gardens', p. 8f.

125. Cf. *Reports of a Joint Commission*, §§ CCCCXI–CCCCXV.

126. This happened on Dow's suggestion. Cf. *Reports of a Joint Commission*, § CCCCXXX.

127. Cf. *Reports of a Joint Commission*, § CCCCXXXVIII–CCCCXLII. The Customs Regulations dated 22.7.1793 can be found in MCR 2540 (TNSA). The proclamation for the local population was declared on 13.9.1793; cf. Logan, *Treaties*, ii, LXII, pp. 202–3.

128. Extract from the Report of Thomas Warden to the Board of Revenue, 19.3.1801, in Panikkar, K.N., *Peasant Protests*, p. 20.

129. Like Baden-Powell, Kunhikrishnan assumes that the *kāṇakkāran* would have claimed the *janmaṃ* for themselves if the janmaṃ had contained property rights in the European sense of the word. He believes that the kāṇakkārans would have passed their demands at the time when the janmakārans had fled on account of the Maisūrian invasions, i.e. when the kāṇakkārans would have had a good chance to take control of the janmaṃ. Instead the kāṇakkārans expanded their kāṇaṃ rights. Cf. Baden Powell, *The Land Systems*, vol. 3, p. 170f., Kunhikrishnan, Vannarth Veettil, *Tenancy Legislation in Malabar (1880–1970): An Historical Analysis*, Calicut, 1993, p. 3.

130. Baden-Powell, *The Land-Systems*, vol. 3, p. 164. Cf. also Logan, *Malabar*, vol. 1, p. 495.

131. For more information on this topic, cf. Dale, *Islamic Society*, pp. 93–104.

Dale cites the British policy of underlining the differences between the Māppiḷḷas and the Hindus as cause for the religious conflict. The Joint Commissioners though had the premiss of affording equal treatment to the Hindus and Māppiḷḷas. Cf. *Reports of a Joint Commisison*, § CCLXIV.

132. The redefinitions can be found in Innes and Evans, *Malabar*, pp. 304–7.

133. Cf. Chapter Two.

134. Luhmann, Niklas, *Legitimation durch Verfahren*, Frankfurt und Main, 7th edn., 1997, p. viif.

135. Cf. Luhmann, *Legitimation*, p. 12, 23, 25.

136. Only in 1907 did the Governor of Madras officially admit that the British interpretation of the land laws in Malabar had been incorrect. Cf. Kunhikrishnan, *Tenancy Legislation*, p. 10.

137. Cf. Logan, *Malabar*, vol. 1, p. 621.

138. Ravindran, *Malabar under Bombay*, p. 4f.

139. Cf. Chopra et al., *History*, vol. 3, p. 177.

140. Cf. Moore, M., 'A New Look', p. 525. What is meant by establishing laws is the enactment of regulations in Malabar by the *men on the spot*, in that case by the commissioners, the trusted administrators of Malabar from 1792–1800. Contrarily, the legislation represents a departure from laws made by the government in Bombay or London.

141. Summary of events in Kōṭṭayaṃ from 1796–1978 (miscellaneous), in HMS, OIOCH/607. Cf. also *Reports of a Joint Commission,* § CCLXII; Transcript of Alexander Dow dated 2.10.1976, in BRP, OIOC P/366/19.

142. Logan, *Treaties*, comment on ii, VII, p. 150f.

143. Cf. also Letter by Vira Varmma to the Governor of Kōḻikōṭu dated 31.12.1795, in BRP, OIOC P/366/18: 'I shall leave to assure your honor that I shall ever be proud to execute with zeal, & to the best of my abilities all such orders as your honor shall be pleased to impose upon me.'; Letter by W.G. Farmer to Vira Varmma dated 16.10.1793, in SPP, OIOC P/E/6.

144. Cf. Transcript of Alexander Dow dated 2.10.1796, in BRP, OIOC P/366/19.

145. Cf. for example the letter by Paḷaśśi Rājā to John Smee dated 3.11.1799, in BRP, OIOC P/366/25; Chapter Three.

146. '[...] the old Coteangary Rajah, who is likewise living at the advanced Age of 70 or 80 years. [...] he is the legal and undisputed inheritor of the Rauye. Being Superannuated, his infirmities induced him to a voluntary abdication of the authority [...]; but he sometimes even now, exerts the Chief Authority.' Transcript of Alexander Dow dated 2.10.1796, in BRP, OIOC P/366/19.

147. Cf. extract from the letter by the Supravisor dated 3.3.1796, in SPP, OIOC P/E/9.

148. Cf. Logan, *Treaties*, ii, LXXXVI, p. 227f.; ii, XCI, pp. 231–3.

149. Cf. Instructions by W.G. Farmer to A.W. Handley dated 30.12.1794, in BRP, OIOC P/366/16.

150. At a later date in 1796 Vira Varmma explained to the Northern Superintendent that peace and order could be instilled in Kōṭṭayaṃ only if British troops were stationed there. Cf. PR 33 A&B.

151. He was by then President and Governor in Council in Bombay.

152. Letter by Alexander Walker to Jonathan Duncan dated 10.8.1800, Walker of Bowland Papers, NLS MS 13602. But by December 1801 Alexander Walker had turned 180 degrees: He now strongly advised the seizing of Paḷaśśi Rājā. Letter by Alexander Walker to Arthur Wellesley, Walker of Bowland Papers, NLS MS 13602.

153. Logan, *Malabar*, vol. 1, p. 505.

154. PR 39 A&B, Cf. also PR 117 A&B.

155. A mosque had been destroyed in the centre of Kōṭṭayaṃ in April 1793. In September of the same year the Māppiḷḷas asked Paḷaśśi Rājā's permission to rebuild the mosque, and they promised him a gift in return. Since they began the construction of the mosque without the requested gift, Paḷaśśi Rājā sent one of his followers with armed men into the town to bring the leader Tahib Kuṭṭi Ali before him. Paḷaśśi Rājā's supporter and also the Māppiḷḷa leader were killed in the fight that ensued. As a consequence of this unrest, six Māppiḷḷas were taken prisoner, of whom two were killed and four wounded. The EIC's only reaction was to station one troop in Kūṭāli and one in Paḷaśśi respectively. The matter was thus settled for the time being. Cf. Logan, *Malabar*, vol.1, p. 497. It is likely that the aforementioned Māppiḷḷas were executed by Paḷavīṭṭil Cantu, an agent of Vira Varmma. Cf. PR 57 B, section of a translated Ola by Kēraḷa Varmma to Vinketa Telean dated 6th Karkkaṭaṃ 970 (July 1795), in SPP, OIOC P/E/8.

156. Cf. Rajayyan, 'Kerala Varma', p. 550.

157. Besides day-to-day objects, sums of money in different currencies, and also swords and jewellery were found in and taken from the palace. An inventory of objects can be found in BC, OIOC F/4/34.

158. Cf. PR 5A; Logan, *Malabar*, vol. 1, p. 510.

159. Cf. the correspondence by Alexander Dow with the Malabar Commission and with Paḷaśśi Rājā dated July 1796, in PCB, OIOC P/342/26. In Duncan's mind these agreements were sealed, and in May 1796 he had sent instructions to the commissioners regarding the matter of 'Paḷaśśi Rājā': in addition to the rules to which Paḷaśśi Rājā was to adhere, he was also to live outside of Kōṭṭayaṃ. Vira Varmma's power was to remain in its entirety over the whole district so as to assure tax collection. Letter by Jonathan Duncan to the commissioners, 8.5.1796, in SPP, OIOC P/E/9. Cf. Logan, *Treaties*, ii, CXVIII, p. 255; Rajayyan, 'Kerala Varma', p. 550. Dow was impressed by Paḷaśśi Rājā's conduct during the meeting—he showed appropriate respect for the EIC. Report by A. Dow dated 5.7.1796, in PCB, OIOC P/342/25.

160. Cf. Logan, *Treaties*, ii, CXXII, p. 257f., cf. also Logan, *Malabar*, vol. 1, p. 511.

161. Cf. PR, 29 A&B, 32 B: Letters by Peile, the Northern Superintendent, which express his astonishment that Paḷaśśi Rājā had not been returned his property in its entirety. He then asked Vira Varmma to explain to him how this had happened.

162. Cf. PR 22 A&B, 23 A&B, 24 B.

163. PR 20 B.

164. Cf. PR 56 B.

165. Cf. PR 57 B: Petition by the noblement of Kōṭṭayaṃ dated 10.11.1796, in which they describe their state in the days of Ṭippu. Likewise the *arjī* by the noblemen of Kōṭṭayaṃ dated 19.11.1796, in BRP, OIOC P/366/19.

166. Cf. PR 39 A&B, 61 A&B, 62 A&B. The mediation was to have been undertaken by Divān Bālājirāyan.

167. Cf. PR 25 A&B, 35 A&B, 50 A&B, 58 B.

168. Cf. PR 36 A&B, 37 A&B.

169. Cf. PR 42 B, 43 B, 44 B, 45 A&B, 46 A&B, 47 A&B, 48 A&B.

170. For example in PR 102 A&B.

171. PR 106 A&B.

172. Cf. PR 119 A.

173. PR 121 A&B.

174. Cf. Logan, *Treaties*, ii, CXXXI, p. 268f.; PR 123 B.

175. Cf. PR 126 B.

176. Cf. PR 137 B; Logan, *Malabar*, vol. 1, p. 515.

177. Cf. PR 138 B, 149 B.

178. Cf. Logan, *Malabar*, vol. 1, p. 513; Datta, Kalikinkar, 'The Malabar Rajahs an the East India Company', *Bengal Past and Present* 57 (1939), pp. 1–9, p. 3f. Large sections of the Bombay army were kept active in Malabar for years on end with the task of suppressing the rebellions. Cf. Muir, Ramsay (ed.), *The Making of Britsh India 1756–1858*, London, 2nd edn., 1917, p. 208.

179. Cf. PR 150 A&B.

180. Cf. Logan, *Malabar*, vol. 1, p. 540.

181. Cf. Chopra et al., *History*, vol. 3, p. 121. For information on the Kuṟiccyars and Kuṟumbars cf. Aiyappan, A., *Report on the Socio-Economic Conditions of the Aboriginal Tribes of the Province of Madras*, Madras, 1948, pp. 93–5.

182. Cf. Report by Paḻavīṭṭil Cantu dated 28.12.1797 in BC, OIOC F/4/33; report by Shamaya Shiney dated 3.5.1797, in MCR 1723 (TNSA); report by Sheenoo about a mission of Eman Nāyar for Ṭippu Sulttān, no date (probably mid-1797), in MCR 1725 (TNSA); report by the senior rājā of Kōṭṭayaṃ dated 26.12.1797, in MCR 1787 (TNSA); Letter by A. Dow to James Rivett dated 19.3.1797, in BC, OIOC F/4/33; Logan, *Malabar*, vol. 1, p. 516; Rajayyan, 'Kerala Varma', p. 551.

183. Cf. Rajayyan, 'Kerala Varma', p. 552f.; idem, *History of Tamilnadu 1565–1982*, Madurai, 1982, p. 212; Chopra et al., *History*, vol. 3, p. 119. Dua sees the rebellions of the *pāḷaiyakkārar*s as the greatest challenge to British rule in Malabar, today's Karnataka and today's Tamiḻnāṭu, one whose influence had to be broken before a British system of administration could be set up. Cf. Dua, J.C., *Palegars of South India: Forms and Contents of Their Resistance in Ceded Districts*, New Delhi, 1996, p. 255.

184. Report on the British defeat by A. Disney (commandant in Vāyanāṭu) to A. Dow dated 18.3.1797, in BC, OIOC F/4/33; Cf. Rajayyan, 'Kerala Varma', p. 552.

185. In April 1797 the commissioners were still stressing the impossibility of giving in Paḻaśśi Rājā, even if peace was the greatest gain. The EIC's honour had to

be respected at all times. Letter by commissioners to Alexander Dow dated 7.4.1797, in MCR 1722 (TNSA).

186. Cf. Logan, *Treaties*, ii, CXLII, p. 276.

187. Cf. ibid., ii, CLII, p. 281f.

188. Cf. Letter by Alexander Dow to John Spencer dated 2.8.1798, in MCR 1729 (TNSA).

189. Cf. Letter by Paḻaśśi Rājā to John Spencer dated 7 Tulāṃ 973, in MCR 1731 (TNSA).

190. Cf. Letter by John Spencer and John Smee to James Stevens dated 4.3.1799, in MCR 1733 (TNSA).

191. Transcript of commission meeting dated 6.10.1799, in BC, OIOC F/4/62.

192. Cf. Information by Devresh Bhundary dated 17.3.1799 and 23.3.1799 as well as report by two *harkārā*s dated 24.3.1799 to the president of the commissioners, in MCR 1734 (TNSA). Letter by Paḻaśśi Rājā to John Spencer dated 27. Mīnaṃ 974/6. or 7.4.1799, in MCR 1735 (TNSA).

193. Cf. Logan, *Malabar*, vol. 1, p. 526; Logan, *Treaties*, ii, CXCIII, pp. 319–22. Förster considers the defeat of the Maisūrians as the beginning of the British policy of expansionism. Cf. Förster, *Die mächtigen Diener*, p. 156.

194. Letter by George Waddell to John Spencer dated 25.2.1800, Walker of Bowland Papers, NLS MS 13608.

195. Letter by Palaśṣi Rājā to the government in Bombay dated 6.12.1799, in HMS, OIOC H/458; Letter by John Smee and John Spencer to James Stevens dated 18.2.1800, in HMS, OIOC H/471; Cf. Logan, *Malabar*, vol. 1, p. 528; Rajayyan, 'Kerala Varma', p. 552f.

196. Edward Clive (1754–1839), son of Robert Clive, was Governor of Madras from 1798 to 1803.

197. Letter by Clive to the resident in Maisūr dated 3.2.1800 and 17.3.1800, in HMS, OIOC H/458. The resident of Maisūr was responsible at this time for administration in Vāyanāṭu, cf. extract from a letter from Bombay dated 14.12.1799, in BC, OIOC F/4/62.

198. Letter by Alexander Walker to Stuart dated 14.10.1800, Walker of Bowland Papers, NLS MS 13605.

199. Letter by Paḻaśśi Rājā to Manjery Allum dated 30 Mēṇaṃ 975/20.4.1800, in HMS, OIOC H/461.

200. Letter by Paḻaśśi Rājā to Kolady Kottah Rājā 16 Mithunaṃ 975/26.6.1800, Walker of Bowland Papers, NLS MS 13602. Cf. Rajayyan, 'Kerala Varmma', p. 553; idem, *South Indian Rebellion: The First War of Independence: 1800–1801*, Mysore, 1971, pp. 175–8.

201. In a letter to Alexander Walker Jonathan Duncan reflecting on the reasons of the attacks concluded 'That this chieftain proclaims his attack on our people at Montana to proceed from the Order of the Gods, to free that sacred spot from the Presence of the white Men'. Letter by Jonathan Duncan to Alexander Walker dated 12.8.1800, Walker of Bowland Papers, NLS MS 13604. At Maṇattaṇa about 250 men were lost on the British side. Walker of Bowland Papers, NLS MS 13605.

202. Arthur Wellesley (1769–1852), Brother of Governor General Richard Wellesley, was British administrator in Maisūr and regent of Śrīraṅgapaṭṭaṇaṃ from 1799 to 1802, and later became famous as the Duke of Wellington.

203. Minute by Alexander Walker dated 31.10.1800, Walker of Bowland Papers, NLS MS 13609.

204. Arthur Wellesley to Henry Dundas dated 18.3.1799, in: Ingram, *Two Views*, p. 250f. Wellesley's main motive was preventive imperialism. Cf. Förster, *Die mächtigen Diener*, p. 157.

205. Pallur Eman Nāyar received services in return for the information which he supplied the British. It is likely that in previous years he had provided Paḷaśśi Rājā with news about planned British actions, since he had access to their offices. Cf. Logan, *Malabar*, vol. 1, p. 530. Cf. Rajayyan, *South Indian Rebellion*, p. 179. Alexander Walker mentions the information given by Eman Nāyar as being a great help to the British cause. Letter by Alexander Walker to Osborne dated February 1801(?), Walker of Bowland Papers, NLS MS 13611.

206. Cf. Rajayyan, 'Kerala Varma', p. 553; idem, *South Indian Rebellion*, p. 186.

207. Logan, *Malabar*, vol. 1, p. 532.

208. Wilson's report dated 15.2.1801, in MCR 2546 (TNSA).

209. Letter by Alexander Walker to John Spencer dated 19.3.1801, Walker of Bowland Papers, NLS MS 13611; Letter by Alexander Walker to Montgomery dated 30.3.1801, Walker of Bowland Papers, NLS MS 13612.

210. Cf. Extract of a secret letter by Fort St. George dated 1.4.1801 and dated 2.5.1801, in BC, OIOC F/4/117; *History of the Madras Army*, 5 vols., Madras 1883, vol. 3, p. 29, in MDR, OIOC L/MIL/17/3/511.

211. Letter by Sartorius to the commissioners dated 25.5.1801, in BC, OIOC F/4/120.

212. Letter by the commissioners to Fort St. George dated 29.6.1801, in BC, OIOC F/4/120.

213. Letter by the commissioners to William Petrie dated 11.6.1801, in BC, OIOC F/4/120.

214. Cf. Logan, *Treaties*, ii, CCXXIX, p. 343f.

215. Cf. Logan, *Malabar*, vol. 1, p. 533.

216. Cf. Extract from a letter from Fort St. George dated 15.10.1801, in BC, OIOC F/4/126.

217. Cf. Report by Wilson dated 15.2.1801, in MCR 2546 (TNSA); Logan, *Malabar*, vol. 1, p. 532.

218. For example, the British had received elephants from local people but not paid them. Letter by J. Kunda Panikkar to the commissioners dated 5.7.1799, in MCR 1697 (TNSA).

219. Proclamation by William Macleod dated 30.1.1802 in BC, OIOC F/4/156.

220. Letter by Wellesley to Stuart dated 24.1.1802, in BC, OIOC F/4/126.

221. Proclamation by James Stevenson dated 16.2.1802, in BC, OIOC F/4/126.

222. Letter by James Stevenson to Clive dated 16.2.1802, in BC, OIOC F/4/126.

223. In 1807 W. Thackeray criticized Macleod's proclamation and cited two

reasons for its failure: firstly, the new exchange rate came into conflict with the exchange rates of the markets and, secondly, the tax payments were not adjusted to the new exchange rate which meant that the farmers had to pay more by percentage. Report by William Thackeray dated 8.9.1807, in MCR 2559 (KSA).

224. Cf. Rajayyan, 'Kerala Varma', p. 555.

225. Cf. *History of the Madras Army*, vol. 3, pp. 55–8, in MDR, OIOC L/MIL/17/3/511; Abdurahiman, 'Macleod's Paimash', p. 68.

226. Transcript by J. Stuart (Commander in Chief) dated 26.10.1802, in BC, OIOC F/4/154.

227. Letter by William Macleod to Fort St. George dated 16.12.1802, in MCR 2309 (KSA).

228. Letter by William Macleod to the Chief Secretary of the government dated 5.3.1803, in MCR 2309 (KSA).

229. Cf. Logan, *Treaties*, ii, CCXXXIX, p. 352f.

230. Letter by Clive to the Chairman dated 12.3.1803, Letter by the government in Fort St. George to William Petrie dated 15.3.1803, Letter by J. Watson and T.H. Baber to William Macleod dated 29.4.1802, in BC, OIOC F/4/156; Letter by Harvey to the Principal Collector dated 27.6.1803, in MCR 2158 (KSA).

231. Cf. Report by Robert Rickards, probably dated 4.7.1803, in MCR 2158 (KSA).

232. Letter by T.H. Baber to the Principal Collector dated 26.2.1804, in MCR 2160 (KSA).

233. Cf. Letter by Wilson to the Northern Subcollector dated 13.1.1804, in MCR 2235 (KSA); Logan, *Treaties*, ii, CCXLVIII, p. 362.

234. Cf. Logan, *Malabar*, vol. 1, p. 541.

235. Cf. Logan, *Treaties*, p. 363.

236. Cf. Logan, *Malabar*, vol. 1, p. 540.

237. The organizational form of the Nāyars was well suited to the guerrilla war, which they successfully led for many years against the European invaders. Cf. Fuller, *The Nayars*, p. 7.

238. Cf. Rajayyan, 'Kerala Varma', p. 556.

239. Letter by T.H. Baber to the Principal Collector dated 9.8.1804, in MCR 2385 (KSA).

240. Proclamations by Macleod dated February 1805 and 13.5.1805, in BC, OIOC F/4/199.

241. Māvilāntōṭu (near to Pulpaḷḷi) on the border with Kurg is reckoned to be the place where the mysterious death of Paḷaśśi Rājā is said to have happened. A memorial stone is located there with the inscription 'Kēraḷasiṃhaṃ / vīrapaḷaśśitam-purānte raktasākśi smārakaṃ / māvilāntōṭu'—roughly translated as 'The lion of Kēraḷa / memorial site to the martyr king Vīra Paḷaśśi / Māvilāntōṭu.'

242. Cf. Menon, A.S., *Kerala History*, p. 186; Leela Devi, *History*, p. 301.

243. Information by K.K. Marar dated 11.9.1998. It is alleged that Baber confiscated this dagger.

244. Kēraḷa Varmma Paḷaśśi Rājā's family was also expropriated; his palace

had to give way for a road. Cf. Gough, Kathleen, 'Indian Peasant Uprisings', *EPW* 9 (1974), pp. 1391–1412, p. 1396, col. 3.

245. Letter by Thomas Warden to Baber dated 8.12.1805, in BC, OIOC F/4/191.

246. Letter by Thomas Warden to the government in Fort St. George dated 2.2.1806, in BC, OIOC F/4/239. Innes and Evans, *Malabar*, p. 337.

247. Letter by T.H. Baber to the Chief Secretary in Fort St. George dated 13.12.1805, in BC, OIOC F/4/191.

248. Cf. Logan, *Malabar*, vol. 1, p. 540.

249. Proclamation by Thomas Warden dated 8.12.1805, in BC, OIOC F/4/191.

250. Cf. *Census of India 1961*, Census District Handbook 1, Cannanore, s.l. 1965, p. 77, col.1; Chopra et al., *History*, vol. 3, p. 121.

251. The inscription on the gravestone reads: 'Vīra Kēraḷa Paḷaśśirājāvu iviṭe antyaviśramaṃ koḷḷunnu. Mānantavāṭi 1805 November 30.'—roughly translated as 'Vīra Kēraḷa Paḷaśśi Rājā found here his last resting-place. Mānantavāṭi 30.11.1805.'

252. Cf. Innes and Evans, *Malabar*, p. 426.

253. He described his 'younger brother' as 'misguided' but did not do anything to make Paḷaśśi Rājā change his course. Cf. PR 16 B.

254. Logan, *Treaties*, comment on ii, VII, p. 150f.

255. For example, in PR 19 A&B: '[...] I shall inform the Company accordingly and then act according to the act of the Company—this is my decision and practice. [...] I request your kind consideration and patronage for everything concerning me.' and 21 B: 'Further, I shall be bound by your orders.' Cf. PR 121 A&B.

Five

Concept of Rule in Malabar

This chapter will examine whether the models of the *little kingdom* and the *contact zone*, which were described in Chapter Two, are of analytical use to the situation in Malabar in the late eighteenth century. The first questions to be addressed are whether the model of the *little kingdom* can be applied in its modified form to Kōṭṭayaṃ at the end of the eighteenth century, and whether any additional parameters must be put in place for its application to the whole of Malabar. Within this context we may also ask what form Paḻaśśi Rājā's legitimation and manifestation of rule actually took, and what status they were afforded in the political arena of the country. The subsequent section is devoted to the processes of negotiation between the colonizers and the local people within the *contact zone* of Malabar, and the consequences of these processes. Finally, a number of events that took place in the nineteenth century will be investigated, especially those regarding the nature of the negotiating processes between the ruling British colonial power and the indigenous population.

Kōṭṭayaṃ—A Little Kingdom?

A brief recapitulation of the main characteristics of a *little king* seems in place in order to decide whether Paḻaśśi Rājā can be considered a *little king*. A *little king* is a ruler who is able to react independently when it comes to internal politics, since he is in control of appropriate financial sources of income, has the means to assert his wishes—by military force if necessary—and is responsible for carrying out political and ritual actions to legitimize his rule within his territory. Parallel to his internal autonomy, the *little king* acknowledges an external ruler of superior standing, who is able to support his higher status in political and ritual terms by military superiority. The system of ritual redistribution allows for the *little king* to share in the *great king's* power, and he is dependent on the *great king* to legitimize his rule in his own territory.

To what extent does Paḻaśśi Rājā match up to the first criterion of a *little king*, that of internal political independence? Paḷaśśi Rājā's finances were made up of the income from his *janmaṃ*, the *cuṅkaṃ*, trade taxes, mint rights, cash punishments for criminal actions, and the property of those people who died without heirs. In addition, there were the gifts given at festival times and ceremonies, such as Oṇaṃ and Viṣu, as well as royal prerogatives. An independent financial basis was thus guaranteed for the king. The officials Paḷaśśi Rājā had at his disposal were the *nāṭuvāḷi*s and *dēśavāḷi*s; they exercised similar authority at their own levels as the king did at the highest level. Paḷaśśi Rājā saw the nāṭuvāḷis and dēśavāḷis as officials with particular spheres of authority, and they in turn regarded themselves as bearers of a higher authority in relation to those who were subordinate to them. The status of the respective partners, as well as the social, political and ritual context of the relationship between these partners, was determined by the relations they developed with each other.[1] Paḷaśśi Rājā was responsible to the *nāṭṭukūṭṭaṃ*, which meant that he could not make decisions at his own discretion. Thus he did not enjoy the position of an absolute ruler. Yet although the levels of authority below Paḷaśśi Rājā did amount to some significance, most notably in everyday matters of administration, Paḷassi Rājā's sacred legitimation ensured that he occupied the central position in Kōṭṭayaṃ, and he underpinned this through ritual legitimation (see below). The structure, which supported the exercise of power in Kōṭṭayaṃ, was thus characterized by 'a center (or centers) exhibiting an ideal sovereignty that is primarily ritual; but actual executive authority is distributed at many lower sites of the structure, where there are multiple, scaled-down replicas of the king.'[2] If necessary, an army could be assembled quickly from within the ranks of the Nāyars, who had themselves undertaken military training. Military intervention was thus an option when it came to defending the king's claim to power.

In the same vein as his neighbouring rulers Paḷaśśi Rājā legitimized his rule symbolically through political and ritual actions. In the Paḷaśśi Rēkhakaḷ, for example, explicit reference is made to Kēraḷa Varmma Paḷaśśi Rājā only having arrived in Talaśśēri for a meeting with Christopher Peile and Vira Varmma once the Navarātri Pūjā ceremonies had been completed.[3] This nine-day festival in reverence of the goddess Bhagavati was said to empower the king—Bhagavati's power was thought to pass to him.[4] In a similar context David Shulman describes the ritual legitimation of a ruler through the *durgga* festival:

> His embodiment of a sacrificial persona is more decisive for his kingdom than any action he may take or any decision he may make. In a sense, the king is most 'real', most palpably present, in the context of ritual drama, as the leading protagonist in the periodic re-creation of a dramatically visible social order—for example, when he receives his investiture from the goddess during the annual Durga festival; [...].[5]

Paḷaśśi Rājā attached importance not only to the Navarātri festival, but also to other religious festivals and ceremonies because their observance was imperative for his sacral legitimation. The rājā manifested his rule in public representations as the donor and protector of the religion of his kingdom and the maintainer of cosmic order.[6]

Paḷaśśi Rājā was supported by the *senior rājā* of Kōṭṭayaṃ in matters relating to the practice of religious ceremonies, for example in discussions with the British as to how the costs of the festivals would be met.[7] Paḷaśśi Rājā also supported the construction of temples and shrines, which displayed not only a sense of charity but was also a manifestation of his rule.[8]

The general acknowledgement of Paḷaśśi Rājā received its symbolic representation in the gifts of the local people at festivals such as Oṇaṃ, Viṣu and other annually occurring festivities, as well as at royal weddings and deaths.[9] The interlinked nature of religion and politics in Kōṭṭayaṃ is brought out clearly by the fact that the rebels, who were led by Kerala Varmma Paḷaśśi Rājā, consulted the oracle in the temple of Bhagavati in Maṇattaṇa prior to their conflicts with the British in 1800,[10] and that they gathered at the temple of Pulpaḷḷi on other occasions. Having carried out a raid, the rebel leader Kaiteri Ampu had a rice offering sent to the temple in Manantēri so as to please the gods.[11] The oracle of the temple of Bhagavati in Pālakkāṭu was valued very highly as well.[12] However, the great store which Paḷaśśi Rājā set by his religious obligations brought him into conflict with the British, who generally displayed little understanding of the importance of the religious and ritual customs in Malabar. Thus his behaviour incurred their wrath.

Paḷaśśi Rājā received another kind of legitimation from the local élite groups within his country: the noble people of Kōṭṭayaṃ expressed in a letter that Paḷaśśi Rājā had committed himself to the welfare of the population despite the rather chaotic conditions which had prevailed during and after Ṭippu's invasion: '[…] His Majesty Paḷaśśi Rājā agreed to look after the country and us people. […] Then His Majesty Paḷaśśi Rājā came with us to the forest and there looked after us and our children. After that the king borrowed for us rice and seeds and thus saved us.'[13]

Paḷaśśi Rājā himself adds:

> I was called for and the country and the people were entrusted to my care. An agreement in writing was also given to this effect. How I looked after the people of the country according to this order, this you can hear from the chieftains and the people if they are summoned. I made the agreement according to the command of my elder brother to look after the Kōṭṭayaṃ country. I am looking after the country according to the traditions of my elders.[14]

With reference to the welfare of his people and his obligations to them, Paḷaśśi Rājā acted in accordance with the *rājādharma.* This was the source the *great king* used to legitimize his rule—qua status as the *little king*, Paḷaśśi Rājā enjoyed a proportion of the power that was exercised by the *great king*, and he was also able to use the same source to legitimize his own rule, although naturally to a lesser degree. In my opinion the rājādharma should also be taken into consideration as a motivational factor to explain the actions of the *little king* since he shared in the same ritual legitimation act as the *great king*. In his correspondence with the British, Paḷaśśi Rājā referred on several occasions to a responsibility for his people: The king could only be content when his people were content. In this attitude Paḷaśśi Rājā was in line with the Arthaśāstra: 'In the happiness of the subjects lies his happiness; in their welfare his welfare. He shall not consider as good only that which pleases him but treat as beneficial to him whatever pleases his subjects.'[15] The solidarity that bonded the people and their king became highly apparent in the resistance movement, and can be described as an interdependency of king and people as parts of a unit. Kēraḷa Varmma Paḷaśśi Rājā saw that neither the British nor Vira Varmma's intentions lay with the welfare of 'his' people, and he forbade the British from collecting taxes because he regarded the ban as a measure of support for his people's well-being. He also expected his political opponents to be concerned with addressing and satisfying the needs of the people: 'I have prohibited collection in the country but for one thing: even if the English Company is very strong they are not to proceed without considering truth and justice. I must ascertain this before permitting collection in the country. That is the reason for the prohibition.'[16]

Although Paḷaśśi Rājā did recognize the EIC's military strength, he expected their conduct to conform to the virtues of Indian ideals of governance of the state, such as truth and justice. The British must have cited the very same virtues in their attempts to convince local rulers of the moral legitimation of their own claim to power. Yet the way of implementing the ideals was a very different one: whereas the local rulers tried to comply with the rājādharma, thereby following the need to ritually legitimate and share their power, the British imposed their system on India considering themselves to be superior in administrative affairs, and therefore more legitimate to rule.

Another indication of just how firmly rooted Paḷaśśi Rājā was in the traditional Indian concept of rule is displayed in his constant reminders to the British that they reimburse him for the state treasury, which was plundered at the palace in Paḷaśśi in 1796.[17] The treasury is one of the seven elements that form the nature of the Indian state according to traditional state doctrine.[18] These elements play an additional role in the concept of the rājādharma, and Paḷaśśi Rājā was aware of this. Within his framework, i.e. as a *little king* at the meso-level, he strove to hold together the seven elements in his kingdom.

It is thus clear that Paḷaśśi Rājā exerted internal independence, was able to assert himself using military means where necessary, and was able to legitimize his rule within his own territory through political and ritual actions, as well as through policies towards the local people which conformed to the traditional concept of a ruler. He can therefore be considered a *little king* in this respect.

We can now turn to the second criterion of a *little king*, his relationship to a *great king* above him. The supreme ruler in Malabar during the ninth century was known as the Cēramān Perumāḷ. Since the *great king* from the Cēramān Perumāḷ line was the most successful rājā, he was able to assume the status of a *mahārājā*. Military success amongst the rulers in Malabar and the expansion of conquered land were prerequisites for this achievement. At the end of the last Cēramān Perumāḷ's reign, there arose the question of a successor. Since the Nāyars in Malabar to which the rulers belonged followed a matrilineal line of succession, the *marumakkattāyaṃ*, it was the son of the last Cēramān Perumāḷ's sister, and not his own son, who inherited the kingdom. Only a subordinate position of power fell to the actual son of the *great king* under this system—something which could lead towards conflict with his theoretically superior cousin. Thus the marumakkattāyaṃ (see Fig. 5.1) caused a structural opposition between the *great king's* son and the *great king's* sister's son.

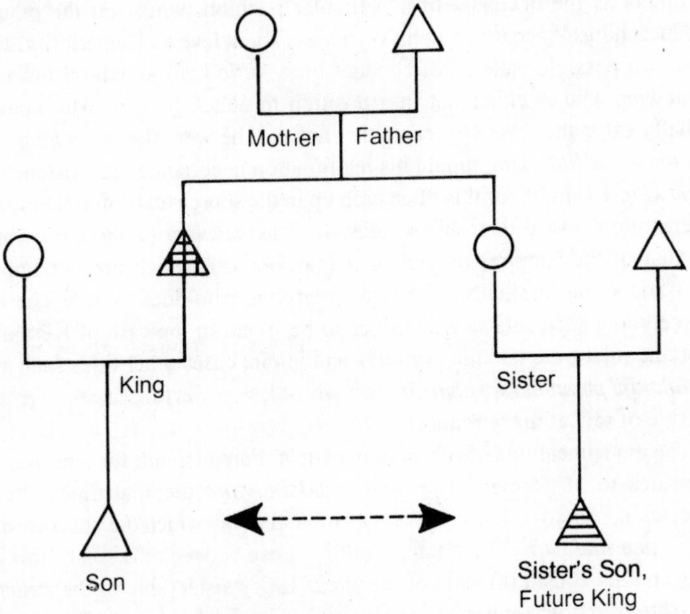

Fig. 5 1. Structural Opposition between a King's Son and a King's Sister's Son

Despite some elements of uncertainty, the end of the last Cēramān Perumāḷ's reign is commonly associated with the beginning of the Koḷḷaṃ era. The calendar known as the Koḷḷaṃ era and later also as the Malayāḷaṃ era—which began in AD 825—is one of the local epochs that was used in Kēraḷa, besides counting the number of years of a king's reign. Śaka time, which was customary elsewhere in India, was not employed in Kēraḷa. Contrary to the kinds of calendars which were generally linked to the founding of a temple, the Koḷḷaṃ era starts with the founding of the town of Koḷḷaṃ.[19] This calendar is also marked by the end of supremacy for the ruler who occupied the highest position: the *little kings* who resided in Malabar took over the responsibility of the land jointly in the absence of the *great king*, always keeping alive the memory of the mahārājā and waiting for his return.[20]

The relationships of power in Malabar in the eighteenth century show a distinctive feature: despite the fact that there had not been a mahārājā since the ninth century, titles, inscriptions and oral records tell us that the legitimation of local princes was hinged on a supreme ruler. The thesis goes that the status of those parties involved depends upon the particular stature of the *little kings* or *great king*; i.e. that a ruler can be both a *great king* in the eyes of somebody weaker than himself, whilst also being a *little king* in the eyes of somebody more powerful than himself. On the one hand he is perceived by others as the occupant of a particular position, whilst on the other he conducts himself according to his own ideas about levels of superiority. There exist two possible patterns of conduct for a *little king* to exhibit towards a *great king* who is either not in a position to attack him, or who does not actually exist: the *little king* can either act as if he were the *great king*, or he can remain a *little king* should his legitimation necessitate the existence of a *great king*. Examples of this often crop up in the source texts of Indian history where rulers award themselves titles, such as *talavāra* (bailiff), *rāṣṭrakūṭa* (Regent of the Empire) or *pratihāra* (gatekeeper), which are not imperial titles and so do implicitly refer to a *great king* who does exist.[21] There are scarcely any such self-awarded titles to be found in the case of Kēraḷa: the supreme ruler bore the title *perumāḷ*, and in rare cases other titles such as *śrī rājādhirājā paramēśvara bhaṭṭāraka*,[22] whilst less powerful princes were given the title of rājā at the very most.[23]

The matrilineal line of succession made it more difficult for long-reigning dynasties to be formed. The *marumakkattāyaṃ*, the matrilineal line of succession, passed on the status of mahārājā in a way which did not correspond to the *dharmaśāstra*.[24] In practice conflict arose between the son of the *great king* and his cousin (the son of the *great king's* sister) due to the structural opposition that was inherent in this system. Its final consequence proved to be the breaking up of the mahārājā's kingdom. From these considerations the following hypothesis can be derived: on a long-term basis a matrilineal society can only support a 'virtual' *great king*, since the rules of succession make it impossible for an actual kingdom of a mahārājā to span several generations. In Malabar the Tāmūtiri had tried to assume the position of the *great king* after the discontinuation of Cēramān Perumāḷ dynasty, but was not accepted by the *little kings* as such.[25]

Another characteristic of matrilineal society is the low level of importance attached to genealogies. In this context, it is considerably more significant to be able to trace back a taṟavāṭu to an ancestress.[26] In the case of Paḷaśśi Rājā, for example, the only thing to be discovered from research in numerous archives and conversations with descendants of Paḷaśśi Rājā in Kēraḷa was the name of his mother and grandmother—the attached comment being that nothing else was of importance.[27] Apparently, there is no *vaṃśāvali*.[28] A possible explanation for this fact is that vaṃśāvalis are a typically north Indian phenomenon, based on and geared towards hierarchies in line with the purāṇic tradition. This in turn is connected with the authority of the father of the family, who constitutes the decisive authority in a patrilineal society, such as was (and is still) to be found in the majority of cases in north India. In Malabar, however, the matrilineal concept meant that the mother's brother had a greater decision-making power than the children's father. Consequently, the vaṃśāvali is dropped as a source of status legitimation, because it does not correspond to the social norm of the Nāyars who were appointed as the *little kings* in Malabar. A purāṇic tradition as known from north India is not found in Malabar. Oral traditions were far more important than any recorded written texts.[29]

Colin Mackenzie's collection of manuscripts from the nineteenth century constitutes a significant contribution to the otherwise scant array of source texts. Mackenzie had local people in south India collect and record historical documents. Malayāḷaṃ manuscripts are not represented in any great number even here, however, since the majority of them were destroyed at the time of the Maisūrian invasions: 'On returning home in the year 966 (M.E.) after the invasion by Tippu Sultan, they found that all their records were destroyed.'[30] The documents tell of the acceptance of an eighteenth-century *great king* in Malabar who no longer existed but who continued to live in the people's memory, and who was important to the practical legitimation of rule: the respective documents mention Cēramān Perumāḷ as the most powerful ruler in Malabar. In a manuscript about the rājās of Kōḻikkoṭu, mention is also made of the rājās of Kocci who had received their crown and a sword passed on as insignia from Cēramān Perumāḷ.[31] There are also records of a report about Cēramān Perumāḷ, which reveals that he was the eighteenth king in his line of Perumāḷs and had ruled for thirty-six years before he became interested in Islam and journeyed to Mecca. The transfer of power to his subordinate rulers is described thus: 'At the time of his departure to Mecca, Cēramān Perumāḷ distributed his kingdom among his subordinates.'[32]

The distribution of power is expressed in similar terms in the report of the Kaṭattanāṭu rājās: '[…] Cēramān Perumāḷ distributed the kingdom amongst his subordinates, […].'[33] A different version of Cēramān Perumāḷ's transfer of power is given in another report: Cēramān Perumāḷ is said to have promised his wife's maidservants, two Vellala girls, that any sons born to them would enjoy the status of independent rulers. Their descendants are said to have ultimately produced four branches.[34] Cēramān Perumāḷ is reported to have made his son ruler of Kōlattunāṭu.[35] Thus he belonged to the circle of Malabar princes, but was not master of the circle of *little kings* as his father had been. Even the Nambyars of Iruvaḻināṭu, who ruled over 1000 Nāyars, traced their regin back to Cēramān Perumāḷ: '[…] the kingdom granted to them by Cēramān Perumāḷ extended north to south […].'[36] The even smaller principality of Payyermola, whose rulers could only call upon 500 Nāyars, was apparently created by Cēramān Perumāḷ before his departure.[37] When Cēramān left for Mecca, the rulers of Kurumpranāṭu received confirmation that they were legally entitled to rule over their area.[38] One of the early rulers of Kōḻikkōṭu was apparently given a piece of land as a gift in return for the services which he had rendered to Cēramān Perumāḷ:

> One of the early kings of Koḻikkōḍu, Konnilakkonadiri by name had done great personal service to Cēramān Perumāḷ for which he, at the time of his departure to Mecca (?) [sic], granted him a piece of land around Koḻikkōḍu over which he was asked to rule and extend his rule over the adjacent territory.[39]

The Malabar princes in the aforementioned cases attributed the establishment of rule, or their participation in rule, to the initiative of Cēramān Perumāḷ. He was obviously keen to put his land in good hands before leaving for Mecca—the recipients seem to have been his *little kings*. With regard to the situation in eighteenth-century Malabar, then, it appears that while no *great king* actually existed, a 'virtual' *great king* was prevalent in the minds of the *little kings* and this concept had far-reaching consequences within the principalities of Malabar. Since most documents were destroyed at the time of the Maisūrian invasions, we can only assume that the surviving documents date from after this period. Thus, if Malabar rulers in the eighteenth century still fell back on the personage of Cēramān Perumāḷ as a *great king*, i.e. legitimator of rule, the logical conclusion is that he served as a 'virtual' *great king* to the *little kings* of Malabar. A parallel to this phenomenon is the concept of rule of the Nāyakas in seventeenth-century Tamil̤ land, who legitimated their rule by relating it to the rājās of Vijayanagara. Their political vocabulary apparently was borrowed from the Kakātiyas.[40] In the context of temples, priests even today legitimize their priestship in the Mīnākṣi temple in Maturai through descendants from a royal appointee; neither the British nor the succeeding government of Tamilnāṭu is accepted as a legitimate successor of the Nāyaka dynasty that during the sixteenth and seventeenth centuries appointed the temple priest.[41]

Pal̤aśśi Rājā, along with other *little kings,* such as the rājā of Ciṟakkal and Vira Varmma of Kurumpranāṭu, and a *little queen*, the Bibi of Kannūr, formed a circle of neighbouring rulers with similar strengths who monitored one another within the Malabar *kūṭṭaṃ*. Pal̤aśśi Rājā's behaviour towards the Malabar *little kings* and *little queen* was expressed in two ways: on the one hand he might join together to form a family relationship, but on the other he might also form changing alliances. This meant that he sometimes had amicable and at other times hostile relations with the neighbouring rulers, depending on the political and economic situation. These fluctuating relations can be attributed to the ever shifting socio-economic, political, and cultural process along with its attendant circumstances. For example, Vira Varmma of Kurumpranāṭu was related to Pal̤aśśi Rājā and yet relations between him and Pal̤aśśi Rājā were decidedly strained on account of Pal̤aśśi Rājā's desire to resist large-scale British interventions in matters of domestic policy. Pal̤aśśi Rājā only resisted intervention, however, once the British broke the agreements that they had made with him. Vira Varmma, on the other hand, opted to cooperate with the British. If we take this as an example of forming alliances, it becomes evident that scenarios in which political power was grouped in a certain way would have caused Pal̤aśśi Rājā to look around for new allies. This search for new allies was a traditional element in Indian government. It was also considered to be a practicable solution to the ongoing establishment of British colonial power at the end of the eighteenth century. In this, Kēral̤a Varmma Pal̤aśśi Rājā found himself facing political opponents who disputed his authority within his *little kingdom* and who intended to exploit his people economically. He seized every possible opportunity to prevent this.

In their minds, Pal̤aśśi Rājā and the other rulers in Malabar still recognized Cēramān Perumāḷ; though no longer alive, he figured as the rightful holder of the title of a *great king*, i.e. as their superior ruler. They derived their legitimation from their participation in his rule. Having considered the main criteria for a *little king*, I have come to the conclusion that the model of the *little kingdom* may indeed be applied to the rājās in Malabar in its modified form. However, a new element must be included for Kēraḷa: the *great king* does not necessarily have to be a living ruler; rather, he can exist in the minds of those rājās considered to be *little kings* and carry out his function as a *great king* in a 'virtual' capacity. It was possible for a *great king* to 'live on' as a 'virtual' *great king* in case he had no actual successor, provided that *little kings* relied on him as the basis for their legitimation of rule in their own territory. In Europe, Charlemagne was given a function similar to the 'virtual' *great king* in Malabar: even after his death he was seen as the *pater Europae*, and he became a force for integration for the counts' lands and the duchies in Europe.[42] Taking into account the elements constituting the concept of rule in Malabar presented so far, Paḻaśśi Rājā was positioned at the meso-level—between the virtual *great king*, at the highest level, and the *nātuvāḻis* or *dēśavāḻis* at levels below his own. From the point of view of Paḻaśśi Rājā, nātuvāḻis and dēśavāḻis had to be regarded as *little kings*, and they in turn considered themselves to be *little kings* in relation to their subordinates. The relations between these parties was determined by the status of respective partners and also by the social, political and ritual context.

The indigenous structures of Malabar became most evident where there was contact with powers from outside Malabar. The invasions by Ṭippu Sulttān, which were accompanied by forced conversions to Islam and high taxes, along with the British attempt at conquest—with its European conception of bureaucracy and equally high taxes—contradicted the local conception of the state and the traditional methods that governed how power was shared amongst the *little kings*. Furthermore, neither Ṭippu Sulttān nor the British could bring forward any sacral legitimation for their claim to power, since they were not integrated into the ritual system in Malabar. The *little kings* in Malabar considered the merchants and employees of the EIC to be ritually inferior, something which they themselves must scarcely have realized.[43] This explains why Paḻaśśi Rājā was unable to accept either power as a superior authority in spite of the initially temporary and later conclusive military supremacy of the British. Since Paḻaśśi Rājā considered his role to be *little king* in relation to the 'virtual' *great king* of Malabar, as did the other *little kings* in Malabar,[44] he recognized neither Ṭippu Sulttān nor the British as supreme rulers or the new *great king*.

Paḻaśśi Rājā's resistance was sparked off by Ṭippu Sulttān's and the British intention to seize sovereignty in Malabar for themselves and to assume the position of *great king*. Ṭippu Sulttān's drive for supremacy in Malabar came with heavy tax burdens and forced conversions. Paḻaśśi Rājā thus felt obliged to take action against Ṭippu Sulttān in order to preserve his authority and to protect his people. Ṭippu Sulttān's invasions in Kōṭṭayaṃ were of such considerable strength as to force Paḻaśśi Rājā to seek assistance against the occupiers, and he turned to the British for help. In doing this, however, he did not realize that they had an entirely different idea of the state and of the exercise of power, and that with his request he was getting into a spiral of increasing suppression and eventual subjugation. After 1792, this was brought home to him in no uncertain terms through the administrative and military actions taken by the British. Once the British had breached the treaty of 1790, which guaranteed Paḻaśśi Rājā and the other rājās in Malabar their freedom following their support in the successful British conflict with Ṭippu Sulttān, and had tried to bring Paḻaśśi Rājā's land under their sovereignty, Paḻaśśi Rājā felt that he was left with only one option for his next action: resistance to the British. He did not stand alone as large sections of the population of Kōṭṭayaṃ supported him in this move.[45]

A further point of conflict with the British was the entirely different conception of state held by both parties. In the Indian context the state certainly had a theoretical definition—one can think of works such as the Arthaśāstra—and yet, in practice, it was manifested in an entirely different way than in Europe. Social and religious institutions formed a plural structure marked by movement and contours which were not always clear—plurality headed by the *great king* at the macro-level, the *little king* at the meso-level and the nātuvāḻis and dēśavāḻis at the micro-level.[46] The Western concept of the state, however, assumes a state unit which is held together by bureaucratic administrative actions and legislation. For Paḻaśśi Rājā to have recognized the British as the *great king* he would have had to leave his traditional circle of rulers who were positioned below the 'virtual' *great king*. As a part of the British system, Paḻaśśi Rājā would not have been able to be anything other than a British subject, since there was no provision for participation in power within the British system, nor would the British have been interested in introducing participatory rule into their concept. His basis of legitimation would thus have been taken away by outside forces.

A different picture is drawn by Dilip Menon, who characterizes political phenomena in Malabar as 'multiple authorities' taking their legitimation from commercial well-being. Menon's notion of kingship is a rather strict one, oriented to the European concept of an absolute monarchy but not taking into account the flexibility and processuality of the *little kingdom* model. According to Menon the turn of the Malabar authorities towards the notion of kingship resulted from the conflict with the British, but did not succeed in stabilizing the country after the Maisūrian invasions. This attitude does not correspond to the aforementioned argument concluding that the political landscape of Malabar was shaped by *little kingdoms*.[47]

To sum up, it is evident that Kēraḷa Varmma Paḻaśśi Rājā held the position of a *little king* in Kōṭṭayaṃ towards the end of the eighteenth century. He legitimized and manifested his rule through political and ritual actions, for example through the patronage of temples and the upkeep of religious ceremonies. Paḷaśśi Rājā's main concern was to exercise his power for the welfare of the people—a goal firmly in accordance with the traditional canon of duty for a king. His status was determined by his ever-shifting relationship to local authorities at the micro-level, to his fellow *little kings*, and to the 'virtual' *great king*. By taking into account the matrilineal structure of society in Malabar, and including a 'virtual' *great king* in the equation, the model of the *little kingdom* could be modified in such a way as to make it applicable to the region of Malabar.

Contact Zone Malabar

This section will examine the processes of negotiation which took place between the local people and the new arrivals to Malabar. The *contact zone* in Malabar exhibits a wide range of different forms of negotiation right up to active, armed resistance. In the sixteenth and seventeenth centuries, Malabar rulers and the British largely accepted one another as trading partners and sought to conduct their business conjointly and in a mutually peaceful fashion. However, the increasing demands for monopolies, tax collections, and territorial control of the land made by the British from the mid-eighteenth century, led to conflicts which were not merely confined to trade interests and were drawn out over a considerable number of years. Which of the two parties would succeed in dominating the discourse and taking power? We can observe different actions and reactions to the British policy of monopolization in Malabar from 1790 to 1805, and it is pertinent here to highlight and consider more closely the following two examples: on the one hand—at least as far as one can see from the outside—the smooth coming together of Vira Varmma of Kurumpranāṭu and the British and, on the other hand, the clash between Kēraḷa Varmma Paḷaśśi Rājā and the British, which was marked by numerous conflicts.

At the beginning of the 1790s the prospects for mutual dialogue-based negotiation in the *contact zone* of Malabar seemed relatively good for local rulers and the British. They had formed an alliance in the three Anglo–Maisūrian wars against Ṭippu Sulttān up until 1792. In return for their support, the British promised the rājās that they would be able to claim back their independence once the war was over. However, the British did not keep this promise and in the treaties of 1792 which they concluded with the Malabar rājās they instead declared that the rājās were only to hold posts as tax-collectors and administrators of the British government and that their sovereignty was to be negated. After a certain time of indecision most local rulers did actually give in to the conditions set by the British, but the previous trust in the integrity of the British diminished visibly. Thus began the 'dialogue of misunderstanding' in Malabar.[48]

The British considered the conduct of the Malabar princes to be rebellious and ungrateful—the aim for which the British strove was to bring 'civilization'. The single characteristic of the Malabar rulers and local magnates that is mentioned again and again by British source texts is their desire for freedom. In one of his letters about the Nambyars of Iruvaḻinäṭu,[49] W.G. Farmer, the supravisor in Malabar at the time, describes and complains about this very trait: the rājās insisted that they collect taxes themselves and without supervision by employees of the EIC, something which Farmer regarded as impudent. Ultimately, Farmer withdrew to the position where the Nambyars were allowed to nominate one of their own as a contact person for the EIC, via whom Farmer would be able to agree on tax collection in Iruvaḻinäṭu.[50] The self-governance which had been practised up until that point and which was now demanded by the Nambyars of Iruvaḻinäṭu, and also by the rājās and other local élite groups in Malabar, caused the British to comment that the Malabaris were a people with a particularly pronounced sense of freedom. Already by the early years of the nineteenth century, a British employee of the EIC known as Harvey, one of Baber's successors, had made the following notes about the rājās and the population of Malabar:

> I have only to observe, that the peculiar habits and prejudices of the People, and a spirit of independence, which, the difficult nature of the country, and their mode of Life, has enabled them in a greater comparative degree, to preserve, renders them less subservient to authority, and always prone to avail of the advantages they possess, to relieve themselves from the operation of such measures, as materially affect their Interests, and which they conceive to be burthensome, or have been unaccustomed to sustain.[51]

William Bentinck, the president in Fort St. George, commented in a similar vein:

> Independence of Mind, seems to be the Characteristic which distinguishes them from our other Subjects. [...] But the independence in Malabar is said to be generally diffused, through the Minds of the people. They are described of being extremely sensible of good treatment and impatient of oppression. To entertain a high respect for Courts of Judicature and to be extremely attracted to their Old Customs.[52]

This description could probably have been applied to the majority of the people of Malabar. With their sense of independence, the Malabar rājās were opposed to the British view that they must submit to the new government. As a result, the processes of negotiation between the local people and the rising colonial power proved to be fractious. Local rulers and the élite used different ways to counter the challenge posed by the British. It was not just in the *contact zone* of Malabar but in other regions of India as well where contact between local rulers and the EIC gave cause for conflict and regularly culminated in armed combat.[53]

The focus of attention can now be turned to the situation in Malabar in the last years of the eighteenth century and the early years of the nineteenth century. How were negotiations running between Vira Varmma of Kurumpranāṭu and the British? Vira Varmma appeared to be open-minded about the proposed British treaties: he was one of the first rājās to sign them. The considerable advantage which Vira Varmma had enjoyed since the very first treaties with the British was that he was not only appointed as tax-collector for Kurumpranāṭu but also for Kōṭṭayaṃ. In this way he was indirectly given the opportunity of gaining another Malabar principality under his sovereignty—albeit a sovereignty which was restricted by the British.[54] The advantage in this for the British was that Vira Varmma played the part of a cooperative middleman for them, who was able to furnish them with insider information and recommendations. Thereby they gained access to details of internal affairs in Malabar, which would otherwise have remained hidden from them, and which helped them to move closer towards achieving their goal of full control over Malabar. A casual assessment of the situation may indicate that Vira Varmma and the employees of the EIC were both pulling in the same direction, particularly over tax collection in Kurumpranāṭu and Kōṭṭayaṃ. Nevertheless, one can safely assume that they were motivated by differing goals. As a *little king* Vira Varmma used his alliance with the British in order to extend the area over which he exerted power, but it is still unclear as to whether he wished to advance to the status of *great king*. For their part, however, the British strove for an absolute sovereignty in Malabar which fitted the European-British model, and they used the aforementioned treaties in order to attain this objective.

Paḷaśśi Rājā's relationship with the British was formed in an entirely different way: he called upon the British to acknowledge his sovereignty in Kōṭṭayaṃ, to take into account the needs of the local people, and to grant him rule over the part of Vayanāṭu to which he had been entitled for ages. Paḷaśśi Rājā's insistence on his rights of sovereignty inevitably led to conflict with the British, who were intent on stabilizing their economic dominance in Malabar; their chief concern lay in the creation of a monopoly over the pepper trade through territorial supremacy and in improvements to administration—

'their euphemism for raising the level of taxation'.[55] The British demand for sovereignty in Malabar and Paḷaśśi Rājā's defence of his sovereignty in Kōṭṭayaṃ and Vāyanāṭu collided at this point. This *clash of sovereignty* came to an end only in 1805,when the British resolved the question of sovereignty through military force and the elimination of Paḷaśśi Rājā.

The question arises here, as to how the British came by the notion that they would claim sovereignty in a country which was foreign to them. Were there motives other than purely economic ones behind their actions? The British claim to sovereignty in Malabar can be attributed partly to their view that they were the 'better', superior civilization.[56] At the same time they also claimed to have a moral obligation, on account of their superiority, to liberate the Indian people from the rule of 'despots'. This self-image gave the British the idea that their law was superior to other systems, and that it was therefore quite unnecessary to take any notice of the existing law of a conquered country.[57] The British were only able to justify their claim to rule, and its associated sovereignty, by preserving the difference between colonizers and colonized, by stressing the 'savageness' of the colonized. There is also the fact that no codified, written system of law existed in Malabar, something which relegated the position of Malabar society to one of the lower levels within the 'ranking' of societies. Furthermore, their own 'gentlemanliness' gave the British ample reason to justify their imperialistic behaviour to themselves.[58]

One of the inherent problems within the *contact zones* was the question of mutual comprehension: which language should be used for communication? The British, at least in the early years of their rule, were reliant on translators. The majority of them were actually loyal to their employers, but they also knew how to turn translation to their advantage.[59] After all, Thomas H. Baber was apparently the only EIC employee in Malabar to have some command of Malayāḷaṃ. Since the beginning of the nineteenth century, in order for them to carry out their business without translators, EIC employees were said to have learned the language of the country.[60] Actually, however, British employees were frequently more reliant on local officials than they wanted to be. The level of dependency varied according to the particular relationship of power between the British and the local élite. The centre of British power in Malabar was situated on the coast, particularly in towns such as Talaśśēri and Kōḻikkōṭu, where colonial discourse dominated proceedings. On the outskirts, however, for example in the jungles of Vāyanāṭu, indigenous models of conduct controlled the processes of negotiation.

The British strategy in seeking to reach their economic and political objectives through negotiations with the different rājās was characterized by a policy of playing off the individual rulers, and also local authorities such as nātuvālis and dēśavālis, against one another.[61] They hoped that this would maximize tax collection in Malabar. The question remains as to why the British strove for direct control of Malabar and why they did not establish an indirect rule[62] with the rājās of Malabar as they did in Tiruvitāṃkūr, for example. This form of rule could have resulted from the process of negotiation in the *contact zone* Malabar. Christopher Bayly gives the following reasons as to why the British did not establish indirect rule in Malabar at the end of the eighteenth century: the British felt that the Māppiḷḷa traders were treated unfairly by Hindu rulers, and this explains why they did not wish the Hindu rājās to rule. Moreover, the British would have feared an endangerment of the pepper trade and the political stability of the country if the Hindu rājās had received indirect rule.[63] The first counter to this line of argument is that the British themselves had great problems with the rājās, since not all of them were prepared to accept the conditions that the British laid down. Therefore, the setting up of an indirect rule would have been fraught with uncertainties. Secondly, the Māppiḷḷa merchants and the rulers cooperated with one another; this is exemplified in the case of Paḷaśśi Rājā and the trader Covakkāran Mūssa, who resided in Talaśśēri, both of whom were united in their opposition to the British. Thus it would not be correct to explain why the British chose to establish direct rule in Malabar by just referring to any concern of the British over a possibly disadvantaged section of the local population. Considerably more probable are motivations such as the British desire to control the pepper and spice trade, as well as to control the numerous rājās in the fragmented country of Malabar. The multitude of rājās and the resulting fragmentation of power proved to be a hindrance to building a counterbalance against the British. Therefore the rājās were not able to oppose the British with sufficient might and unity, and it was this which encouraged and allowed the British to pursue a policy of playing them against one another.

Even where the British did strive to achieve a uniform policy towards the rājās, individual cases led to disputes within their own camp. As was the case in other parts, EIC employees in Malabar often had differing ideas as to how policy should be pursued in India. The discrepancies arose partly between the Board of Control in London and the government in Bombay, and partly between the government in Bombay and the commissioners in Malabar. In certain cases the commissioners did not consider themselves obliged to carry out orders from Bombay if these did not concur with their own interests, or if the commissioners felt that they, as *men on the spot*, had a clearer view of things and were thus in a better position to make the right decisions over any emergent problems.[64] This was the case, for example, in 1796, when the commissioners ignored clear instructions from Bombay to hand over the palace treasures and compensation payment to Palaṡṡi Rājā.[65] Nevertheless, the British were united about one thing: the extension of their power. The objective as such was never in question, only the means by which it might be attained.

As one of the few British people who strove for constructive and non-violent negotiations between the colonial power and the local rulers, Alexander Dow sought to understand the rājās to some extent, and even to cooperate with them where possible. He was the official with the closest contact to the Malabar rājās during the mid-1790s. Contrary to his colleague James Stevens, who felt that any progress towards the goal of British supremacy in northern Malabar could only be achieved by force,[66] Dow rejected the violent subjugation of the rājās: 'Colonel Dow [...] was fully convinced that tranquillity could not, for a long time at least, be re-established in that district by compulsive measures. The example of Tippo's administration, he judged a sufficient warning to the Company's Government [...].'[67]

Yet his opinion on how the rājās in Malabar should conduct themselves remained unambiguous. The rājās were to submit to British orders, for he too was convinced of the legitimacy of British trade. When it came to seizing power Dow was simply prepared to use more moderate methods than some of his colleagues.

In a letter to John Smee, one of the commissioners in Malabar, Palaṡṡi Rājā expresses his disappointment over the British policy pursued during the 1790s. The following quotation underlines how the very basis of Palaṡṡi Rājā's preconceptions about the British and the basis of British demands were frequently at odds with one another:

> It was thought and universally believed, that whenever the whole of the Kingdoms of Malabar should devolve in peaceful Sovereignty to the Honourable the English East India Company, the religious and charitable Instructions of the Gods and Brahmins, the honours, dignities and rights of the Rajahs, and the prosperity, ancient Customs and Laws of all the People and Inhabitants of them, would be happily insured and maintained, but to the Evil destiny of all the Rajahs of Malabar, we owe our disappointment in seeing all our Concerns and most Sacred institutions neglected none of them regarded as they hitherto have been.[68]

Palaṡṡi Rājā laid great emphasis on the upkeep of religious and social obligations, as he did by the rights of a ruler and by the welfare of the local people.[69] In the years during which the British strove to obtain rule over Malabar he observed that the British did not comply with these obligations. His disappointment over this discovery, and his fear that perhaps the worst was yet to come, led him to mount opposition to British policy, which culminated in active resistance from 1796.

From Smee's reply to Paḷaśśi Rājā's letter it is noticeable that the British had different ideas as to how Malabar was to be governed, and that they tried to justify and legitimize their interventions into the existing administrative and social structure by their own 'just way' of government.

The uprightness of the Honourable Company's Government, and the invariable anxiety it has always and forever will manifest to protect and support their Subjects of every denomination, together with the expense and attention the Government bestow towards preserving the various Sacred religious Instructions of India in their ancient purity, are such well authenticated circumstances as to excite universal administration and revenue of the natives throughout the Company's Dominions to their ruling authority, and which from its *wise and just exercise diffuses a degree of happiness and prosperity unknown* to the ancestors of those who have long lived under a British Government. If you consult your own reason and inform your mind of the *very happy and flourishing State of the Company's Dominions in general,* you will no doubt be persuaded of the truth of this relation, while you will no longer wonder at the Circar's Resumption of the entire administration of its Sovereignty in Malabar *for the good of the natives.*[70]

Smee does give brief mention to the traditional right of the rājās and he also cites the consideration which the British would give the religious make-up of India, and yet he only employs this argument in order to make the actual British assumption of government in Malabar more palatable to Paḷaśśi Rājā. By 1797, with the consent of the other commissioners, Smee had already drawn up a draft for the administrative reform in Malabar in which he called for the continual weakening of the rājās' influence at the same time as an increase in the commissioners' influence.[71] He emphasizes the 'wise and just' practice of EIC employees as his argument in favour of the British takeover of government, which for him not only justified the EIC's rule and sovereignty simply in Malabar but in the whole of India. The commander of the British troops in Malabar, James Stevenson, expresses a similar sentiment when he writes of the principles of 'justice and moderation, which distinguish the British Government in India',[72] freeing the country from the 'despots', who ruled the country with 'selfishness' and 'an authority that they constantly abuse'.[73] Another line of argument used by EIC employees was that the country had been prosperous since the EIC took power, and that this had not been the case in a very long time. The opinions expressed here by British administrative and military officials correlate with the aforementioned British view that Indian society was in a state of administrative and moral collapse, which could only be stopped and turned around for the better by British intervention.

The cited example from Palaśśi Rājā's correspondence with different EIC employees is symptomatic of a dialogue that neither goes into what the other party has expressed nor tries to comprehend their intellectual world, but regards one's own stance as the correct one and attempts to show one's own actions in the best light. As far as the British were concerned Stevenson, among others, assured the rājās of a 'determined spirit of opposition'.[74] It is clear that this would inevitably lead to a hardening of the lines of discussion between the two parties.

The British felt that what they considered to be the chaotic and alien situation in Malabar was caused by the institutions within Malabar society and by the rights of the Nāyars, which were associated with these 'unsatisfactory' institutions. As a result the British cut back their rights as far as was possible and in some cases even did away with them completely. The EIC issued a ban of considerable consequence which outlawed the carrying of weapons—they pointed out that since their army was now protecting the country it was no longer necessary to carry weapons.[75] Furthermore, over the course of the nineteenth century, the matrilineal system of the Nāyars was also replaced systematically by the patrilineal British concept. Besides, the legal powers enjoyed by Nāyars and rājās were given into British administrative institutions, for instance courts. Seen in this respect, the establishment of European law proved to be the ruin of former structures of society, as a different language, mode of conduct, and idea of morality were employed in daily life.[76]

The Talaśśēri Rēkhakaḷ originate from the *contact zone*, and can be classed in the category of auto-ethnographic literature in accordance with Pratt's concept. This collection of correspondence and governmental reports was supposed to make it easier for the British to rule because it provided them with information about indigenous affairs and relations. Once the British were established, however, they no longer required the Talaśśēri Rēkhakaḷ, ceased using it and gave it away to a German missionary.[77]

A 'dialogue of misunderstanding' was the order of the day within the *contact zone* of Malabar. From outside there may appear to have been some unity between Vira Varmma of Kurumpranāṭu and the British when it came to short-term administrative and tax measures, but each had very different motivations for signing the treaties. Peaceful negotiation over sovereignty in Kōṭṭayaṃ between Palaśśi Rājā and the British ended in failure, which initially led to verbal hostility and later turned into active resistance on the part of Palaśśi Rājā and the population of Kōṭṭayaṃ and Vāyanāṭu. The dialogue between Palaśśi Rājā and the British came to an abrupt end in 1805, with the death of the rājā. By the end of the negotiation process there was scarcely any more mutual understanding between EIC employees and the local population in Kōṭṭayaṃ and Vāyanāṭu than there had been at its beginning. The ultimately violent enforcement of British administration shook the very foundations of the pre-colonial social structures in Malabar. British dominance was accompanied by the emergence of state structures that were intended to be as similar as possible to those found in Europe and which disregarded local structures. This was exemplified by the suppression of traditional matrilineal succession as well as the legitimation basis of the nobility and the adoption of the European patrilineal system, thus changing the whole social construction.

The Aftermath in the Nineteenth Century

Once the British had rounded off their areas of rule in India, something which had been completed by the mid-nineteenth century, they concentrated all their efforts on consolidating their power. The British conviction that a stable government could only emerge from the foundations of a state which was essentially European and bureaucratic by nature resulted in fundamental changes being made to the social, political, and economic structure of India. This conviction dictated their perspective on India, making them look at the different representations of India and its population, through their own uniform cultural filter.[78]

But there were contradictions in their own representations—they had treated their subjects conveniently, focussing on aspects that suited their purposes and interpreting them so that they created the impression that they wanted. In fact they had taken the same characters and depicted them as heroes and villains to suit the political needs of the time. And those political needs dictated that those rulers who were 'more likely' to cooperate were made 'moral' (or at least semimoral) and those that weren't were demonized. Even the dead were not immune, especially as they were unlikely to need recreation. Memories were selective and convenient, serving the end of proving that in the final reckoning British rule was the only stable, and therefore the preferable, mode of government of otherwise unstable Indians.[79]

Thus the British took great pains to consolidate their rule by seeking to establish an administration that was based on the Western model. At the same time, they provided for themselves economic frameworks with the most profitable parameters, and endeavoured to occupy the position of supremacy in society. An outline of one example of British intervention in the field of educational policy and one in the field of law will now follow by way of further clarification.

One measure taken to help stabilize British control over the country was the introduction, in the nineteenth century, of British training centres for the Indian Civil Service. By training Indian officials in the British way they hoped to integrate different elements of the Indian social structure, something which at the same time intended to bind competing loyalties and transform them into a sense of loyalty towards the British.[80] Educational policy in Malabar was also geared towards the memorandum of Thomas B. Macaulay (1800–59), which called explicitly for the anglicization of the school system.[81] Thus the British held the dominant, colonial discourse in the sphere of social policy as well.

An example of the restructuring of society, specific to Malabar, is the changes made to the rights of the taravāṭus, and thereby to the matrilineal system of the Nāyars. There was a gradual redefinition of the taravāṭu; the definition of a taravāṭu at the end of the nineteenth century was entirely different from the same concept a hundred years previously. The essential features of the 'original' taravāṭu—the equality of each of its members in votes over questions of property, the freedom of female members in their choice of spouse and in the founding of new *tāvaḷi*s—were replaced by the primacy of the oldest male member, who, according to English law, was the only person who was legally entitled to make decisions about the property of the taravāṭu. According to the new law women were only entitled to occupy the position of *kāraṇavarti* or to open tāvaḷis, new branches of a taravāṭu, under certain exceptional circumstances which were laid down in the law. The woman's role was reduced to that of the decorous housewife and mother who stayed at home, similar to the norm in Victorian England. Indeed, during the course of the nineteenth century, there was a sequence of legal proceedings in which women fought for their rights, yet the outcome was usually in favour of the kāraṇavar, whom the British defined as the oldest male member of a taravāṭu. A system that was open to unconventional solutions had thus been turned into a codified, fixed legal system which restricted the legal rights of women in the relationship between husband and wife and in the sphere of authority and property.[82] British judges of the nineteenth century, such as Herbert Wigram, stressed that they were following the ancient Malabar law. However, they overlooked the fact that their love of textual foundations generally led them to regard brahminical customs as the normative standard for all Hindu groups. British judges in Malabar had been treating the common rights of the patrilineal Nampūtiri Brahmins as the legal norm since the 1850s. Thus a patrilineal codification of the matrilineal customs was established.[83] From the 1870s the taravāṭu was defined as an inseparable unit within which all rights over matters of property and management were assumed by the appointed head, who in law was defined as the oldest male member, comparable to a Roman *paterfamilias*.[84] This example shows that the British assumed in the first place that their rule over India would be best guaranteed if they preserved indigenous practices—and yet they frequently overlooked the diversity of customs and simply applied a custom which they regarded as Indian to the entire country. In this vein Bernard Cohn speaks of the British having appointed themselves curators of what they saw as an enlarged outdoor museum.[85]

The influence of colonial policy is still evident in Malabar to the present day. It is most noticeable in the antiquated state of agricultural development and industrialization in Kēraḷa. In addition to more recent problems, such as the strong position of trade unions, there are deeper underlying reasons which go back to the time of colonial rule: the preference for *janmakāran*s as landowners; Maisūrian and British tax structures, which hindered the development of an agricultural market and an increase in productivity; and the restriction of the *kāṇakkāran*s' rights.[86] The imports to Malabar which the British promoted also had a negative effect on the local commercial sector. For example, the import of large quantities of machine-spun cotton decimated sales of the handwoven cotton products sold by smaller firms in Malabar. This in turn had the effect that those working in agriculture could not be motivated to move into the commercial sector.[87] There is hardly any industry in Kēraḷa even today. A major setback for Malabar, as for Bengal and Madras, was the priority of private trading interests of different colonial administrators and merchants, who exploited their power in order to satisfy their own commercial goals. This 'policy' can be regarded as one of the main reasons for the social upheavals as well as the economic decline in nineteenth-century Malabar.[88]

The restructuring of Indian society gave rise to a series of conflicts which erupted in various rebellions in Malabar—above all by the Māppiḷḷas—throughout the nineteenth century.[89] These rebellions reached their peak in 1921/2.[90] As always, the causes of the rebellions continue to be areas of heated debate in the academic field. One line of argument cites the objective and reason for the rebellions as the improvement to the economically impoverished situation of the farmers, who were for the most part Māppiḷḷas. Another line claims that religious motives were the chief cause of the rebellions. It is likely that the truth lies somewhere between the two; often economic factors were veiled in religious ones. Not as well known as the Māppiḷḷa rebellions is the 1812 rebellion by the Kuṟiccyars and Kuṟumbars in Vāyanāṭu, which had its roots in the suppression of these ethnic groups after the defeat of Paḷaśśi Rājā in 1805. The British had forbidden the Kuṟiccyars and Kuṟumbars to trade with merchants on the coast, had imposed excessive tax demands, and their troops had regularly plundered the Kuṟiccyars and Kuṟumbars since the beginning of the nineteenth century. All of these measures created the potential for unrest among these groups. Ultimately, at the beginning of 1812, a rebellion broke out against the British under the leadership of a few Nāyars, but the colonial power succeeded in inflicting defeat upon them within a few months.[91]

Although the British were able to crush each and every rebellion by people of Malabar, they could eliminate neither their desire for freedom nor their ability to remember. The memory of the various rebellions of the eighteenth and nineteenth centuries is still very much alive today. The difficulty, however, lies in the classification of Paḻaśśi Rājā within the ranks of 'freedom fighters', which has been made by a host of historians who glorify him as being a patriot and the very first 'freedom fighter' and who stylize the rebellions under his leadership as 'national revolts against the British authority'.[92]

He [Paḻaśśi Rājā] was the last great Kēraḷa patriot who sacrificed his all for the freedom of his people and refused till the last to bend his knee to the foreigner. [...] but his true greatness lay in the unquenching love of liberty which made him choose the wilds of Kēraḷa, while his brother princes accepted the decision of the Company to annex their little states.[93]

A. Sreedhara Menon believes that Paḻaśśi Rājā deserves a special place 'in the gallery of great freedom fighters of India' on account of his 'heroic' fights for a 'just cause'.[94] Further glorification of Paḻaśśi Rājā has been made through the founding of a museum in his memory in Mānantavāṭi, which was opened in 1995, as well as through the erection of a memorial stone in the 1990s at the presumed site of his death in the jungle of Vāyanāṭu, near the border with Karnataka.

In my opinion, a clear distinction must be made between the 'freedom fighters' of the twentieth century, who fought for India's independence, and the rebels of the eighteenth and nineteenth centuries. The former took up arms against an established colonial power, which had already exerted a strong influence over them, whereas the latter sought to prevent a foreign power from successfully gaining control over their country. One has to bear in mind that these are different categories of action: during the eighteenth and nineteenth centuries the indigenous structures were still intact—at least to a certain extent—out of which the motivation to resist emerged, whereas in the twentieth century, so-called 'Western' motives like self-determination began to play a role.

NOTES

1. Inden also establishes an order for India in medieval times, in which a number of *little kings* existed alongside a *king of kings*. Inden, Ronald, 'Hierarchies of Kings in Medieval India', in: T.N. Madan (ed.), *Way of Life: King, Householder, Renouncer: Essays in Honour of Louis Dumont*, New Delhi, 1982, pp. 99–125, p. 99.

2. Freeman, J. Richardson, 'Purity and Violence: Sacred Power in the Teyyam Worship of Malabar', unpublished dissertation, University of Pennsylvania, 1991, p. 715.

3. Cf. PR 12 A.

4. Gough observes: 'She is the fount of human, animal, and crop fertility, of war, smallpox, and other pestilence—in short, of good and evil happenings which may strike all men, regardless of their caste.' Gough, Kathleen, 'Pālakkara: Social and Religious Change in Central Kerala', in: K. Ishwaran (ed.) , *Change and Continuity in India's Villages*, New York and London, 1970, pp. 129–64, p. 132.

5. Shulman, David D., *The King and the Clown in South Indian Myth and Poetry*, Princeton, 1985, p. 22. Navarātri was royal in nature and had an integrating effect on the state, as noted for Vijayanagara and also Ramnad. Stein, Burton, 'Mahanavami: Medieval and Modern Kingly Ritual in South India', in: Bardwell L. Smith (ed.), *Essays on Gupta Culture*, Delhi, 1983, pp. 67–90, p. 85.

6. Cf. Heitzman, James, *Gifts of Power: Lordship in an Early Indian State*, Delhi, 1997, p. 125.

7. Letter by the senior rājā to the commissioners on 20 Karkkaṭakaṃ 973/ 1.8.1798, in SPP, OIOC P/380/72.

8. Cf. Nair, C.G., *Malabar Series*, p. 18f.: Kēraḷa Varmma had shrines to Bhagavati erected in two districts in Vāyanāṭu, which were still in use in 1911. Cf. also Bayly, *Saints*, p. 56.

9. Cf. *Reports of a Joint Commission*, § CCCI; Extracts from the Minute of Sir John Shore, in: K.N. Panikkar, *Peasant Protests*, p. 12. Cf. also Nair, C.G., *Malabar Series*, p. 23.

10. Cf. Rajayyan, 'Kerala Varmma', p. 553. A detailed description of the consultation of the oracle can be found in Rajayyan, *South Indian Rebellion*, pp. 175–8.

11. Cf. PR 23 A&B.

12. *Reports of a Joint Commission*, § CCII.

13. PR 57B.

14. PR 16B.

15. Kautilya, *Arthashastra*, Book I, Chapter 19, verse 34.

16 Cf. PR 45 A&B.

17. Cf. Chapter Five. Cf. also Kane, Pandurang Vaman, *History of Dharmaśāstra (Ancient and Medieaval Religious and Civil Law in India)*, 5 vols., Poona, 1962–1975 (Government Oriental Series Class B, No. 6), vol. 3, pp. 17–19.

18. Cf. Chapter Three.

19. Sircar, Dipesh Chandra, *Indian Epigraphy*, Delhi, 1965, reprint Delhi, 1996, p. 269f; Narayanan, M.G.S., *Perumals of Kerala: Political and Social Conditions of Kerala under the Cera Perumals of Makotai (c. 800–1124 A.D.)*, Calicut, 1996, p. 34f. The founding of Koḷḷaṃ took place after liberation by the Pāṇḍyas.

20. Logan, *Malabar*, vol. 1, pp. 243, 245.

21. Cf. Berkemer, *Little Kingdoms*, p. 157.

22. Roughly translated as the highest ruler, king of kings.

23. Cf. Narayanan, *Perumals*, p. 79.

24. Claus argues against Hocart, that the socio-religious complex of southern

India is not derived from Aryan sacrificial rituals, but is the result of an unmistakably southern Indian development. Claus, Peter. 'Oral Traditions, Royal Cults and Materials for a Reconsideration of the Caste System in South India', *JIF* 1,1 (1978), pp. 1–25, p. 18.

25. Menon, K.P.P., *History of Kerala*, vol. 1, p. 263.

26. 'As descent and succession within the kin-group was organized on matrilineal principles, it was important for these taravads to trace their lineage from an ancestress', Arunima, G., 'A Vindication of the Rights of Women: Families and Legal Change in Nineteenth-Century Malabar', in: Michael R. Anderson and Sumit Guha (eds.), *Changing Concepts of Rights and Justice in South Asia*, Delhi et al., 1998 (SOAS Studies on South Asia Understandings and Perspectives Series), pp. 114–39, p. 117

27. Research trip to London, Tamilnāṭu, and Kēraḷa, 1998.

28. Summary of events from 1796–8 in Kōṭṭayaṃ (miscellaneous), in HMS, OIOC H/607. The Santals do not have a *vaṃśāvali* tradition either.

29. Cf. Claus, 'Oral Traditions', p. 1.

30. MLTMT Ms. 77, No. 9, in: Mahalingam, *Mackenzie Manuscripts*, vol. 1, p. 298.

31. MLTMT Ms. 75, No. 4, in: Mahalingam, *Mackenzie Manuscripts*, vol. 1, p. 282.

32. MLTMT Ms. 75, No. 6, in: Mahalingam, *Mackenzie Manuscripts*, vol. 1, p. 285.

33. MLTMT Ms. 75, No. 11, in: Mahalingam, *Mackenzie Manuscripts*, vol. 1, p. 288.

34. MLTMT Ms. 75, No. 8, in: Mahalingam, *Mackenzie Manuscripts*, vol. 1, p. 287.

35. MLTMT Ms. 75, No. 7, in: Mahalingam, *Mackenzie Manuscripts*, vol. 1, p. 285.

36. MLTMT Ms. 75, No. 10, in: Mahalingam, *Mackenzie Manuscripts*, vol. 1, p. 288.

37. MLTMT Ms. 75, No. 12, in: Mahaligam, *Mackenzie Manuscripts*, vol. 1, p. 289.

38. MLTMT Ms. 75, No. 13, in: Mahaligam, *Mackenzie Manuscripts*, vol. 1, p. 289.

39. MLTMT Ms. 75, No. 4, in: Mahaligam, *Mackenzie Manuscripts*, vol. 1, p. 283.

40. Narayana Rao, Velcheru, Shulman, David and Subrahmanyam, Sanjay, *Symbols of Substance: Court and State in Nayaka Period Tamilnadu*, Delhi, 1992, pp. 7, 12, 38. See also Subrahmanyam, Sanjay and Shulman, David, 'The Men Who Would Be King? The Politics of Expansion in Early Seventeenth-Century Northern Tamilnadu', *MAS* 24, 2 (1990), pp. 225–48.

41. Fuller, Christopher J., *Servants of the Goddess: The Priests of a South Indian Temple*, Delhi, 1991, pp. 109, 111

42. Cf. Fleckstein, Josef, 'Karl der Große', in: *Lexikon des Mittelalters*, vol. 5, München and Zürich, 1991, pp. 955–9; Becher, Matthias, *Karl der Große*, München, 1999, p. 118.

43. Cf. Deyell and Frykenberg, 'Sovereignty', p. 21.

44. The Cēramān Perumāḷ dynasty is still recalled by the Malayalees even today, which serves as an indicator that the *little kings* had fixed themselves firmly to the intellectual world and patterns of conduct of that dynasty even almost 900 years after its end.

45. Nair reports that the local population still speak of Palaśśi Rājā in complete reverence as *Śaktan rājā* (mighty king) even a hundred years after his death. Nair, C.G., *Malabar Series*, p. 40.

46. Contrarily, Arunima assumes that the state in Malabar was a 'nebulous and

unstable entity', which was dependent on external influences. Arunima, 'Multiple Meanings', p. 288. Frykenberg describes the state as a box-within-a-box principle. Frykenberg, Robert E., 'Traditional Processes of Power in South India: A historical Analysis of Local influence', *IESHR* 1 (1963), pp. 122–42, S. 137. In my opinion, however, this principle is too rigid. I feel that the exchange between the levels and the opportunity to change levels depending on the situation is more significant, i.e. the flexibility of the system. This is not expressed in the box principle.

47. Menon, D.M., 'Houses by the Sea'.

48. Even in active forms of dialogue, in the majority of cases this could be seen as a dialogue of the deaf and dumb, characterized at the least by misunderstandings. Heesterman, Johannes C., *The Inner Conflict of Tradition: Essays in Indian Ritual, Kingship and Society,* Chicago, 1985, p. 159.

49. The Nambyars appear to have fallen under the protection of Paḷaśśi Rājā: Letter by Jonathan Duncan dated 2.3.1797, in BC, OIOC F/4/32; Letter by James Stevens to John Spencer dated 6.3.1800, in HMS, OIOC H/471.

50. Cf. Letter by W.G. Farmer to A.W. Handley dated 30.12.1794, in BRP, OIOC P/366/16.

51. Letter by Harvey to the Principal Collector of Malabar dated 27.6.1803, in MCR 2158 (KSA).

52. Report by William Bentinck dated 22.4.1804, in MCR 2384 (KSA).

53. Peter J. Marshall considers that the British only resolved emerging conflicts in the eighteenth century through peaceful means because they did not have sufficient military power. Indeed the government in London did not plan any enlargement of their areas in India by the EIC, but the lack of ways by which they could control *the men on the spot* meant that development became geared towards expansion. Marshall, 'British Expansion', p. 32., 42f. According to Förster the *men on the spot* inflicted great damage to the EIC at the turn of the eighteenth century. Cf. Förster, *Die mächtigen Diener*, p. 73.

54. A brief recapitulation: Vira Varmma had originally grown up in the Kōṭṭayam dynasty but had been adopted into the family of the Kurumpranāṭu Rājās, because they (presumably) did not have any successors who were fit to govern. As a result, however, he was excluded from the line of succession in Kōṭṭayam. Yet he was able to pass over the old conventions in the treaties he made with the British once they had arrived and changed the situation in Malabar accordingly—this was thanks to the loyalty which he had shown towards the British.

55. Ingram, *Empire-Building*, p. 9.

56. The English 'mission' to the world, which they wanted to liberate from its chains, became the transfer of their parliamentary system characterized by freedom and progress. Dewey, Clive, 'Images of the Village Community: A Study in Anglo-Indian Ideology', *MAS* 6 (1972), pp. 291–328, p. 300.

57. Cf. Mann, Michael, *Flottenbau und Forstbetrieb in Indien 1794–1823*, Stuttgart, 1995 (Beiträge zur Südasienforschung 175), p. 56.

58. Cf. Skaria, Ajay, 'Shades of Wildness: Tribe, Caste, and Gender in Western India', *JAS* 56, 3–4 (1997), pp. 726–45, pp. 727, 731, 735.

59. Cf. Bayly, *Empire and Information*, p. 6; Irschick, *Dialogue*, p. 73f.

60. Report by H. Clephane, J.W. Wye dated 11.2.1801, in OIOC F/4/118.

61. Cf. Letter by John Spencer and Alexander Walker dated 26.6.1801 and 13.7.1801, in BC, OIOC F/4/121.

62. Indirect Rule can be defined as 'indirect control over other peoples through indigenous political structures.' The term was actually only in use from the twentieth century; in previous centuries, terms like 'British' paramountcy, and similar expressions were employed. Fisher, Michael H., *Indirect Rule in India: Residents and the Residency System* 1764–1858, New Delhi et al., 1998, pp. 2,4; R. Jeffrey studies the situation in Tiruvitāṃkūr from 1800–1947. Jeffrey, Robin, 'The Politics of "Indirect rule": Type of Relationship among Rulers, Ministers and Residents in a "Native State"', *Journal of Commonwealth and Comparative Studies* 13 (1975), pp. 261–81.

63. Bayly, C., *Indian Society*, p. 63.

64. Marshall describes the individual actions of the EIC employees who were *on the spot* as sub-imperialist. Cf. Marshall, 'British Expansion', p. 37. Contrary to the men in the London government, Förster characterizes the men in the Bombay government, who had relatively large scope for action on account of distanced paths of communication, as *men on the spot*. Cf. Förster, *Die mächtigen Diener*, p. 35f. The local officials in Malabar should also be understood as *men on the spot* in this context.

65. Cf. Chapter Five; Cf. Logan, *Malabar*, vol. 1, p. 512f.

66. In a letter to Bombay, Stevens asked as a precaution for troops to be deployed to Kōṭṭyaṃ, Ciṟakkal, and Kaṭattanāṭu in case he felt that the taxes were not being accepted. He also stressed that the government of the EIC was considerably better for the local people than that of the rājās. Letter by James Stevens to Bombay dated 20.8.1794, in SPP, OIOC P/E/7. For more information on the use of violence, cf. Letter by James Stevens to Bombay dated 20.12.1974, quoted in Nightingale, *Trade and Empire*, p. 111.

67. For information on Dow's opinions: Summary of events in Kōṭṭayaṃ from 1796–1798 (miscellaneous), in HMS, OIC H/607.

68. Letter by Paḻaśśi Rājā to John Smee dated 20 Tulaṃ 975/3.11.1799, in BRP, OIOC P/36/25.

69. Cf. Chapter Six.

70. Letter by John Smee to Paḻaśśi Rājā dated 9.11.1799, in BRP, OIOC P/366/25. Italics mine.

71. Letter by the commissioners to John Spencer dated 19.11.1797, in MCR 1712 (TNSA).

72. Proclamation by James Stevenson dated 16.2.1802, in BC, OIOC F/4/126.

73. Letter by Scott to Alexander Walker dated 31.5.1797, Walker of 13.5.1797, Walker of Bowland Papers, NILS MS 13004.

74. Letter by James Stevenson to John Spencer dated 23.6.1801, in BC, OIOC F/4/121.

75. Proclamation by James Stevenson dated 16.2.1802, in BC, OIOC F/4/126.

76. Cf. Mayer, *Land and Society*, p. 32f.

77. See below: Chapter One.

78. Cf. Cohn, 'The Past', p. 20. Metcalf argues that the British constructed an 'Indian' reality. Metcalf, *Ideologies*, p. 15.

79. Chatterjee, *Representations*, p. 194.

80. Cf. Frykenberg, Robert E., 'Modern Education in South India, 1784–1854: Its Roots and its Role as a Vehicle of Integration under Company Raj', *The American Historical Review* 91, 1 (1986), pp. 37–65, p. 40.

81. The Macaulay Minute can be found in Sharp, H., *Selections from Educational Records, 1789–1839*, Calcutta, 1920, pp. 107–17. Cf. also Trevelyan, George Otto, *The Life and Letters of Lord Macaulay*, 4 vols., Leipzig, 1876, vol. 2, pp. 181–4; Jones, Kenneth, *Socio-religious Reform Movements in British India*, Cambridge, 1989 (The New Cambridge History of India III, I); Nair, P.R. Gopinathan, 'Education and Socio-economic Change in Kerala, 1793–1947', *Social Scientist* 4,8 (1976), pp. 28–43, p. 31.

82. Arunima, 'Vindication', p. 114. For information on the development of policies regarding the matrilineal system in the twentieth century cf. Jeffrey, Robin, *Politics, Women and Well-Being: How Kerala Became a 'Model'*, Basingstoke and London, 1992.

83. Cf. Arunima, 'Vindication', pp. 115, 120.

84. Report by Judge Strange dated 25.9.1852, quoted in Moore, L., *Malabar Law*, p. 95.

85. Cohn, 'The Past', pp. 17, 35.

86. Cf. Prakash, B.A., 'Agricultural Backwardness of Malabar During the Colonial Period: An Analysis of Economic Causes', *Social Scientist* 16, 6–7 (1988), pp. 51–76, pp. 56–9. Cf. also the essay by Shea, Thomas W., 'Barriers to Economic Development in Traditional Societies: Malabar, a Case Study', *Journal of Economic History* 19 (1959), pp. 504–22 and Kurup, K.K.N., 'British Colonial Policy in Malabar and its Impact on Land Settlement and Revenue (1792–1800)', *Journal of Kerala Studies* 3, 3–4 (1976), pp. 421–30. N. Ram takes a Marxist approach, which regards the backwardness in southern India as the reason why the British were able to conquer the land and exploit it economically. Ram, N., 'Impact of Early Colonisation on Economy of South India', *Social Scientist* 1,4 (1972), pp. 47–65.

87. Cf. Prakash, B.A., 'Agricultural Backwardness', p. 64.

88. Cf. Nightingale, *Trade and Empire*, p. 241.

89. Susan Bayly believes that colonial culture created the military conflict between individual groups. Bayly, S., *Saints*, p. 460. Nightingale attributes the unrest in Malabar in the nineteenth century to the policies of the EIC. EIC merchants carried out their trade in order to make themselves money, and in doing so they ruined domestic economic resources. Nightingale, *Trade and Empire*, p. 241.

90. For more details see Panikkar, K.N., *Against Lord and State: Religion and Peasant Uprisings in Malabar 1836–1921*, Delhi et al., 1992; Radhakrishan, P., *Peasant Struggles, Land Reforms and Social Change: Malabar 1836–1982*, New Delhi, Newbury Park and London, 1989. For more detailed information on the

rebellions of 1921/22, cf. Menon, M. Gangadhara, *Malabar Rebellion (1921–22)*, Allahabad, 1989.

91. Cf. Ravindran, *Institutions*, pp. 158, 175; idem, 'The Kurichya Rebellion of 1812', *Journal of Kerala Studies* 3, 3–4 (1976), pp. 533–44, pp. 533, 543.

92. Panikkar, K.M., *History of Kerala*, p. 394. Cf. also Chopra et al., *History*, pp. 121–3. Rajendran, *Establishment*, p. 258.

93. Panikkar, K.M., *History of Kerala*, p. 421.

94. Menon, A. Sreedhara, *Kerala and Freedom Struggle*, Kottayam, 1997, p. 31.

Six

Transformation of Rule in Malabar

A key issue that has been addressed in this study is the construction and legitimation of rule by local élites in Malabar. In this context we examined whether Kēraḷa Varmma Paḻaśśi Rājā of Kōṭṭayaṃ can be considered a *little king*. It was possible to determine that Paḻaśśi Rājā did legitimize his rule by ritual actions—as was customary for a *little king*—and that he expressed this legitimation, for example, by extending patronage to temples and by performing ceremonies in the Bhagavati temples. As a *little king* he drew the sacral legitimation of his rule from his observance of religious ceremonies, to which he did his utmost to adhere and to which he assigned far greater importance than any meeting with British employees of the EIC. This network of temples, which extended over his entire kingdom, played a significant part in Paḻaśśi Rājā's legitimation of rule. In addition to the religious and ritual function which the temples of Kōṭṭayaṃ and Vāyanāṭu provided, they also formed a network that was of considerable importance for Paḻaśśi Rājā's rule. When he was forced to retreat into the jungle areas of his kingdom during the conflicts with the British, the network of temples played an even more important role by serving as places of refuge and sanctuaries for the *rājā*. The acceptance of Paḻaśśi Rājā as a *little king* was expressed symbolically by the gifts that the local people bestowed upon him at festivals, such as Oṇaṃ and Viṣu. It was on account of the sacral legitimation that Paḻaśśi Rājā occupied the central position in the *little kingdom* of Kōṭṭayaṃ. Paḻaśśi Rājā for his part was also aware of his duties towards the local people; the *rājādharma* can be seen as a source for his motivation.

Paḻaśśi Rājā and the other Malabar rulers formed a circle of *little kings* and a *little queen*. They shared in the superior *great king*'s sovereignty and legitimized their rule through political and ritual acts. The relationships of the *little kings* in Malabar to one another were characterized, on the one hand, by blood relations, and by constantly changing alliances on the other. New allies were sought according to the spread of political power, and since this was formed by the socio-economic, political and cultural set-up, the whole system was in constant flux. Yet it is important to bear in mind that the *little kings* of Malabar did not consider themselves to be rebels in this context as the Europeans generally believed them to be; instead they saw themselves as legitimate rulers who were constantly redefining their sovereignty through the *modus vivendi* of battle. The *little kings* occupied a position at the meso-level of the political structure; below them on the micro-level were local functionaries, such as *nāṭuvāḻis* and *dēśavāḻis*, who in turn considered themselves to be *little kings* in relation to their subordinates. In the *kūṭṭaṃs*, the local authorities formed an opposite pole to the *little kings* which meant that the *little kings'* position could not assume an absolute status. The relationship between the respective partners on the micro-, meso-, and macro-level was determined by status, as well as by the ritual, political, and social conditions that constituted the milieu of the parties concerned. What was distinctive about the construction of rule in Malabar was the fact that since the ninth century, the *great king* at the macro-level had been a 'virtual' *great king*. We have set up the hypothesis that under the *marumakkattāyaṃ*, the matrilineal system of inheritance, it was impossible for any *mahārājā* to succeed in securing an actual, i.e. non-virtual, kingdom for his family over a period of many generations. The logical conclusion is that only a 'virtual' *great king* could have existed on a long-term basis in a matrilineal society. The 'virtual' *great king* constitutes a fresh element for the model of the *little kingdom*. The advantages of a 'virtual' *great king* were significant: *little kings* could legitimize their power according to the redistributive system over a body above them, i.e. a *great king*, on the one hand, but could act relatively independent of a superior king on the other hand. At the same time, the idea of a 'virtual' *great king* united the *little kings* and *queen* of Malabar under a joint head; at least for certain decisions they had to meet and consult each other. Amongst themselves, the *little kings* and *queen* had to negotiate, and the *little king* also had to consult his elders, thereby acting in the 'internal' *contact zone* Malabar.

The process of negotiation, which takes place when different cultures—in this case those of Britain and Malabar—come into contact with each other was another point this study has focused on. Various models can be used to describe the phenomenon of conflicting cultures. The negotiation of new values within the spheres of politics, society and the economy has in this study been projected as such an encounter, occurring in the field that was termed the *contact zone*. In the case of Malabar the forms of interaction ranged from peaceful negotiation right through to military conflict. The analysis of the various constructions of rule and exercise of rule is key to deeper understanding of events in Malabar. It emerges that a relationship of tension had prevailed for many years between the Europeans and local forces and that this was reflected in both of their respective patterns of negotiation: dialogic negotiation between the Malabar rājās and the British broke down with the treaties of 1792, since the Malabar rulers no longer trusted in the integrity of the British once they had failed to keep to their promise of 1790, under which the rājās were to be returned their independence. Thus arose a 'dialogue of misunderstanding'. In addition to the question of freedom, which constituted one of the main areas of conflict between colonial officials and the indigenous élite, the differing perceptions of rule stood in the way of any constructive dialogue. The rājās were not prepared to simply give the British their sovereignty and the self-government which they themselves had been practising, whilst at the same time the British were adamant in their claim for sovereignty. The problematic nature of this clash of contrary views lay in the inherent incompatibility of the firmly established Eurocentric concept of state with the complex Indian structure. The differing constructions of rule turned the conflicts between colonizers and colonized in Malabar into an (almost) never-ending story.

During the process of establishing their rule in the Malabar province, the British stuck to the Western concept of state which assumed a rigidly defined system that embraced political, economic, and administrative structures. The dominance of the colonial discourse, which in the case of Malabar prevailed chiefly in the coastal towns of Kōḻikkōṭu and Talaśśēri, was especially evident in British attempts to establish an efficient administrative apparatus. Here the British used the implementation of suitable procedures and an attitude of supremacy as legitimation for their rule. However, since it was the indigenous discourse that dominated in the periphery, the Indian concept of state continued to be used as the model for rule in these parts. Whilst the king occupied the highest position within this Indian model he was nevertheless placed within and not outside of the state structure, something which could also be said for Paḻaśśi Rājā's position in Kōṭṭayaṃ. A king was always linked to other elements of the state by a structure of relationships which was itself defined by political and ritual actions. Institutionalized committees and advisors served as a corrective to the rājā. A key factor within this model was the concept of the *rājādharma*, which assumes an interdependency between society and king and which goes to ensure that social order is maintained. The British were not integrated into this political and ritual system. Therefore, in spite of their military superiority, Paḻaśśi Rājā was unable to accept that the British might have greater authority than he when it came to matters of state. At the same time he considered himself to be a *little king* vis-à-vis the *great king* Cēramān Perumāḷ, which rendered impossible any acceptance of Ṭippu Sulttān or a European power as a supreme authority. These factors acted as a catalyst for the ensuing conflict, which ultimately led to Paḻaśśi Rājā's resistance. I described the resulting conflict between the British colonial power and local rulers as a *clash of sovereignty*. This should be understood as a clash which took place within the *contact zone* of Malabar between the acutal, proportional sovereignty exercised by local rulers and the abstract claim to sovereignty made by the EIC.

When it came to conflicts with the British the Malabar rulers often reacted very differently . The behaviour of two rājās who adopted completely opposite stances towards the British was given as an example of this phenomenon: Kēraḷa Varmma Paḻaśśi Rājā of Kōṭṭayaṃ, who opted in favour of resistance, and Vira Varmma of Kurumpranāṭu, who found it more favourable to cooperate with the British. We can at least make assumptions about the motivation for each respective decision. Vira Varmma of Kurumpranāṭu appeared to hope that contact with the British would bring gains either to his finances or to his political power. He did not become embroiled in open conflict when faced with difficult situations, but instead preferred to use middlemen and to scheme against others, Paḻaśśi Rājā included. Once Paḻaśśi Rājā had mounted resistance to the British, Vira Varmma was then able to label himself the 'good' rājā, eager to agree with the British—at least on matters of tax and administration. He did this in spite of the fact that in any joint agreement his reasons and those of the British were at odds with one another. At the other end of the spectrum Paḻaśśi Rājā clung firmly to his sovereignty in Kōṭṭayaṃ and Vāyanāṭu, and insisted that he be allowed to perform his duties towards the local people. After a lengthy and ultimately unsuccessful attempt to assert his position with the British through diplomatic means he concluded that it was impossible to negotiate with the British on equal terms. It is also noteworthy that the British were quite successful in their tactic of playing the two rājās off against one another. The cause for dispute in Kōṭṭayaṃ ultimately erupted into armed clashes between Paḻaśśi Rājā with his followers and the British. This marked the failure of all attempts at peaceful negotiation between Paḻaśśi Rājā and the British. The example of these two rājās shows just how varied a form the processes of negotiation between the British and the local people actually took. Returning to the debate of 'orientalism' versus 'dialogue' mentioned at the beginning of this study, we have to conclude that not only parts but always the full spectrum of forms and consequences of negotiations with each other has to be taken into consideration. Playing off the different attitudes against each other is not necessarily helpful in the analysis. As we could show, however, the use of *contact zone* as an analytical framework enables us to investigate different perspectives and come to new conclusions. Here we land up in Malabar again, a striking example for exchange and change over centuries.

As previously illustrated, contact between the colonial power and the Malabar people resulted in fundamental changes at the socio-political and economic level: the transformation into a patrilineal, hierarchical social system had altered broad sections of Malabar society by the end of the nineteenth century. Above all, the British failed to recognize the function of the *tar̲avāṭus* within Malabar society and, whilst not destroying them in a physical sense, they did destroy them as political, social, and ritual units. The British can be seen as responsible for the increasing abrogation of the pre-colonial Malabar state structure, which had already been weakened by Maisūrian invasions and administrative changes. They compounded this even further through their misinterpretation of the structures relating to land law in Malabar. They failed to recognize that the basis for these structures was not that of European property law, but a system in which the parties involved lived within a complex structure of social and economic relationships stipulating mutual conditions that were profitable for all sides. The crucial point about the distribution of land in Malabar was not the idea of property itself, but the political, economic and ritual functions of the *janmakāran* associated with land and represented in the distributive system by the *sthānamānaṅṅaḷ*. It was a serious mistake on the part of the British not to have recognized the closely interlinked relationships of society and economy in Malabar, and to have undone these relationships by splitting up the two areas; as was exemplified by their establishment of codified property law. In place of what had been the customary *maryyāda,* the British introduced the concept of codified law.

At the violent end of the negotiation process, i.e. the death of Paḷaśśi Rājā in 1805, there was obviously no greater level of understanding between the British and the Malabar rājās than there had been at the beginning of the dialogue. The British simply implemented European, bureaucratic ideas of a functioning administrative system in Malabar which took no account of either the indigenous social and economic structures or the pre-colonial legal and state systems. British dominance in the *contact zone* of Malabar resulted in the almost complete disappearance of pre-colonial structures over the course of the nineteenth century.

The rebellions of Kēraḷa Varmma Paḷaśśi Rājā of Kōṭṭayaṃ and his supporters had seriously endangered the British position of power in Malabar, and the British only succeeded in eradicating them through large-scale disarmament drives and the neutralization of Paḷaśśi Rājā in 1805. With the unrest over, the British were able to consolidate their rule in the province of Malabar, eliminate traditional structures to a large extent and change society according to their way of thinking. Vira Varmma of Kurumpranāṭu lost his status as a ruler and became a subject, as was clear through his cooperation with the British. Paḷaśśi Rājā's death meant that he never lost his status as a ruler, since he had never swapped his position as *little king* with that of a British subject. Consequently, he became a symbol of freedom in the mid-twentieth century for the Indian people in their struggle for independence.

Notes on Sources and Transliteration

Incomplete sources on Malabar make it difficult to form a clear impression of its political and economic structure and of the events that took place there in the eighteenth century. Many textual sources were destroyed during Maisūrian invasions in the second half of the eighteenth century.[1] The Paḻaśśi Rēkhakaḷ, part of the Talaśśēri Rēkhakaḷ, and British records provide a unique corpus of sources as to how the British established supremacy in South India. The Talaśśēri Rēkhakaḷ are a collection of administrative documents and decrees by the British administration, as well as its correspondence with the rulers of Malabar in Malayāḷaṃ between 1796 and 1800. Part of this collection, the Paḻaśśi Rēkhakaḷ, refers directly to the events surrounding the ruler of Kōṭṭayaṃ, Kēraḷa Varmma Paḻaśśi Rājā. The British provided the impetus for collating these documents to compensate for the lack of written sources in Malabar. The fact that these documents were handed over to a missionary working in Malabar suggests that they were no longer of use to the British after they had consolidated their rule.[2] The originals of the collection have been kept in the university library of Tübingen (Germany) since the end of the nineteenth century, but they only became available as a reference work when rediscovered in 1986 by Scaria Zacharia. Subsequently, he and his colleagues made the documents accessible to a wider public.[3] During my stay in India in 1995, I had the opportunity to translate a section of the Paḻassi Rēkhakaḷ documents jointly with Scaria Zacharia.[4] The manuscripts of Colin Mackenzie (1753–1821), collected by local officials in southern India on his instructions, are an additional source of Malayāḷaṃ documents, as well as Telugu and Tamiḻ documents, on Malabar.[5] Nevertheless, there are still only a small number of written texts in existence on the history of Kōṭṭayaṃ or its royal family.

Documents of the British colonial administration are located in the Tamil Nadu State Archives (TNSA), Ceṉṉai, the Kerala State Archives (KSA), Tiruvanantapuraṃ, and the Regional Archives, Koḻikkōṭu (RAK). They are mainly taken from the Malabar Collectorate Records (MCR), which provide a record of the correspondence between the various levels of British administration, of military and economic files, minutes of parliamentary sessions and recordings of interviews with local people. During my stay in India in 1998, I studied the Malabar Collectorate Records kept in the TNSA and KSA.

However, poor preservation has now rendered certain volumes of the Malabar Collectorate Records in the TNSA illegible. The RAK primarily contains documents from the British administration dating from the nineteenth century. Additional source texts, the files of the Bombay and Madras Presidency, are kept in the Oriental and India Office Collections (OIOC) at the British Library in London. The Bombay Revenue Proceedings (BRP), the Public Consultations Bombay (PCB) and parts of the Home Miscellaneous Series (HMS) are of particular pertinence to files recorded in Malabar from 1790 to 1805, and it was to their study that I devoted my stay in London in spring 1998. In summer 2000, I had the opportunity to see and work with the Walker of Bowland Papers in the National Library of Scotland in Edinburgh (NLS).

When using British source texts, one must always bear in mind that the British attitude to Malabar was marked by its desire to attain sovereignty there. The difficulty in any analysis is that the written documents usually reflect the opinion of a group, in this case the British, who happened to be the predominant power in Malabar by dint of their supremacy since the beginning of the nineteenth century. Hardly any other written records exist about historical events and the British documents only reflect a fraction of this complex reality. We largely depend on existing, written source texts. However, oral traditions, where recorded, must also be included in the research so that a more comprehensive picture of Malabar history is presented.[6] During my visit to India in 1998, I located and visited the temples in Kōṭṭayaṃ and Vāyanāṭu, which were significant to Kēraḷa Varmma Paḷaśśi Rājā's legitimation of rule, and I was able to speak with descendants of the royal family and with some prominent public figures.

A significant printed source is the Joint Commissioner's report, which constituted an overview of the historical and political situation in Malabar from 1792 to 1793. The British used this report to extract information on the land and its people, and thereby to furnish themselves with the necessary background knowledge for the establishment of their rule.[7] Also worthy of note is Buchanan's report of his travels through southern India, which can be used as a general source of information although it does necessitate consultation with alternative sources.[8] Files dating back to the eighteenth century between local rulers and the British colonial administration give a valuable insight into the political events of the time. These files were compiled in the nineteenth century by William Logan (1841–1914), who, amongst other things, was a member of the Board of Revenue in Fort St. George in Madras.[9] At the beginning of the nineteenth century, the British colonial administration in the ranks of the Madras District Gazetteers published a volume on Malabar.[10]

The British generally used the European calendar but they had to take note of the Malayāḷaṃ or Koḷḷaṃ era, starting with the year AD 825, which was common to Malabar. This calendar can also be found in British documents, often in the abbreviated form 'M.E.', particularly after the province of Malabar was taken over in 1792.[11] Kēraḷite personal names and place-names were changed to make them palatable for European tongues. Thus, it is possible to find several English names for a place or a person, and the relation between these names is often far from clear. An example is the town of Paḷaśśi, which was also known as 'Pychy', 'Peychey', and 'Paychy'. To avoid confusion, and consequent misunderstanding, I followed the conventional transcription used in Gundert's dictionary when spelling *termini technici* and people- and place-names in Malayāḷaṃ.[12] The English terms introduced into the administrative language of Malabar have been maintained as they are found in the records.

NOTES

1. MLTMT, Ms. 77, No. 9, Ms. 79, No. 7, Ms. 79, No. 10, in: Mahalingam, *Mackenzie Manuscripts,* vol, I, pp. 298, 318.

2. The missionary Hermann Gundert mentions the Talaśśēri Rēkhakaḷ for the first time in a diary entry after his visit to the administrative office of the British in Kōḷikkōṭu on 17.1.1842, Gundert, Hermann, *Tagebuch aus Malabar 1837–1859,* ed. by Albrecht Frenz, Ulm, 1983, p. 83. In 1861 he reports to have read the Talaśśēri Rēkhakaḷ and to have incorporated its lexicon into his dictionary. Letter by Hermann Gundert to the Committee of the Basel Mission in Basel dated 21.6.1861, Deutsches Literaturarchiv Marbach A: Hesse-Gundert.

3. Zacharia, Scaria (ed.), *Tuebingen University Library Malayalam Manuscript Series* (TULMMS), 5 vols., Kottayam, 1994–6.

4. This translation of parts of the Paḷaśśi Rēkhakaḷ (PR) is printed in the German version of the book.

5. Mahalingam, *Mackenzie Manuscripts.*

6. The difficulty involved in reconstructing the history of Malabar was already determined when the Archaeological Survey was written up in the nineteenth century. Sewell, Robert (ed.), *Lists of Inscriptions and Sketch of the Dynasties of Southern India,* Madras, 1884 (Archaeological Survey of Southern India 2), p. 195.

7. *Reports of a Joint Commission.*

8. Buchanan, *Journey.* Buchanan's report on southern India was primarily a political document, which was intended to serve towards the justification of Lord Wellesley's conquest of Maisūr. In addition, the inventory was also meant to help Buchanan's rise up the career ladder of the EIC. Cf. Vicziany, Marika, 'Imperialism, Botany and Statistics in Early Nineteenth-Century India: The Surveys of Francis Buchanan (1762–1829)', *MAS* 20,4 (1986), pp. 625–60.

9. Logan, *Treaties.* For information on Logan, cf. Kurup, K.K.N., *William Logan: A Study in the Agrarian Relations of Malabar,* Calicut 1981, pp. 110–18.

10. Innes and Evans, *Malabar.*

11. This era presumably goes back to the foundation of the town of Koḷḷaṃ in 825. Cf. Chapter Six.

12. Gundert, *Dictionary*, transliteration, s.p.

Appendix

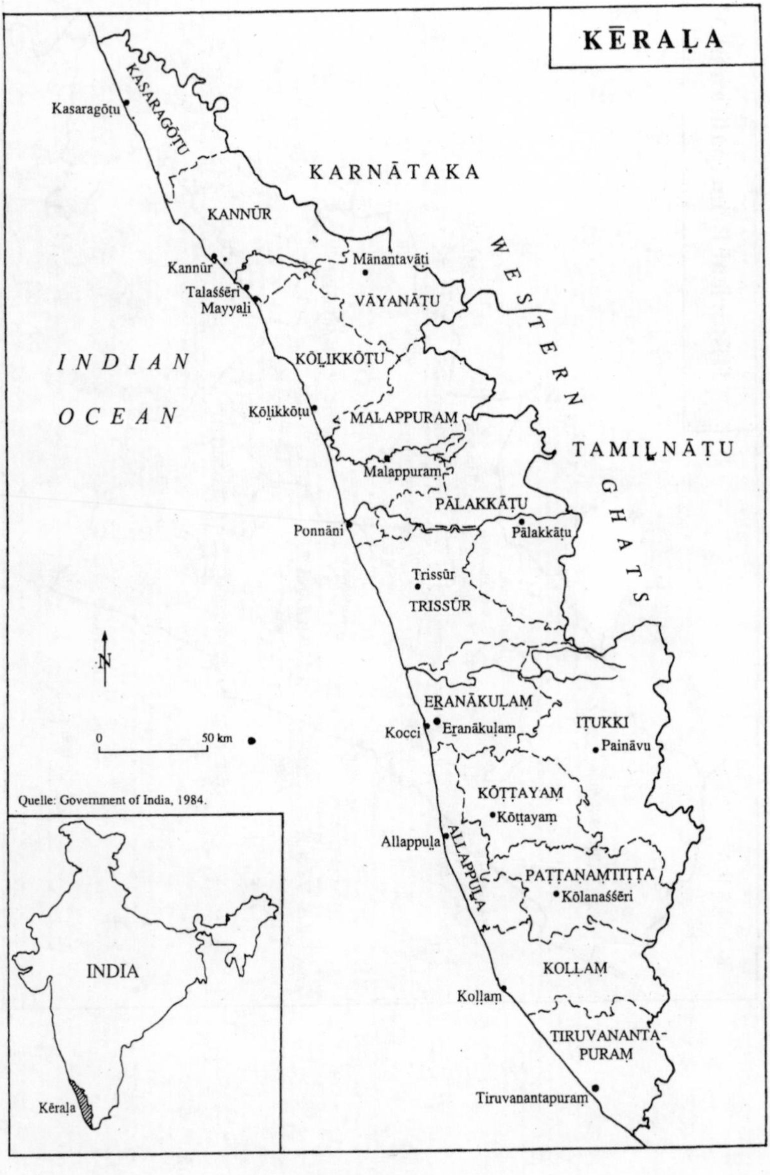

KĒRAḶA
KASARAGŌṬU
Kasaragōṭu
KARNĀTAKA
KANNŪR
Kannūr
Talaśśēri
Mayyaḻi
Mānantavāṭi
VĀYANĀṬU
WESTERN GHATS
INDIAN OCEAN
KŌḺIKKŌṬU
Kōḻikkōṭu
MALAPPURAM
Malappuram
TAMIḺNĀṬU
PĀLAKKĀṬU
Pālakkāṭu
Ponnāni
Trissūr
TRISSŪR
N
0
50 km
ERANĀKUḶAM
Kocci
Eranākuḷam
IṬUKKI
Painävu
Quelle: Government of India, 1984.
KŌṬṬAYAM
Kōṭṭayam
Allappuḻa
ALLAPPUḺA
PAṬṬANAMTIṬṬA
Kōlanaśśēri
INDIA
KOḺḺAM
Kollam
TIRUVANANTA-PURAM
Tiruvanantapuram
Kēraḷa

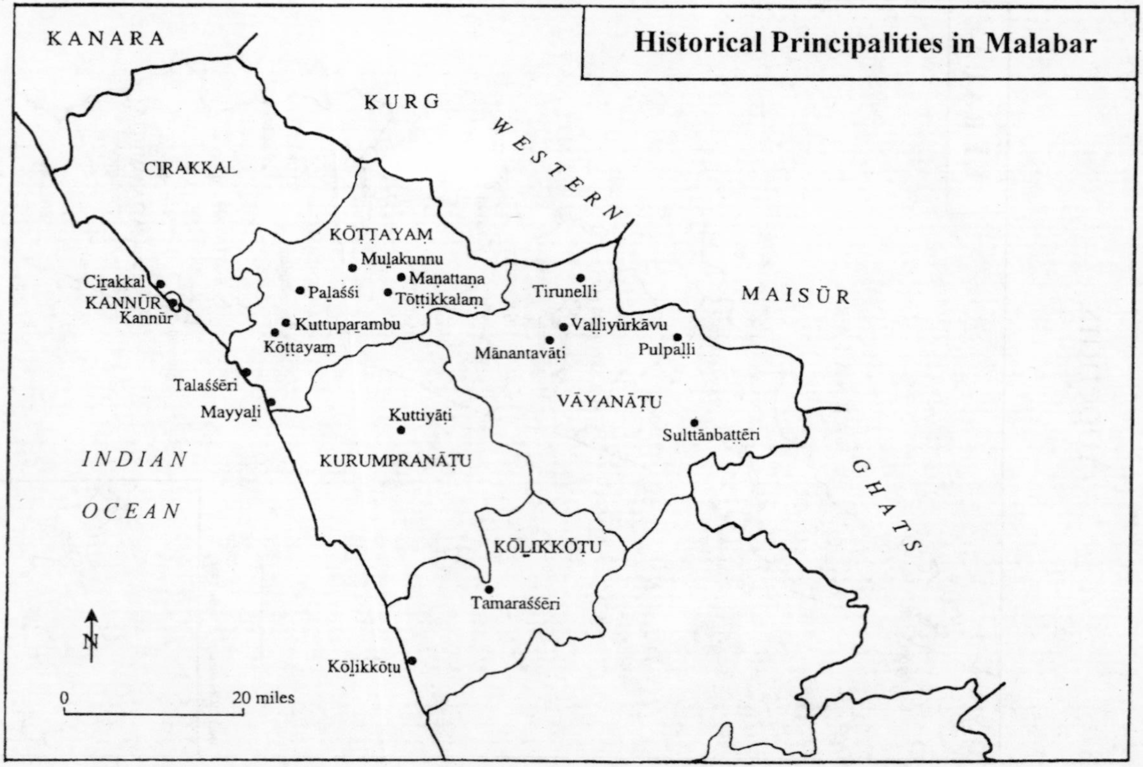
Historical Principalities in Malabar
KANARA
KURG
WESTERN
GHATS
MAISŪR
CIRAKKAL
KŌṬṬAYAM
Muḻakunnu
Maṇattaṇa
Paḻaśśi
Tōṭṭikkalam
Cirakkal
KANNŪR
Kannūr
Kuttuparambu
Kōṭṭayam
Tirunelli
Valliyūrkāvu
Mānantavāṭi
Pulpaḷḷi
Talaśśēri
Mayyaḻi
VĀYANĀṬU
Kuttiyāṭi
Sulttānbattēri
INDIAN
OCEAN
KURUMPRANĀṬU
KŌḺIKKŌṬU
Tamaraśśēri
Kōḻikkōṭu
N
0
20 miles

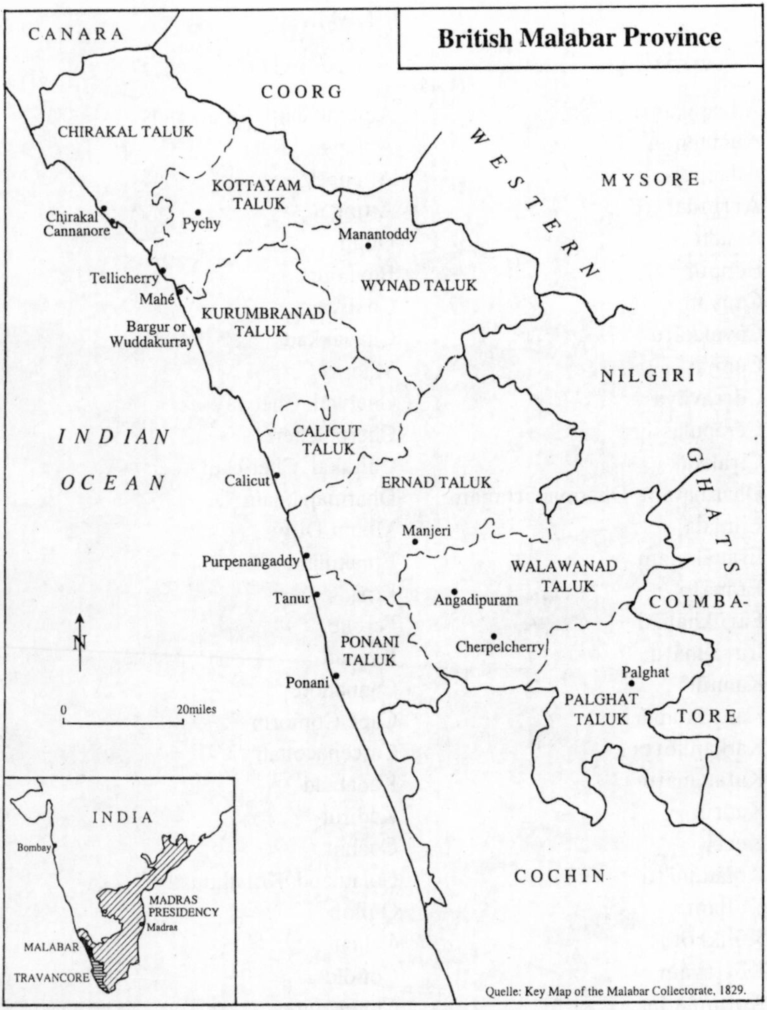
British Malabar Province
CANARA
COORG
MYSORE
WESTERN
GHATS
NILGIRI
COIMBA-
TORE
COCHIN
INDIAN
OCEAN
CHIRAKAL TALUK
KOTTAYAM TALUK
WYNAD TALUK
KURUMBRANAD TALUK
CALICUT TALUK
ERNAD TALUK
WALAWANAD TALUK
PONANI TALUK
PALGHAT TALUK
Chirakal
Cannanore
Pychy
Manantoddy
Tellicherry
Mahé
Bargur or
Wuddakurray
Calicut
Manjeri
Purpenangaddy
Tanur
Angadipuram
Cherpelcherry
Ponani
Palghat
N
0
20miles
INDIA
Bombay
MADRAS
PRESIDENCY
Madras
MALABAR
TRAVANCORE
Quelle: Key Map of the Malabar Collectorate, 1829.

Place names

Indian spelling	*English spelling*
Añcarakaṇṭi	Anjerakandy, Anjarkandy
Añcuteṇṇa	Anjengo
Allappuḻa	Alleppey
Āṟṟiṅṅal	Attingal
Avadh	Oudh
Bēppūr	Beypore
Caliyaṃ	Chaliyam
Cāvakkāṭu	Chavakkad
Ceṉṉai	Madras
Cēṟṟavāya	Chetwai, Chetway
Cērapuḻaśśēri	Cherpelcherry
Ciṟakkal	Chirakal, Chericaul
Dharmaṭaṃ, Dharmapaṭṭaṇaṃ	Dharmapatnam
Ēḻimala	Mount Dilly
Eṟanākuḷaṃ	Ernakulam
Ēṟanāṭu	Ernad
Fāṟūkhābād	Feroke
Iruvaḻināṭu	Irvenad
Kannūr	Cannanore
Kanyākumārī	Cape Comorin
Karkaṇkōṭṭa	Carcenacottah
Kaṭattanāṭu	Kadatnad
Katirūr	Kadirur
Kocci	Cochin
Kōlattunāṭu	Colatnaud, Kolathunad
Koḷḷaṃ	Quilon
Kōḻikkōṭu	Calicut
Kōṭṭayaṃ	Cotiote
Koṭuṅṅalūr	Cranganore
Kōyamputtūr	Coimbatore
Kurumpranāṭu	Kurumbranad, Kurumbanad
Kūtiyāti	Kuttyadi, Kuttiyadi
Kūttupaṟambu	Cuttaparamba
Maisūr	Mysore
Mānantavāṭi	Manantoddy, Manantody
Maṇattaṇa	Mantana, Montana
Maṅgalūr	Mangalore

Mayyaḻi	Mahé
Muḻakunnu	Molencoon
Mumbai	Bombay
Nīlagiri	Nilgiri
Niṭṭūr	Nettur
Pāḻakkāṭu	Palghat
Palaśśi	Pychy, Peychy, Peychey, Paychy, Pyechy
Pantalāyini Koḷḷaṃ	Quilondy
Ponnāni	Ponani
Pulpaḷḷi	Pulpally
Putukkōṭṭai	Poodoocottah
Raṇṭutaṟa	Randaterra, Randatarra
Śrīraṅgapaṭṭaṇaṃ	Seringapatam
Sulttānbaṭṭēri	Sultan's Battery, Gunapuddyvattom
Talaśśēri	Tellicherry
Talippaṟambu	Taliparamba
Tamaraśśēri	Tamarcherry
Tamiḻnāṭu	Tamilnad
Taṅṅaśśēri	Tangacherry
Tanūr	Tanur
Tiṇṭukkal	Dindigul
Tirunāvāya	Tirunavayi
Tirunelli	Tirunelly
Tiruraṅṅāṭi	Tirurangady
Tiruvanantapuraṃ	Trivandrum
Tiruvaṅṅāṭu	Tiruvengad
Tiruvitāṃkūr	Travancore
Tōṭṭikkaḷaṃ	Thodicalum
Vāyanāṭu	Wynad
Veṅkatakōṭṭa	Venkatacottah
Veṭṭattanāṭu	Bettatnad, Vettatnad

Glossary

Abbreviations: Arab. = Arabic, Hind. = Hindi, Mal. = Malayāḷaṃ, Pers. = Persian, Port. = Portuguese, Skt. = Sanskrit, Tam. = Tamiḻ

adhikāri	official, magistrate (Mal.)
ādiparaśakti	in the Śaivasiddhānta, the female original force from which the world emerged (Skt.)
amātya	minister (Skt.)
aṃśadhikāri	official, magistrate of an *aṃśaṃ* (Mal.)
aṃśaṃ	administrative unit (an order above *dēśaṃ*) (Mal.)
aṅṅāṭi	weekly bazaar, market square (Mal.)
arji (arzee)	petition (Arab.)
cartaz	Portuguese permit to trade in the Indian Ocean (Port.)
cuṅkaṃ	customs route (Mal.)
daṇḍa	power, control; symbol of legal authority; army (Skt.)
dēśaṃ	village (Mal.)
dēśavāḻi	village head, local authority, responsible for the *nāṭuvāḻi* (Mal.)
dēvasvaṃ	temple property (Mal.)
dēvī	goddess (Skt.)
dharma	ritual and social norms (Skt.)
durga	fortress, fort (Skt.)
durgga	goddess Durgā (Mal.)
fanam	gold or silver coins of differing value (Arab.)
harkārā	messenger (Hind.)
hōbali, hōvali	department within a district (Mal.)
hūn	Maisūrian gold coins
iṭaṅṅaḻi	liquid measure on the west coast: 1 *iṭaṅṅali* equals 1.8696 litres (Mal.)
jamā	collection, capital (Hind.)
jamābandī	tax assessment, state revenue of land (ownership) (Hind.)
janapada	territory (Skt.)

janmakāran	landowner, proprietor (Mal.)
janmakāran-kuṭiyān-saṃpradāyan	owner-tenant /proprietor-farmer regulations (Mal.)
janmaṃ	birth, hereditary ownership (Skt.)
janmaṃ-kāṅaṃ-maryyāda	ownership-leasehold regulations (Mal.)
janmanīr	to part with all rights of a landowner (Mal.)
janmappaṇayaṃ	mortgage on a property, on which an additional advance is given; the owner relinquishes his rights (Mal.)
kaḷari	school for the art of fencing (Mal.)
kaḷarippayaṟṟu	the art of fencing (Mal.)
kaḷaripparadēvata	deity of the art of fencing (Mal.)
kāṇakkāran	leaseholder (Mal.)
kāṇaṃ	purchase of a *janmaṃ*, mortgage, credit (Mal.)
kaṇṭi	unit of measure for weight, between 500lb and 560lb (Mal.)
kānūṅgo	registrar (Pers.)
kāraṇavar	(male) head of the family, dignitary directly after the head administrators of a temple (Mal.)
kāraṇavarti	(female) head of the family (Mal.)
kāyal	lagoon (Mal.)
kāyar	rope made from coconut fibre (Mal.)
kāvu	shrine (Mal.)
kōvilakaṃ	branch of the royal family (Mal.)
kośa	treasure, treasure chamber (Skt.)
kuladaivaṃ	protective deity (Mal.)
kuḻikkāṇaṃ	rent for the cultivation of jungle land (Mal.)
kuṭiyān	inhabitants, leaseholders (as opposed to the *janmakāran*) (Mal.)
kūṭṭaṃ	assembly, court (Mal.)
lakh	numeral for 100,000
mahārājā	great king (Skt.)
mahārājādhirājā	king of kings (Skt.)
makkattāyaṃ	inheritance by the son (Mal.)
marumakkattāyaṃ	inheritance by the sister's son (Mal.)
maryyāda	social custom (Mal.)
mitra	ally (Skt.)
nāṭu	district (Mal.)
nāṭuvāḻi	head of a *nāṭu*, who led approximately 100 Nāyars (Mal.)

nāṭṭukūṭṭaṃ	a *nāṭu* assembly (Mal.)
navarātri	nine-day festival in reverence of the goddess Durgga (Skt.)
nazrānā	charge (Hind.; of Pers. origin, derived from Arab.)
nīrmutal	property (Mal.)
oṭi	a piece of land; also *uṭa*; proportional right to land (Mal.)
oṭṭikuṃ purameyullakāṅaṃ	mortgage on a piece of land and a house (Mal.)
ɔṭṭipuraṃ	abbreviation of *oṭṭikuṃ purameyullakāṅaṃ* (Mal.)
pāḷaiyakkārar	local ruler (Tam.)
paṟa	liquid measure: 1 *paṟa* equals 10 *iṭaṅṅaḷis*, i.e. 18.696 litres (Mal.)
pārapatti	Mal. lower-level administrative official (Mal.)
pāṭṭaṃkār	leaseholder (Mal.)
pāṭṭaṃ	lease (Mal.)
prakṛti	nature, original matter (Skt.)
pratihāra	gatekeeper (Skt.)
rājā	king (Skt.)
rājādharma	king's ethics, canon of duty for a king (Skt.)
rāṣṭrakūṭa	regent of the empire (Skt.)
ṣāmanta	original title of a Nāyar, a caste name in Kēraḷa from approx. 18th century. Neighbouring prince in inter-state areas.
sepoy	English for Pers. *sipāhī*; local soldier recruited by the British
seristtadār	administrative official (Hind.)
sthānamānaṅṅaḷ	honours, legal titles (Mal.)
sulttānṭōṭu	sultan's canal (Mal.)
svāmi	master (Skt.)
tahsildār	head tax official (Hind.)
talavāra	bailiff (Skt.)
tālūkka	Urdu *tālluqā*: administrative unit
taṟa	administrative unit (Mal.)
taṟakūṭṭaṃ	*taṟa* assembly (Mal.)
taṟavāṭu	family unit forming a household and unit of land ownership (Mal.)
tāvaḻi	collateral of the branch of a family unit (*taṟavāṭu*), ownership of this branch (Mal.)

tukri	division, district (Hind.)
tukridār	overseer of division or district (Hind.)
vērumpāṭṭaṃ	simple lease (Mal.)
zamīndār	landowner; pays his taxes directly to the government (Pers.)

Bibliography

Sources

Oriental and India Office Collections (OIOC), British Library, London

Board's Collection (BC): Shelf-mark (Year)

F/4/9 (1796)	F/4/32 (1796/7)	F/4/33 (1797/8)
F/4/34 (1798/9)	F/4/38 (1798/9)	F/4/62 (1799/1800)
F/4/68 (1799/1800)	F/4/90 (1801/02)	F/4/117 (1800)
F/4/118 (1800)	F/4/119 (1800)	F/4/120 (1800)
F/4/121 (1801)	F/4/126 (1802/03)	F/4/154 (1803/04)
F/4/156 (1803/04)	F/4/191 (1806/7)	F/4/199 (1807/08)
F/4/239 (1808/9)		

Home Miscellaneous Series (HMS): Shelf-mark

H/458	H/461	H/471	H/607

Military Department Records (MDR), 1708–1957

L/MIL/17/3/511 (*History of the Madras Army*, 5 vols., Madras 1883.)

Proceedings

Political and Secret Department (SPP): Shelf-mark (Year)

P/E/6 (1792)	P/E/7 (1794)	P/E/8 (1795)
P/E/9 (1796)	P/E/10 (1796)	P/380/68 (1798)
P/380/69 (1798)	P/380/70 (1798)	P/380/72 (1798)
P/381/2 (1799)	P/381/3 (1799)	

Public Consultations Bombay (PCB): Shelf-mark (Year)

P/342/25 (1796)	P/342/26 (1796)

Bombay Revenue Proceedings (BRP): Shelf-mark (Year)

P/366/15 (1793)	P/366/16 (1794)	P/366/18 (1798)
P/366/19 (1796)	P/366/25 (1799)	

Tamil Nadu State Archives (TNSA), Ceṉṉai

Malabar Collectorate Records (MCR): Volume number (same as the shelf-mark)

1697	1712	1715	1716	1722	1723	1725	1729
1731	1733	1734	1735	1787	2540	2546	

Kerala State Archives (KSA), Tiruvanantapuraṃ

Malabar Collectorate Records (MCR): Volume number (same as the shelf-mark)

2158	2160	2235	2309	2384	2385	2559

National Library of Scotland, Edinburgh

Walker of Bowland Papers

13602 13604 13605 13608 13609 13611 13612

Archives of the Basel Mission, Basel

Hermann Gundert's account of his travels to the committee of the Basel Mission, regional files C-1.

Deutsches Literaturarchiv, Marbach

Letter from Hermann Gundert to his parents of 18.11.1838, A: Hesse-Gundert.

Letter from Hermann Gundert to the committee of the Basel Mission in Basel of 21.6.1861, A: Hesse-Gundert.

Published Source Texts

Aitchison, C.U., *A Collection of Treaties, Engagements and Sanads Relating to India and Neighbouring Countries* (Revised and Continued up to 1929), 14 vols., Calcutta, 5th edn., 1929–32.

Baden-Powell, B.H., *The Land-Systems of British India: Being a Manual of the Land-Tenures and of the Systems of Land-Revenue Administration Prevalent in the Several Provinces*, 3 vols., Oxford, 1892, reprint Delhi, 1988.

Barbosa, Duarte, *An Account of the Countries Bordering on the Indian Ocean and Their Inhabitants*, Translated from the Portuguese, 2 vols., reprint New Delhi and Madras, 1989.

Benson, C. and Majoribanks, N.E., *A Statistical Atlas of the Madras Presidency*, Madras, 1908.

British India Analyzed: The Provincial and Revenue Establishments of Tippoo Sultaun and of Mahomedan and British Conquerors in Hindostan, 3 vols., London 1793, reprint New Delhi, 1988.

Buchanan, Francis, *A Journey from Madras through the Countries of Mysore, Canara and Malabar, Performed under the Orders of the Most Noble the Marquis Wellesley, Governor General of India, etc.*, 3 vols., London 1807.

Census of India 1961, vol. 7: Kerala, part 6 H: Village Survey Monographs Tribal Areas, Trivandrum and Kottayam, 1974.

Census of India 1961, Kerala State, Distict Census Handbook 1, Cannanore, s.l., 1965.

Clementson, P., *A Report on Revenue and Other Matters Connected with Malabar: Dated 31st December 1838*, Calicut, 1914.

Devimahatmyam (Glory of the Divine Mother), trans. by Swami Jagadiswarananda, Madras s.a.

Gundert, Hermann, *Tagebuch aus Malabar 1837–1859*, ed. by Albrecht Frenz, Ulm, 1983.

Innes, C.A. and Evans, F.B., *Malabar and Anjengo*, Madras, 1908 (Madras District Gazetteers).

Kautilya, *The Arthashastra*, ed. by L.N. Rangarajan, New Delhi, 1992.

Khirmani, Mir Hussein Ali Khan, *The History of Hydur Naik, Otherwise Styled Shums Ul Moolk, Ameer Ud Dowla, Nawaub Hydur Ali Khan Bahadoor, Hydur Jung, Nawaub of the Karnatic Balaghaut*, trans. by W. Miles, London, 1842.

———, *History of Tipu Sultan: Being a Continuation of the Neshani Hyduri*, s.l. 1864, reprint New Delhi, 1986.

Logan, William, *A Collection of Treaties, Engagements and Other Papers of Importance Relating to British Affairs in Malabar*, s.l., 2nd edn., 1891, reprint New Delhi and Madras, 1989.

Mahalingam, T.V. (ed.), *Mackenzie Manuscripts: Summaries of the Historical Manuscripts of the Mackenzie Collection*, 2 vols., Madras, 1972.

Periyapurāṇam, trans. by T.N. Ramachandran, Thanjavur, 1995.

Ravenstein, E.G. (trans. and ed.), *A Journal of the First Voyage of Vasco da Gama 1497–1499*, London 1898, reprint New Delhi and Madras, 1995.

Reports of a Joint Commission from Bengal and Bombay, Appointed to Inspect into the State and Condition of the Province of Malabar, in the Years 1792 and 1793. With the Regulations thereon Established for the Administration of that Province, 3 vols., Bombay n.d., reprint: 2 vols., Madras, 1862.

Sewell, Robert, *Lists of the Antiquarian Remains in the Presidency of Madras*, vol. 1, s.l. 1882, reprint Delhi and Varanasi s.a. (Archaeological Survey of Southern India 7).

——— (ed.), *Lists of Inscriptions and Sketch of the Dynasties of Southern India*, Madras, 1884 (Archaeological Survey of Southern India 2).

Sharp, H., *Selections from Educational Records, 1789–1839*, Calcutta, 1920.

Spencer, J., Smee, J., and Walker, A., *A Report on the Administration of Malabar: Dated 28th July 1801*, Calicut, 1910.

Strachey, J., *Report on the Northern Division of Malabar. Dated 7th March 1801*, Calicut, 1908.

The Śatapatha-Brāhmaṇa, According to the Text of the Madhyandina School, transl. by Julius Eggeling, part 1, Oxford 1882, reprint Delhi, 1963 (Sacred Books of the East 12).

Wilson, H.H., *The Mackenzie Collection: A Descriptive Catalogue of the Oriental Manuscripts, and Other Articles Illustrative of the Literature, History, Statistics and Antiquities of the South of India; Collected by the Late Lieut. Col. Colin Mackenzie, Surveyor General of India*, Madras, 2nd edn., 1882.

Yule, Henry and Cordier, Henri, *The Book of Ser Marco Polo*, 2 vols., Paris, 3rd edn., 1903, reprint New Delhi, 1993.

Zacharia, Scaria (ed.), *Tuebingen University Library Malayalam Manuscript Series* (TULMMS), 5 vols., Kottayam, 1994–6.

Secondary Literature

Abdurahiman, A.P., 'Macleod's Paimash and the Malabar Rebellion of 1803', *Journal of Kerala Studies* 4,1 (1977), pp. 65–71.

Aiyappan, A., *Report on the Socio-Economic Conditions of the Aboriginal Tribes of the Province of Madras*, Madras, 1948.

Appadurai, Arjun, 'Kings, Sects and Temples in South India, 1350–1700 A.D.', *IESHR* 14,1 (1977), pp. 47–73.

———— and Breckenridge, Carol A., 'The South Indian Temple: Authority, Honour and Redistribution', *CIS* (n.s.) 10,2 (1976), pp. 187–211.

Arasaratnam, Sinnappah, 'India and the Indian Ocean in the Seventeenth Century', in: Ashin Das Gupta and Michael N. Pearson (eds.), *India and the Indian Ocean, 1500–1800*, pp. 94–130.

————, *Pre-Modern Commerce and Society in Southern Asia: An Inaugural Lecture Delivered at the University of Malaya on December 21, 1971*, Kuala Lumpur, 1972.

Arunima, G., 'A Vindication of the Rights of Women: Families and Legal Change in Nineteenth-Century Malabar', in: Michael R. Anderson and Sumit Guha (eds.), *Changing Concepts of Rights and Justice in South Asia*, Delhi et al., 1998 (SOAS Studies on South Asia Understandings and Perspectives Series), pp. 114–39.

————, 'Multiple Meanings: Changing Conceptions of Matrilineal Kinship in Nineteenth- and Twentieth-Century Malabar', *IESHR* 33, 3 (1996), pp. 283–307.

Balakrishnan, P.V., *Matrilineal System in Malabar*, Kannur, 1981.

Banerjee, Ruchira, 'A Wedding Feast or Political Arena? Commercial Rivalry between the Ali Rajas and the English Factory in Northern Malabar in the 18th Century', in: Rudrangshu Mukherjee and Lakshmi Subramanian (eds.), *Politics and Trade in the Indian Ocean World: Essays in Honour of Ashin Das Gupta*, Delhi, 1998, pp. 83–112.

Bayly, Christopher A., *Empire and Information: Intelligence Gathering and Social Communication in India, 1780–1870*, Cambridge, 1996 (Cambridge Studies in Indian History and Society 1).

————, *Indian Society and the Making of the British Empire*, Cambridge, 1988, reprint, 1997 (The New Cambridge History of India II, 1).

————, 'The British Military-Fiscal State and Indigenous Resistance, India 1750–1820', in: Lawrence Stone (ed.), *An Imperial State at War: Britain from 1689 to 1815*, London and New York, 1994, pp. 322–54.

Bayly, Christopher and Bayly, Susan, 'Eighteenth-Century State Forms and the Economy', in: Clive Dewey (ed.), *Arrested Development in India: The Historical Dimension*, Delhi, 1988, pp. 66–90.

Bayly, Susan, 'Hindu Kingship and the Origin of Community: Religion, State and Society in Kerala, 1750–1850', *MAS* 18,2 (1984), pp. 177–213.

————, *Saints, Goddesses and Kings: Muslims and Christians in South Indian Society, 1700–1900*, Cambridge, 1989 (Cambridge South Asian Studies 43).

Becher, Matthias, *Karl der Große*, München, 1999.

Bennell, Anthony S., *The Making of Arthur Wellesley*, Hyderabad, 1997.

Berkemer, Georg, *Little Kingdoms in Kalinga: Ideologie, Legitimation und Politik regionaler Eliten*, Stuttgart, 1993 (Beiträge zur Südasienforschung 156).

Bernier, Ronald M., *Temple Arts of Kerala: A South Indian Tradition*, New Delhi, 1982.

Bitterli, Urs, *Die 'Wilden' und die 'Zivilisierten': Grundzüge einer Geistes– und Kulturgeschichte der europäisch-überseeischen Begegnung*, 2., ext. edn., München, 1991.

Bouchon, Geneviève, *'Regent of the Sea': Cannanore's Response to Portuguese Expansion, 1507–1528* (French Studies in South Asian Culture and Society 11), Delhi, 1988.

———, 'Sixteenth Century Malabar and the Indian Ocean', in: Ashin Das Gupta and M.N. Pearson (eds.), *India and the Indian Ocean 1500–1800*, Calcutta, 1987, pp. 162–84.

Bowring, Lewin B., *Haidar Alī and Tipū Sultān and the Struggle with the Musalmān Powers of the South*, Oxford, 1899, reprint New Delhi and Madras, 1997.

Brittlebank, Kate, *Tipu Sultan's Search for Legitimacy: Islam and Kingship in a Hindu Domain*, Delhi, 1997.

Caldwell, Sarah L., 'Bhagavati: Ball of Fire', in: John Stratton Hawley and Donna Marie Wulff (eds.), *Devī: Goddesses of India*, Delhi, 1998, pp. 195–226.

———, *Oh Terrifying Mother: Sexuality, Violence and Worship of the Goddess Kāli*, New Delhi, 1999.

Callahan, Raymond, *The East India Company and Army Reform, 1783–1798*, Cambridge (Massachusetts), 1972.

Casson, Lionel, *The Periplus Maris Erythraei: Text with Introduction, Translation, and Commentary*, Princeton, 1989.

Chatterjee, Amal, *Representations of India, 1740–1840: The Creation of India in the Colonial Imagination*, London and New York, 1998.

Chaudhuri, Kirti N., *Trade and Civilisation in the Indian Ocean: An Economic History from the Rise of Islam to 1750*, Cambridge, 1985.

Chopra, Pran N., Ravindran, T.K. and Subrahmaniam, N., *History of South India*, 3 vols., New Delhi, 1979.

Claus, Peter, 'Oral Traditions, Royal Cults and Materials for a Reconsideration of the Caste System in South India', *Journal of Indian Folkloristics* 1,1 (1978), pp. 1–25.

Coburn, Thomas B., *Devi Māhātmya: The Crystallization of the Goddess Tradition*, Delhi, 1984, reprint 1997.

Cohn, Bernard S., 'Political Systems in Eighteenth-Century India: The Banaras Region', in: *An Anthropologist Among the Historians and Other Essays*, New Delhi, 1990, pp. 483–99.

———, 'Some Notes on Law and Change in North India', in: idem, *An Anthropologist Among the Historians and Other Essays*, New Delhi, 1990, pp. 554–74.

———, 'The Past in the Present: India as Museum of Mankind', *History and Anthropology* 11,1 (1998), pp. 1–38.

Conermann, Stephan, 'Muslimische Seefahrt auf dem Indischen Ozean vom 14. bis zum 16. Jahrhundert', in: idem (ed.), *Der Indische Ozean in historischer Perspektive*, Hamburg 1998 (Asien und Afrika. Beiträge des Zentrums für Asiatische und Afrikanische Studien (ZAAS) der Christian-Albrechts-Universität zu Kiel 1), pp. 143–80.

Copland, Ian, 'The Historian as Anthropologist: 'Ethnohistory' and the Study of South Asia', *South Asia* 11 (1988), pp. 101–16.

Dale, Stephen Frederic, *Islamic Society on the South Asian Frontier: The Māppiḷas of Malabar 1498–1922*, Oxford, 1980.

———, 'Trade, Conversion and the Growth of the Islamic Community of Kerala, South India', *Studia Islamica* 71 (1990), pp. 155–75.

Das Gupta, Ashin, 'Malabar in 1740', *Bengal Past and Present* 80 (1960), pp. 90–117.

———, *Malabar in Asian Trade 1740–1800*, Cambridge, 1967 (Cambridge South Asian Studies 1).

Datta, Kalinkinkar, 'The Malabar Rajahs and the East India Company', *Bengal Past and Present* 57 (1939).

De Lannoy, Mark, *The Kulasekhara Perumals of Travancore: History and State Formation in Travacore from 1671 to 1758*, Leiden, 1997.

Deloche, Jean, *Transport and Communications in India Prior to Steam Locomotion*, 2 vols., Delhi, 1993/94 (French Studies in South Asian Culture and Society 7).

Dewey, Clive, 'Images of the Village Community: A Study in Anglo-Indian Ideology', *MAS* 6 (1972), pp. 291–328.

Deyell, John S. and Frykenberg, Robert E., 'Sovereignty and the "SIKKA" under Company Raj: Minting Prerogative and Imperial Legitimacy in India', *IESHR* 19,1 (1982), pp. 1–25.

Dickson, P.G.M., *The Financial Revolution in England: A Study in the Development of Public Credit 1688–1756*, New York, 1967.

Dirks, Nicholas B., *Castes of Mind: Colonialism and the Making of Modern India*, Princeton, 2001.

———, 'From Little King to Landlord', in: idem (ed.), *Colonialism and Culture*, Ann Arbor, 1992, pp. 175–208.

———, *The Hollow Crown: Ethnohistory of an Indian Kingdom*, Ann Arbor, 2nd edn., 1993.

———, 'The Pasts of a *Pālaiyakkārar*: The Ethnohistory of a South Indian Little Kingdom', *JAS* 41 (1982), pp. 655–83.

———, 'The Structure and Meaning of Political Relations in a South Indian Little Kingdom', *CIS* 13 (1979), pp. 169–206.

Dua, J.C., *Palegars of South India: Forms and Contents of Their Resistance in Ceded Districts*, New Delhi, 1996.

Elamkulam, Kunjan Pillai, *Studies in Kerala History*, Kottayam, 1970.

Fisher, Michael H., *Indirect Rule in India: Residents and the Residency System 1764–1858*, Oxford, 1991, New Delhi et al., 1998.

———, *The First Indian Author in English: Dean Mahomed (1759–1851) in India, Ireland, and England*, Delhi, 1996.

———, (ed.), *The Politics of the British Annexation of India, 1757–1857*, Delhi, 1993.

Fleckstein, Josef, 'Karl der Große', in: *Lexikon des Mittelalters*, vol. 5, München and Zürich, 1991, pp. 955–9.

Förster, Stig, *Die mächtigen Diener der East India Company: Ursachen und Hintergründe der britischen Expansionspolitik in Südasien, 1793–1819*, Stuttgart, 1992 (Beiträge zur Kolonial- und Überseegeschichte 54).

Freeman, J. Richardson, 'Performing Possession: Ritual and Consciousness in the Teyyam Complex of Northern Kerala', in: Heidrun Brückner, Lothar Lutze and Aditya Malik (eds.), *Flags of Fame: Studies in South Asian Folk Culture*, Delhi, 1993 (South Asian Studies 27), pp. 109–38.

———, *Purity and Violence: Sacred Power in the Teyyam Worship of Malabar*, unpublished dissertation, University of Pennsylvania, 1991.

Frykenberg, Robert E., 'Modern Education in South India, 1784–1854: Its Roots and its Role as a Vehicle of Integration under Company Raj', *The American Historical Review* 91,1 (1986), pp. 37–65.

———, 'The Emergence of Modern "Hinduism" as a Concept and as an Institution: A Reappraisal with Special Reference to South India', in: Günther-Dietz Sontheimer and Hermann Kulke (eds.), *Hinduism Reconsidered*, 2., ext. ed., New Delhi, 1997 (South Asian Studies 24).

———, 'Traditional Processes of Power in South India: A Historical Analysis of Local Influence', *IESHR* 1 (1963), pp. 122–42.

Fuller, Christopher J., *Servants of the Goddess: The Priests of a South Indian Temple*, Delhi, 1991.

———, 'The Hindu Temple and Indian Society', in: Michael V. Fox (ed.), *Temple in Society*, Winona Lake, 1988, pp. 49–66.

———, 'The Internal Structure of the Nayar Caste', *Journal of Anthropological Research* 31,4 (1975), pp. 283–312.

———, *The Nayars Today*, Cambridge, 1976.

Furber, Holden, 'Asia and the West as Partners before "Empire" and After', *JAS* 28,4 (1969), pp. 711–21.

Gaastra, Femme S., 'Comptetition or Collaboration? Relations between the Dutch East India Company and Indian Merchants around 1680', in: Sushil Chaudhury and Michel Morineau (eds.), *Merchants, Companies and Trade: Europe and Asia in the Early Modern Era*, Cambridge, 1999, pp. 188–201.

Ganesh, K.N., 'Ownership and Control of Land in Medieval Kerala: Janmam-Kanam Relations During the 16th–18th Centuries', *IESHR* 28,3 (1991), pp. 299–323.

Gangadharan, T.K., *Kerala History*, Calicut s.a.

Gonda, Jan, *Die Religionen Indiens*. vol. 2 Der jüngere Hinduismus, Stuttgart, 1963 (Die Religionen der Menschheit vol. 12).

Gopal, Krishna Kanti, 'The Assembly of the Samantas in Early Medieaval India', *Journal of Indian History* 22,1 (1964), pp. 241–50.

Gopal, Lallanji, 'Sāmanta—Its Varying Significance in Ancient India', *JRAS* 5 (1963), pp. 21–37.

Gough, Kathleen, 'Changing Kinship Usages in the Setting of Political and Economic Change Among the Nayars of Malabar', *JRAI* 82 (1952), pp. 71–81.

———, 'Indian Peasant Uprisings', *EPW* 9 (1974), pp. 1391–1412.

———, 'Nayar: Central Kerala', in: idem and David M. Schneider (eds.), *Matrilineal Kinship*, Berkeley and Los Angeles, 1961, pp. 298–384.

———, 'Nayar: North Kerala', in: idem and David M. Schneider (eds.), *Matrilineal Kinship*, Berkeley and Los Angeles, 1961, pp. 385–404.

———, 'Pālakkara: Social and Religious Change in Central Kerala', in: K. Ishwaran (ed.), *Change and Continuity in India's Villages*, New York and London, 1970, pp. 129–64.

———, 'The Nayar Taravad', *Journal of the M.S. University of Baroda* 1,2 (1952), pp. 1–13.

Gundert, Hermann, *A Malayalam and English Dictionary*, Mangalore 1872, reprint Kottayam, 1992.

Heesterman, Johannes C., *The Inner Conflict of Tradition: Essays in Indian Ritual, Kingship and Society*, Chicago, 1985.

Heitzman, James, *Gifts of Power: Lordship in an Early Indian State*, Delhi, 1997.

Henderson, J.R., *The Coins of Haidar Ali and Tipu Sultan*, Madras, 1921, reprint New Delhi and Madras, 1989.

Hjejle, Benedict, 'Slavery and Agricultural Bondage in South India in the Nineteenth Century', *The Scandinavian Economic History Review* 15,1–2 (1967), pp. 71–126.

Huntington, Samuel P., 'Clash of Civilizations?', *Foreign Affairs* 72,3 (1993), pp. 22–49.

———, *The Clash of Civilizations and the Remaking of World Order*, New York, 1996.

Inden, Ronald, 'Hierarchies of Kings in Medieval India', in: T.N. Madan (ed.), *Way of Life: King, Householder, Renouncer. Essays in Honour of Louis Dumont*, New Delhi, 1982, pp. 99–125.

———, 'Ritual, Authority, and Cyclic Time in Hindu Kingship', in: John F. Richards (ed.), *Kingship and Authority in South Asia*, Delhi et al., 1998, pp. 41–91.

Ingram, Edward, *Commitment to Empire: Prophecies of the Great Game in Asia 1797–1800*, Oxford, 1981.

———, *Empire-Building and Empire-Builders: Twelve Studies*, London, 1995.

——— (ed.), *Two Views of British India: The Private Correspondence of Mr. Dundas and Lord Wellesley, 1798–1801*, Somerset, 1970.

Irschick, Eugene F., *Dialogue and History: Constructing South India, 1795–1895*, Berkeley and Los Angeles, 1994.

Iyer, L.A. Krishna, *Social History of Kerala*, 2 vols., Madras, 1970.

Jahn, Beate, 'Globale Kulturkämpfe oder einheitliche Weltkultur? Zur Relevanz von Kultur in den internationalen Beziehungen,' *Zeitschrift für internationale Beziehungen* 2 (1995), pp. 213–36.

Jeffrey, Robin, *Politics, Women and Well-Being: How Kerala Became a 'Model'*, Basingstoke and London, 1992.

——————, *The Decline of Nair Dominance: Society and Politics in Travancore 1847–1908*, New Delhi, 2nd edn., 1994.

——————, 'The Politics of "Indirect rule": Types of Relationship among Rulers, Ministers and Residents in a "Native State"', *Jounal of Commonwealth and Comparative Studies* 13 (1975), pp. 261–81.

Jones, Kenneth, *Socio-religious Reform Movements in British India*, Cambridge, 1989 (The New Cambridge History of India III, 1).

Kane, Pandurang Vaman, *History of Dharmaśāstra (Ancient and Mediaeval Religious and Civil Law in India)*, 5 vols., Poona, 1962–1975 (Government Oriental Series Class B, No. 6).

Kareem, C.K., 'A Probe into the Veracity of the Malabar Edicts of Haider Ali and Tipu Sultan', *South Indian History Congress*, XVIII Session at Sree Sankaracharya University of Sanskrit, Kalady, Kerala, 1998, pp. 33–9.

——————, *Kerala under Haidar Ali and Tipu Sultan*, Ernakulam, 1973.

Kejariwal, O.P., *The Asiatic Society of Bengal and the Discovery of India's Past, 1784—1838*, Delhi et al., 1988.

Kieniewicz, Jan, 'Asian Merchants and European Expansion: Malabar Pepper Trade Routes in the Indian Ocean World-System in the Sixteenth Century', in: Karl Reinhold Haellquist (ed.), *Asian Trade Routes*, Kopenhagen, 1991 (Studies on Asian Topics 13), pp. 78–86.

——————, 'Pepper Gardens and Market in Precolonial Malabar', *Moyen Orient & Océan Indien* 3 (1986), pp. 1–36.

Kolff, Dirk H.A., 'The End of an *Ancien Régime*: Colonial War in India 1798–1818', in: A. de Moor Joop and H.L. Wesseling (ed.), *Imperialism and War: Essays on Colonial Wars in Asia and Africa*, Leiden, 1989 (Comparative Studies in Overseas History 8), pp. 22–49.

Koshy, M.O., *The Dutch Power in Kerala (1729–1758)*, New Delhi, 1989.

Kühnhardt, Ludger, *Stufen der Souveränität: Staatsverständnis und Selbstbestimmung in der 'Dritten Welt'*, Bonn, 1992.

Kulke, Hermann, 'Die frühmittelalterlichen Regionalreiche: Ihre Struktur und Rolle im Prozeß staatlicher Entwicklung Indiens', in: idem and Dietmar Rothermund, (eds.), *Regionale Tradition in Südasien*, Wiesbaden, 1985, pp. 77–114.

——————, 'The Early and the Imperial Kingdom: A Processural Model of Integrative State Formation in Early Medieval India', in: idem (ed.), *The State in India 1000–1700*, Delhi, 1997.

Kulke, Hermann and Rothermund, Dietmar, *Geschichte Indiens*, Stuttgart, 1982.

Kumar, Dharma, *Land and Caste in South India: Agricultural Labour in the Madras Presidency During the 19th Century*, Cambridge, 1965, reprint New Delhi, 1992.

Kunhikrishnan, Vannarth Veettil, *Tenancy Legislation in Malabar (1880–1970): An Historical Analysis*, Calicut, 1993.

Kurup, K.K.N., 'Fort St. Angelo', in: M.G.S. Narayanan and K.K.N. Kurup, (eds.), *Kerala Historical Studies*, Calicut, 1976, pp. 44–6.

———, 'British Colonial Policy in Malabar and its Impact on Land Settlement and Revenue (1792–1800),' *Journal of Kerala Studies* 3,3–4 (1976), pp. 421–30.

———, *The Cult of Teyyam and Hero Worship in Kerala*, Calcutta, 1963.

———, *William Logan: A Study in the Agrarian Relations of Malabar*, Calicut, 1981.

Lingat, Robert, *The Classical Law of India*, California, 1973, reprint Delhi et al., 1998.

Leela Devi, Rangaswami Pillai, *History of Kerala*, Kottayam, 1986.

Lemercinier, Geneviève, *Religion and Ideology in Kerala*, New Delhi, 1984.

Logan, William, *Malabar*, 2 vols., Madras 1887, reprint New Delhi and Madras, 1989.

Luhmann, Niklas, *Legitimation durch Verfahren*, Frankfurt, 7th edn., 1997.

Maclean, C.D. (ed.), *Manual of the Administration of the Madras Presidency*, 3 vols., Madras 1885–93, reprint New Delhi and Madras, 1990.

Mahalingam, T.V., *South Indian Polity*, Madras, 2nd edn., 1967.

Majumdar, Ramesh Chandra, *The Classical Accounts of India: Being a Compilation of the English Translations of the Accounts Left by Herodotus, Megasthenes, Arrian etc.*, Calcutta, 1960.

Malayalam Lexicon: A Comprehensive Malayalam-Malayalam-English Dictionary on Historical and Philological Principles, University of Kerala, Trivandrum, 1970–97 (series not completed).

Malekandathil, Pius M.C., *Portuguese Cochin and the Maritime Trade of India: 1500–1663*, New Delhi, 2001 (South Asian Studies 39).

Mani, Vettam, *Purāṇic Encyclopaedia: A Comprehensive Work with Special Reference to the Epic and Purāṇic Literature*, Delhi, 1975, reprint Delhi, 1996.

Mann, Michael, *Flottenbau und Forstbetrieb in Indien 1794–1823*, Stuttgart, 1995 (Beiträge zur Südasienforschung 175).

Marar, Krishna Kumar, 'Rediscovering a Unique Tradition: Murals of Thodikkalam', *The India Magazine of Her People and Culture* 12 (1992), pp. 50–9.

Marshall, Peter J., 'British Expansion in India in the Eighteenth Century: A Historical Revision', *History* 60 (1975), pp. 28–43.

———, 'Western Arms in Maritime Asia in the Early Phases of Expansion', *MAS* 14,1 (1980), pp. 13–28.

Mathée, Ulrich, '"*Zu den Christen und zu den Gewürzen*"—Wie die Portugiesen den Indischen Ozean gewannen', in: Stephan Conermann (ed.), *Der Indische Ozean in historischer Perspektive*, Hamburg, 1998 (Asien und Afrika. Beiträge des Zentrums für Asiatische und Afrikanische Studien (ZAAS) der Christian-Albrechts-Universität zu Kiel 1), pp. 181–207.

Mathews, Johnsy, *Economy and Society in Medieval Malabar (A.D. 1500–1600)*, Changanacherry, 1996.

Mayer, Adrian C., *Land and Society in Malabar*, Oxford, 1952.

———, 'Rulership and Divinity: The Case of the Modern Hindu Prince and Beyond', *MAS* 25,4 (1991), pp. 765–90.

Mencher, Joan P., 'Namboodiri Brahmins: An Analysis of a Traditional Elite in Kerala', *Journal of Asian and African Studies* 1 (1966), pp. 183–96.

——— and Goldberg, Helen, 'Kinship and Marriage Regulations Amongst the Namboodiri Brahmans of Kerala', *Man* (n.s.) 2 (1967), pp. 87–106.

Menon, A. Sreedhara, *A Survey of Kerala History*, Madras, 1988.

———, *Kerala and Freedom Struggle*, Kottayam, 1997.

———, *Kerala History and its Makers*, 2nd edn., 1990.

Menon, C. Achyuta, 'A Note on Kali or Bhagavati Cult of Kerala', in: *S. Krishnaswami Aiyangar Commemoration Volume*, Madras, 1936, pp. 234–8.

Menon, Dilip M., 'Houses by the Sea: State Experimentation on the Southwest Coast of India 1760–1800', in: Neera Chandhoke, *Mapping Histories: Essays Presented to Ravinder Kumar*, New Delhi, 2000, pp. 161–86.

Menon, K.P. Padmanabha, *History of Kerala: Written in the Form of Notes on Visscher's Letters from Malabar*, 4 vols., reprint New Delhi and Madras, 1989.

Menon, M. Gangadhara, *Malabar Rebellion (1921–22)*, Allahabad, 1989.

Metcalf, Thomas R., *Ideologies of the Raj*, Cambridge, 1995 (The New Cambridge History of India III, 4).

Michaels, Axel and Sharma, Nutan, 'Goddess of the Secret: Guhyeśvarī in Nepal and Her Festival', in: Axel Michaels, Cornelia Vogelsanger and Annette Wilke, *Wild Goddesses in India and Nepal*, Bern et al., 1996 (Studia Religiosa Helvetica 96), pp. 303–42.

Michaud's History of Mysore under Hyder Ali & Tippoo Sultan, transl. by V.K. Raman Menon, Paris, 1801–9, reprint New Delhi, 1985.

Miller, Eric J., 'Caste and Territory in Malabar', *American Anthropologist* 56,1 (1954), pp. 410–20.

Miller, Roland E., *Mappila Muslims of Kerala: A Study in Islamic Trends*, 2nd, ext. ed., Hyderabad, 1990.

Moore, Lewis, *Malabar Law and Custom*, Madras, 3rd edn., 1905.

Moore, Melinda A., 'A New Look at the Nayar Taravad', *Man* (n.s.) 20 (1985), pp. 523–41.

———, *Taravad: House, Land and Relationship in a Matrilineal Hindu Society*, unpublished dissertation, University of Chicago, 1983.

Moorthy, K.K., *The Kovils of Kerala: An 18-Petal Fragrant Rose*, Tirupati, 2nd edn., 1997.

Muir, Ramsay (ed.), *The Making of Britsh India 1756–1858*, London, 2nd edn., 1917.

Mukherjee, Nilmani and Frykenberg, Robert E., 'The Ryotwari System and Social Organization in the Madras Presidency', in: Robert E. Frykenberg (ed.), *Land Control and Social Structure in Indian History*, Madison and London, 1969, pp. 217–26.

Mundadan, A. Mathias, *History of Christianity in India. Volume 1: From the Beginning up to the Middle of the Sixteenth Century (up to 1542)*, Bangalore, 1984.

Nair, C. Gopalan, *Malabar Series. Wynad: Its Peoples and Traditions*, Madras, 1911.

Nair, P.R. Gopinathan, 'Education and Socio-economic Change in Kerala, 1793–1947', *Social Scientist* 4,8 (1976), pp. 28–43.

Narayana Rao, Velcheru, Shulman, David and Subrahmanyam, Sanjay, *Symbols of Substance: Court and State in Nāyaka Period Tamilnadu*, Delhi, 1992.

Narayanan, M.G.S., *Perumals of Kerala: Political and Social Conditions of Kerala Under the Cēra Perumals of Makotai (c. 800 A.D.–1124 A.D.)*, Calicut, 1996.

Nightingale, Pamela, *Trade and Empire in Western India 1785–1806*, Cambridge, 1970 (Cambridge South Asian Studies 9).

Outlook 5, 19 of 24.5.1999.

Panikkar, K.M., *A History of Kerala 1498–1910*, Annamalainagar, 1960.

Panikkar, K.N., *Against Lord and State: Religion and Peasant Uprisings in Malabar 1836–1921*, Delhi et al., 1992.

———, *Peasant Protests and Revolts in Malabar*, New Delhi, 1990.

Panikkar, T.K. Gopal, *Malabar and its Folk: A Systematic Description of the Social Customs and Institutions of Malabar*, Madras, 3rd edn., 1929.

Pieper, Jan, *Die anglo-indische Station oder die Kolonialisierung des Götterberges: Hindustadtkultur und Kolonialstadtwesen im 19. Jahrhundert als Konfrontation östlicher und westlicher Geisteswelten*, Bonn, 1977 (Antiquitates Orientales Reihe B, 1).

Pillai, V.R. Parameswaran, *Temple Culture of South India*, New Delhi, 1986.

Prakash, B.A., 'Agricultural Backwardness of Malabar During the Colonial Period: An Analysis of Economic Causes', *Social Scientist* 16, 6-7 (1988), pp. 51–76, pp. 56–9.

Prakash, Om, *European Commercial Enterprise in Pre-Colonial India*, Cambridge, 1998 (The New Cambridge History of India II, 5).

Pratt, Mary Louise, *Imperial Eyes: Travel Writing and Transculturation*, London and New York, 1992.

———, 'Linguistic Utopias', in: Nigel Fabb et al. (eds.), *The Linguistics of Writings: Arguments Between Language and Literature*, Manchester, 1987, pp. 48–66.

Price, Pamela G., *Kingship and Political Practice in Colonial India*, Cambridge, 1996 (University of Cambridge Oriental Publications 51).

———, 'Raja-dharma in 19th Century South India: Land, Litigation and Largess in Ramnad Zamindari', *CIS* 13,2 (1979), pp. 207–39.

Quaritsch, Helmut, *Souveränität: Entstehung und Entwicklung des Begriffs in Frankreich und Deutschland vom 13. Jh. bis 1806*, Berlin, 1986.

Radhakrishnan, P., *Peasant Struggles, Land Reforms and Social Change: Malabar 1836–1982*, New Delhi, Newbury Park and London, 1989.

Raj, Kaleeswaram and Suchitra, K.P., *Commentaries on Marumakkathayam Law*, Payyanur, 1995.

Rajayyan, K., *History of Tamilnadu 1525–1982*, Madurai, 1982.

———, 'Kerala Varma and Malabar Rebellion', *Journal of Indian History* 47,1 (1969), pp. 549–57.

———, *South Indian Rebellion: The First War of Independence: 1800–1801*, Mysore, 1971.

Rajendran, N., *Establishment of British Power in Malabar (1664 to 1799)*, Allahabad, 1979.

Ram, N., 'Impact of Early Colonisation on Economy of South India', *Social Scientist* 1,4 (1972), pp. 47–65.

Ravindran, T.K., *Cornwallis System in Malabar*, Calicut, 1969.

———, *Institutions and Movements in Kerala History*, Trivandrum, 1978.

———, *Malabar under Bombay Presidency*, Calicut, 1979.

———, 'The Kurichya Rebellion of 1812', *Journal of Kerala Studies* 3,3–4 (1976), S. 533–44.

Rothermund, Dietmar, *Asian Trade and European Expansion in the Age of Mercantilism*, New Delhi, 1981.

———, *Government, Landlord and Peasant in India: Agrarian Relations under British Rule 1865–1935*, Wiesbaden, 1978 (Schriftenreihe des Südasien-Instituts der Universität Heidelberg 25).

Said, Edward W., *Orientalism*, New York, 1979.

Santha, E.K., *Local Self-Government in Malabar (1800–1960)*, New Delhi, 1994.

Schnepel, Burkhard, *Die Dschungelkönige: Ethnohistorische Aspekte von Politik und Ritual in Südorissa/Indien*, Stuttgart, 1997 (Beiträge zur Südasienforschung 177).

Schoff, Wilfried H. (transl. and ed.), *The Periplus of the Eythraean Sea: Travel and Trade in the Indian Ocean by a Merchant of the First Century*, New York, 1912, reprint New Delhi, 1974.

Schweinitz, Karl de Jr., *The Rise & Fall of British India: Imperialism as Inequality*, London and New York, 1983.

Scott, James, *Domination and the Arts of Resistance: Hidden Transcripts*, New Haven and London, 1990.

———, 'Resistance Without Protest and Without Organization: Peasant Opposition to the Islamic *Zakat* and Christian Tithe', *Comparative Studies in Society and History* 19,3 (1987), pp. 416–52.

Shea, Thomas W., 'Barriers to Economic Development in Traditionial Societies: Malabar, a Case Study', *Journal of Economic History* 19 (1959), pp. 504–22.

Shulman, David D., 'On South Indian Bandits and Kings', *IESHR* 17,3 (1980), pp. 283–306.

———, *The King and the Clown in South Indian Myth and Poetry*, Princeton, 1985.

Singh, R.L., *India: A Regional Geography*, Varanasi, 1971, reprint Varanasi, 1998.

Sircar, Dipesh Chandra, *Indian Epigraphy*, Delhi, 1965, reprint Delhi, 1996.

Sivaramakrishnan, K., 'British Imperium and Forested Zones of Anomaly in Bengal, 1767–1833', *IESHR* 33,3 (1996), pp. 243–82.

Skaria, Ajay, 'Shades of Wildness: Tribe, Caste, and Gender in Western India', *JAS* 56, 3–4 (1997), pp. 726–45.

Sridharan, K., *A Maritime History of India*, New Delhi, 1965.

Srinivasan, K.R., *Temples of South India*, New Delhi, 1972 (India—the Land and People).

Stein, Burton, 'Mahānavami: Medieval and Modern Kingly Ritual in South India', in: Bardwell L. Smith (ed.), *Essays on Gupta Culture*, Delhi, 1983, pp. 67–90.

———, *Vijayanagara*, Cambridge, 1989 (New Cambridge History of India I, 2).

Stokes, Eric, 'Traditional Resistance Movements and Afro-Asian Nationalism: The Context of the 1857 Mutiny Rebellion in India', in: idem, *The Peasant and the Raj*, Cambridge, 1978 (Cambridge South Asian Studies 23), pp. 120–39.

Subrahmanyam, Sanjay, *Penumbral Visions: Making Polities in Early Modern South India*, New Delhi, 2001.

———, *The Career and Legend of Vasco da Gama*, Cambridge, 1997.

———, *The Political Economy of Commerce: Southern India 1500–1650*, Cambridge, 1990 (Cambridge South Asian Studies 45).

——— and Shulman, David, 'The Men Who Would Be King? The Politics of Expansion in Early Seventeenth-Century Northern Tamilnadu', *MAS* 24, 2 (1990), pp. 225–48.

Swai, Bonaventure, *The British in Malabar, 1792–1806*, unpublished dissertation, University of Sussex, 1974.

Tarabout, Gilles, *Sacrifier et Donner`a Voir en Pays Malabar: Les Fêtes de Temple au Kerala (Inde du Sud): Etude Anthropologique*, Paris, 1986.

Thomas, P.J., 'The Pepper Trade of India in Early Times', in: *S. Krishnaswami Aiyangar Commemoration Volume*, Madras, 1936, pp. 226–33.

Thurston, Edgar and Rangachari, K., *Castes and Tribes of Southern India*, 7 vols., Madras, 1909.

Trautmann, Thomas R., *Dravidian Kinship*, New Delhi, 1981.

Trevelyan, George Otto, *The Life and Letters of Lord Macaulay*, 4 vols., Leipzig, 1876.

Unni, K. Raman, 'Visiting Husbands in Malabar', *Journal of the M.S. University of Baroda* 5,1(1956), pp. 37–56.

Vaidyanathan, K.R., *Temples and Legends of Kerala*, Bombay, 3rd edn., 1994.

Verghese, T.C., *Agrarian Change and Economic Consequences: Land Tenures in Kerala 1850–1960*, Bombay et al., 1970.

Vicziany, Marika, 'Imperialism, Botany and Statistics in Early Nineteenth-Century India: The Surveys of Francis Buchanan (1762–1829)', *MAS* 20,4 (1986), pp. 625–60.

Vink, Mark, 'Mare Liberum and Dominium Maris: Legal Arguments and Implications of the Luso-Dutch Struggle for the Control over Asian Waters ca. 1600–1663', in: K.S. Mathew (ed.) *Studies in Maritime History*, Pondicherry, 1990, pp. 38–68.

Wiesehöfer, Josef, '*Mare Erythraeum*, *Sinus Persicus* und *Fines India*: Der Indische Ozean in hellenistischer und römischer Zeit', in: Stephan Conermann (ed.), *Der Indische Ozean in historischer Perspektive*, Hamburg, 1998 (Asien und Afrika. Beiträge des Zentrums für Asiatische und Afrikanische Studien (ZAAS) der Christian-Albrechts-Universität zu Kiel 1), pp. 9–36.

Wolf, Eric R., *Europe and the People Without History*, Berkeley, Los Angeles and London, 1982.

Yule, Henry and Burnell, A.C., *Hobson-Jobson: A Glossary of Colloquial Anglo-Indian Words and Phrases, and of Kindred Terms, Etymological, Historical, Geographical, and Discursive*, London, 1903, reprint New Delhi and Madras, 1995.

Zarrilli, Phillip B., *When the Body Becomes all Eyes: Paradigms, Discourses and Practices of Power in Kalarippayattu, a South Indian Martial Art*, Delhi et al., 1998.

Index

Abd-ul-Khalic, 82
Abercromby, Robert, 99
age of partnership, 2
Ali Rājā of Kannūr, 7, 70, 78
Añcarakaṇṭi plantation, 8, 108, 121
Añcarakaṇṭi river, 7–8
Añcuteṅṅa, 74
Anglo–Maisūrian war, 75, 80–3, 120, 152
Arasaratnam, Sinappah, 66
Āṟṟiṅṅal Rāni, 74
Arshed Beg Khan, 93–4, 96
Arthaśāstra, 144, 151
Arunima, G., 13
Avadh, 3
Ayyappan, 36

Baber, Thomas H., 36–7, 123–6, 155
Baden-Powell, B.H., 4
Bayly, Christopher, 2, 53, 156
Benares, 3, 35, 38
Bentinck, William, 153
Bēppūr port, 9
Bēppūr river, 8–9
Berkemer, Georg, 3–4, 42
Bhadrakāḷi, 31
Bhagavati temples, 170
Bhagavati worship, in Malabar, 30–3
Bhatkal, 64
Bibi of Kannūr, 76, 82, 149
Board of Control, 156
Board of Revenue for 1801, 17
Board of Revenue, Fort St. George, Madras, 176
Boddam, Charles, 98
Bombay Presidency, 98, 110
Bombay Revenue Proceedings (BRP), 176
Brown, Murdoch, 108, 110, 121
Buchanan, Francis, 17, 176
bureaucracy, Western-style system of, 41, 45

Caldwell, Sarah, 30
Caliyaṃ port, 9
cardamom, trade in, 63
Cartaz system of trade, 67–9
Cāvakkāṭu, 94
Cēramān Perumāḷ, 145–9, 172
Cērapulaśśēri, 101–2
Charlemagne, 150
Chatterjee, Amal, 50
Chaudhuri, K.N., 64, 71
cinnamon, trade in, 63
Ciṟakkal, 6, 63, 82, 109, 149
Ciṟakkal Rājā, 16, 93–4, 97, 100, 119
Civil Code, 107
civilized nation, 51
civilized people, 50
Clash of Civilizations, 47
Clive, Edward, 121
Code of Bengal, 102
Cohn, Bernard S., 3, 38, 162
Colbert, 72
colonialism, 50–1
Commission of Malabar Affairs, 103
Compagnie des Indes Orientales, 72
contact zone model of interaction, 3, 22
    definition of, 47
    dialogue in, 49–52
    in linguistics, 47
    resistance in, 52–4

Cornwallis, Charles, 75
Cornwallis system of administration, 103
Covakkāran Mūssa, 109, 120, 156
cultivable land, lease of, 18
cuṅkaṃ, 21, 66, 100, 142

Dale, Stephen, 4
Das Gupta, Ashin, 66, 70
dēśavāḷḷi, 14–15, 21, 43, 92, 102, 142, 150–1, 171
dēvasvaṃ, 18
Dharmatam port, 9
Dirks, Nicholas, 2–4
Dow, Alexander, 98, 100, 107, 116, 157
Duncan, Jonathan, 34, 101, 115
Durgga, 3l, 33, 142
Dutch, 1, 9, 62–3, 69–71, 75

East India Company (EIC), 9, 70–1, 73, 82–3, 99–101, 103, 105–10, 113, 116, 120–1, 144, 151, 153–4, 156, 158–9, 170
Eḻimala river, 7
ethnohistory, 38

Farmer, William Gamul, 98, 100–1, 108, 153
French, 1, 62, 72–3, 75, 79, 108
French East India Company, 72
Fuller, Christopher, 4, 13
Furber, Holden, 2

Gama, Vasco da, 1, 7, 67–8
Ganesh, K.N., 4, 20
ginger, trade in, 63
Gordon, James, 115
Gough, Kathleen, 13, 17
great king, 38–45, 141, 144–54, 170–2
Gundert, Hermann, 31, 177

Haidar Ali, 5, 7, 10, 20, 37, 66, 72, 78–84, 92–3, 95, 97–8, 109

Hariścandra Perumāḷ, 34
Harvey, 153
Huntington, Samuel, 47

Indian Civil Service, 160
Indian Ocean, 1, 7, 64–5, 67, 69, 71, 73
indirect rule, 156
Irschick, Eugene F., 2, 49, 51
Iruvaḻināṭu, 148, 153

jamābandī, 105
janmakāran, 18–21, 93, 95, 105, 110–11, 162, 174
janmaṃ, 16–17, 111, 142
janmanīr, 19
janmappaṇayaṃ, 19
Joint Commission/Commissioners, 94–5, 100–2, 105–9, 114

Kaiteri Ampu, 117, 119, 143
Kaḷari, 34
Kaḷaripayyaṟṟu, 34
Kāḷi, 31
Kalinga, 42
kāṇakkāran, 17, 21, 111
Kāṇaṃ, 14, 17–18, 111
Kanara, 64, 120
Kannavam, 117
Kannūr (port), 8, 64, 70
Kannūr (town), 6–7, 14, 21, 68, 70, 76, 78, 83, 102, 123
Kāraṇavar, 12, 14, 161
Kāraṇavarti, 12, 104, 161
Kareem, C.K., 4
Kaṭattanāṭu, Raja of, 80–l, 93–4, 100, 148
Katirūr, 166
Kēraḷa,
  agricultural development and industrialization of, 162
  Brahmins, 11
  calendar used in, 146
  communities, 32

decline in ship-building in, 95
deity of, 31
economic conditions, 4, 67
history of, 4
navigable network of water routes in, 8
political and economic development in, 4
rivers in, 7
trade with Malabar, 64
under Maisūr rule, 4
Kērala State Archives (KSA), Tiruvanantapuraṃ, 175
Kēraḷōḷaṭṭi, 14–15
Kērala Varmma Paḷaśśi Rājā, 6, 12, 77, 107–8, 112–20, 124–7,142–3, 151–2, 170, 173–6
Kocci, 6, 9, 64, 68, 70, 74–5, 147
Koḻikkōṭu (port), 9, 64–5, 67
Koḻikkōṭu (town), 1, 6, 21, 31, 67, 80–3, 94–7, 101–2, 147–8, 155, 172
Kollam, 68, 146, 177
Kōṭṭa river, 8
Kōṭṭayaṃ
British occupation of, 124–5
British treaty (1736), 74
history of, 176
land under cultivation in, 20
little kingdom model applied to, 141–52
Nāyars of, 78–82, 101, 177, 123
pepper-growing areas in, 8, 63, 74
population's resistance against British, 151, 159–60
rājā of, 12, 32, 34, 75–7, 79–81, 93, 97, 100, 170, 174–5
reforms in, 16
royal family of, 11
senior rājā of, 82, 114, 120, 143
sovereignty over, 106, 154–5
tax collection in, 77, 93–4, 106–7, 117–19, 123, 154
temples in, 170
Kōṭṭayaṃ rebellions, 115, 115–20, 120–2, 122–7
Koṭuṅṅalūr, 36, 65, 68, 70
Kōvilakaṃ, 12, 33
Koyamputtur, 6, 10, 96, 120–1
Kulaidevaṃ, 32
Kulke, Hermann, 42–3
Kumar, Dharma, 4
Kurg, 6
Kuṟiccyar, 119, 162
Kurumbar, 119, 162
Kurumpranāṭu, 6, 94, 106, 115, 148
Kurumpranāṭu, Raja of, 6, 12, 77, 106–7, 113–18, 125–7, 148–9, 152, 154, 159, 174
Kurup, K.K.N., 31
Kūṭṭaṃ, 15, 149, 171
Kuṭiyān, 16, 20–1
Kuttupaṟambu, 33–4, 121, 123

land law, 16–22, 110–13
legitimation,
religious, 30–9, 170
ritual, 39–45, 142, 144, 170
see also rule
Lemercinier, Geneviève, 17
little king, 38–45, 141, 144–54, 170–2
little kingdom model of state, 3–4, 6, 22
characteristics of, 43–5
Dirks' approach to, 38–46
processual model, 42–5
rituals significance in, 39–41
structures, 41
Logan, William, 4, 8–9, 105, 114, 176
Luhmann, Niklas, 112

Macaulay, Thomas B., 161
Mackenzie, Colin, 147, 175
Macleod, W., 107, 122
Madras District Gazetteers, 176
Madras Presidency, 9, 103, 110
Mahāmakhaṃ festival, 15
Malabar,
Bhagavati worship in, 30–3

British initial contacts, 73–7
British policy towards, 98–113, 172–3
administrative interventions in, 98–105
courts establishment, 102–3
land law issue, 110–13
plantation in, 108
role of pepper in dispute over, 108–10
tax policy in, 98–105
British province of, 6–7
civil administration, 101
clash of sovereignty, 172
contact zone model, 46–54, 152–60, 171, 173–4
dialogue and resistance in, 49–54
conversion to Islam in, 96
direct British rule in, 5
Dutch in, 69–71
economic attraction of, 62–7
ethnohistory, 38
French in, 72–3
geography of, 6–7
in early modern period, 5
in eighteenth century, 6–11
in nineteenth century, 160–3, 174
invasions of Haider Ali and Ṭippu Sulttān in, 66, 78–84, 92–8, 108–10
Kōṭṭayaṃ rebellions, 115–27, 162
land transport connections, 9–11, 64
legitimation of rule, 170
little kingdom model for, 38–48, 141–52
Dirks' approach, 38–46
local elite and colonial administration conflicts, 113–27
Maisūrian invasion of, 78–84, 92–8, 108–10
pepper role in dispute over, 108–10
political units, 6
ports, 8
Portuguese in, 67–9
pre-colonial,
land law, 16–22, 110–13
social order, 11–16
rebellions in, 162–3
regional trade, 64–5
religious legitimation, 30–8
resistance to Maisūrian policy in, 92–6
restructuring of society in, 161–3, 174
rivers in, 7
road building, 10
rule legitimation, 30–54
rulers' reaction to Maisūrian innovations, 96–8
ruling élite in, 5
social structure of, 104–5
sources and transliteration on, 175–7
sovereignty clashes, 92–127, 154–5
tax assessment and collection in, 93–5, 105
temples in, 33–8
trade, *see* trade between Malabar and
transcontinental trade, 65
transformation of rule in, 170–7
transshipment tonnage from, 9
water-routes network in, 7–9, 64
Malabar, 4
Malabar Collectorate Records, 175–6
Malabar Commission, 110
Malabar Land Tenures Committee, 18
Malabar Province, 103
Malabarkūṭṭaṃ, 15–16
Māṇantavāṭi, temples in, 36–7
Maṇattaṇa, temples in, 35
Mangalūr peace settlement, 93
Māpiḷḷa rebellion, 162
Māpiḷḷa traders, 156
Martanda Varmma, 5, 70
Marumakkattāyam, 13, 142, 146, 171

Maryyāda, 16, 21, 111, 174
matrilineal society, characteristics of, 146–7
matrilineal system, 159, 161, 171
Mayyaḷi, 9, 72, 79, 108–9
Mencher, Joan, 4
Menon, A. Sreedhara, 163
Menon, Dilip, 151
Menon, K.K.P., 4
Miller, Roland, 5
Mir Ibrahim, 94
Moore, Melinda, 4, 13
Mṛdaṃgaśailēśvari, Sri, 33
Muḷakunnu, 33–4

Nambyar, 148, 153
Nampūtiris, Kēraḷa Brahmiṅs, 11, 15
Nāṭṭukūṭṭaṃ, 14–16, 142
Nāṭuvāḷi, 21, 43, 92, 102, 142, 150–1, 171
Nāyars,
community, 4, 11, 96–7
influence in pre-colonial social order, 11
internal structure, 11
kāṇaṃ and, 18
loyal, 15
matrilineal system of, 159, 161
members of royal family, 11
military training, 14, 79, 142
of Kōṭṭayaṃ, 78–82, 101, 117
paṭṭaṃ collection by, 18
rights of, 159
socio-political structures within, 4
taṟavāṭu, 104
Nīlagiri, 6, 8
Nilesvaram river, 7
Nīrmutal, 19
Niṭṭūr, 78, 80, 117–18

Oṅam, 21, 100, 142–3, 170
Oriental and India Office Collections (OIOC), British Library, London, 176
Oṭi, 19
Oṭṭikuṃ Purameyullakāṇaṃ, 19

Page, William, 98
Pāḷaiyakkārar, 38, 42, 119, 121
Pālakkāṭu, 7–8, 10, 93, 102, 143
Paḷaśśi, 106
Paḷaśśi Rājā, *see* Kerala Varmma
Paḷaśśi Rebellion, 112
Paḷaśśi Rēkhakaḷ, 175
Paḷavīṭṭil Cantu, 34–5
Pallur Eman Nāyar, 121, 123
Pantalāyini Kollam, 31, 65, 102
Parvati, 31
patrilineal Namputiri Brahmins, 161
Pāṭṭaṃ, 18–20, 93, 111
Pāṭṭaṃkār, 20
Peile, Christopher, 117, 142
pepper, trade in, 62–3, 108–10
Pēriya, 119, 121
Periyapurāṇam, 31
Polo, Marco, 7
Ponnāni, 7, 102
Pōrkkāḷi, 33
Portuguese, 1, 9, 62, 67–70
Pratt, Mary Louise, 3, 47, 49, 159
Public Consultations Bombay (PCB), 176
Pulpalli, 124, 143
Puraḷimala, 34
Putukkōṭṭai, 3, 40, 42, 46
Rama Varmma, 5
Ranger, Terence, 52
Rajadharma, 46, 114, 143–4,170, 172
Rajendran, 4
Ravi Varmma (of Ciṟakkal), 119–20
Ravi Varmma (of Kōṭṭayaṃ), 12, 93–4
Ravi Varmma (of House of Tāmūtiri), 81–2, 96–7
Ravindran, J.K., 103
Regional Archives Records (RAK), 175–6
resistance,
against British colonial power, 52–4, 76, 106, 126

against Maisūrian policy, 92–6
definition, 52
Rickards, Robert, 123
Rothermund, Dietmar, 67
rule,
colonial, 113–27, 154
conception of, 46, 53–4, 141
construction of, 5, 171
legitimation of, 5, 30–45, 142–52, 170, 172, 176
local élites, 5, 44–5, 54, 73, 113–27, 143, 153–5, 170
manifestation, 6, 42
territorial, 5
transformation of, 170–4

Said, Edward, 2, 50
Śaivasiddhanta, 31
Sāmanta, 11
Schnepel, Burkhard, 3–4
Sepoys, 73, 121
Seristtadar, 92
Shulman, David, 142
Sirdār Khan, 80–1
Śiva, 30–2, 34, 36
Smee, John, 157–8
sovereignty, 41, 45, 50, 53–4, 62, 76, 78, 142, 154, 159, 170
absolute, 41
clash of, 54, 92–127, 154–5, 172
Srinivas Rao, 93
Śrīrangapaṭṭaṇaṃ peace treaty, 77, 83, 98, 101, 120
State,
elements of nature of, 45
Eurocentric concept, 45
Indian conception, 53
model in eighteenth century India, 38
traditional doctrine of, 45
Western concept, 172
Stevens, James, 107, 157–8
Sthānamāññaḷ, 19, 111, 174
Stokes, Eric, 52
Stuart, James, 34
Subrahmanyam, Sanjay, 2
Sulttānbaṭṭēri, temples in, 37
Talaśśēri, 9–10, 72, 74–5, 78–9, 82, 93, 101, 106–10, 116, 120–1, 123, 142, 155–6, 172
Talaśśēri Rēkhakaḷ, 159, 175
Taḷippaṟambu river, 7
Tamaraśśēri, 82
Tamil Nadu State Archives (TNSA), Cennai, 175–6
Tamilnāṭu, 4, 75 49, 64, 149
Tāmūtiri of Kōḻikkōṭu, 15, 67–8, 80, 96, 147
Taṟakūṭṭaṃ, 12, 14
taṟavāṭu, 12–14, 34, 98, 104, 112, 147, 161, 174
temple network, 22, 30, 37, 170
temple patronage, 37
temples in Malabar, location of in,
Kōṭṭayam, 170
Mānantavāṭi, 36–7
Maṇattaṇa, 35
Muḻakunnu, 33–4
Sulttānbaṭṭēri, 37
Tirunelli, 35–6
Tiruvaṅṅāṭu, 37
Tōṭṭikkaḷaṃ, 34–5
Vāḷḷiyūrkāvu, 36
Vayanāṭu, 170
Ṭippu Sulttān, 5, 9–10, 20, 35–7, 66, 72, 75–84, 92–101, 105–6, 108–11, 119–20, 143, 147, 150–2
Tirunāvāya, 15
Tirunelli, temples in, 35–6
Tiruvanantapuraṃ, 1
Tiruvaṅṅaṭu, temples in, 37
Tiruvitāṃkur, in early modern period, 5
Tottikkalam, temples in, 34–5
trade between Malabar and,
British, 73–7
Dutch, 69–71
French, 72–3

Portuguese, 67–9
Travancore lines, 75, 82
Tukri, 92
Tuḳridar, 92, 94
Unni Mūta Mūppan, 123

Valapaṭṭaṇaṃ river, 7
Vaḷḷiyūrkāvu, temples in, 36
Vaṃśāvali, 147
Vāyanāṭu, temples in, 170
Veḷiccappāṭus, 36
Venkatakotta, 10
Verenigde Oostindische Compaigne (VOC), 69–71
Verghese, T.C., 4
Vērumpāṭṭaṃ, 18
Vettaṭṭanāṭu, 94
Vira Varmma, 6, 12, 16, 77, 106–8, 113–20, 125–7, 142, 144, 149, 152, 154, 159, 170, 173
Viśṇu, 30–1, 34–5, 37
Viṣu, 21, 100,142–3,170

Walker, Alexander, 17, 115, 120
Warden, Thomas, 17, 105
Wellesley, Arthur, 121–2
Wigram, Herbert, 161

Zacharia, Scaria, 175